Life Interrupted

In the Aftermath of My Son's Murder

by

Karen Lynne Duffie

Order this book online at www.trafford.com
or email orders@trafford.com

Most Trafford titles are also available at major online book retailers.

Note for Librarians: A cataloguing record for this book is available from Library and Archives Canada at www.collectionscanada.ca/amicus/index-e.html

Printed in Victoria, BC, Canada.

ISBN: 978-1-4269-1895-7

Our mission is to efficiently provide the world's finest, most comprehensive book publishing service, enabling every author to experience success. To find out how to publish your book, your way, and have it available worldwide, visit us online at www.trafford.com

Trafford rev. 1/26/2010

www.trafford.com

North America & international
toll-free: 1 888 232 4444 (USA & Canada)
phone: 250 383 6864 • fax: 812 355 4082

TRIBUTE

This is my tribute to the guy with the sweetest smile, a good friend until the end, a responsible big brother, a wonderful grandson, a cool nephew, a fun cousin~that young man, none other than,

Mr. Kourtney E. Duffie, my son.

Affectionately, called "1st Born"

...not in vain

Kourtney E. Duffie

July 20, 1984 - June 11, 2007

Dedication

This publication, straight from my heart and soul, can only be dedicated to my devoted daughter, Jazmyn and my son, John-John. I don't know that any other person fully understands the dept of how much Kourt is missed other than our small circle. When I say his death hit home…it hit our home. As a family, we have been forever changed, but, hear me when I say it's not the end. We will meet up with him again.

And, now, Your Brother, My Son, Kourtney—waits for us!

Thank you, Jaz and John-John for hanging in there for yourselves, for us, for me—even when I'm not my best and for the Love of your Big Bro.

July 2005

Acknowledgements

THANK YOU TO ALL my supporters and especially to you who love Kourtney! I need to acknowledge and give a special thank you to some people such as: author, Elizabeth Atkins, who cheered me on and believed in me and my story from day one. To my daughter, Jazmyn, thank you for always believing in me and your encouragement, your full support in all that I do, is of the highest importance to me, I love you. To my "sweet-angel", John-John, you are the glue that holds us together and I love you for just being you! Thank you for your endless sense of humor and for being there for me with "your words of wisdom!" Thank you to my sister Kim, we go through what we go through but remember this: sisters by fate and friends by choice! I appreciate your care and concern not only of this book but of me and Kourtney over the years. To my sister Angie, thank you for your total support of what I do and being there for everything from the time Kourt entered this world in 1984 until he departed in 2007—and for still being there to this day for me. To Joseph, you're like a son to me, sometimes it takes a tragedy for us to get where God wants us to be. Joseph, you were one of the first to learn about my book endeavor and you were on board immediately—thank you for letting me lean on you too. To my Auntie Cat, thank you, for always listening and taking a stand for me all my life - genuinely being happy for me for *whatever* I accomplish! To my parents, Honey & Kenneth, without you...there would have never been a Kourtney because there would have never been a me—so thank you. To ALL my cousins, showing up to court, being ever supportive and having faith in me during the creation of this book. THANK YOU cuz (my cousins) for a lifetime of love and friendship. To my spiritual sister and author, Janine Edwards, thank you my sister for your time and generous spirit. I feel very blessed to have had your input on this project at the precise time.

There are other family members and friends of mine as well as friends of Kourtney's that have been helpful to me in one way or another since the tragedy and the creation of this very special publication. And, there are too many names to mention, but, you know who you are. I must say "thank you" for calling, text messages, Facebook, Myspace, emails to check on the status of the book or just to say hello. Believe me I have come to trust that it is the little things we do for each other that register BIG in my mind. Your kind gestures are always noticed.

Friends,

THANK YOU FOR YOUR support. In an effort to put out work that is responsible and not offensive—I must place a **"WARNING"** that my book does contain very strong language (profanity) and some derogatory statements. It is my hope that you are not offended. However, as one might expect, during certain times within in my recovery process, which still continues, my hurt, anger, confusion, and depressed emotional state did not always render me to be mindful of how I said things. When I read my work after the fact I realize I could have used other words. I decided against changing or replacing these words in my journal entries that contain such strong language because I did not want to change anything about what I said day to day—thus affecting the integrity or impact of this project. Replacing certain words, to me, would have meant, I'm covering over things—not being true to my journal or my feelings. Further, I don't want to ever give the impression that I don't fall short of the grace of God or that although I have concrete faith in God and active in church does not mean that I will not say or even think unholy things. My goal every day is to be who I am in all things. So, in the words of my late son, Kourtney..."Keep it 100!"

Most sincerely,

Karen Lynne Duffie

Remember: To Yourself Be True....

Introduction

ON JUNE 11, 2007, at about 1:30am, I heard four words that changed my life from that very moment and forever: "HE DIDN'T MAKE IT." I asked myself, "Did they mean *my son* is the "He"? In the utter confusion that took hold of me, I was trying to make sense of who is the "he" for about 3-5 seconds. I remember feeling the wrinkles around my eyes, raising my eyebrows, and holding my lips together tightly. Well, after all, I was in the emergency room to see about my son Kourtney after receiving a frantic call from my sister Kim. And then, BAM! It (the realization) hit me as if I were hit in the face with a hard snow ball...it stings...oh it hurts! *My* Kourtney didn't make it–meaning that: he is dead.... Yes, he is dead! My Kourtney, or "1st Born," which was my nickname for him, entered this world on July 20, 1984, at 3:17 in the morning. Now, a few weeks shy of his 23rd birthday, he's gone.... My knees started to buckle, I could feel my legs give away, my bones felt like rubber-bands, and I screamed with all my strength "Noooooo!" Everyone in the emergency room was looking at me. "Since you say he's dead, I have to see him," I said. They (a team of two doctors and two other staff) walked me down the hall...and there he lay. One of his friends was leaning over him, crying. Jaz was there, but, I did not notice her immediately. I remember feeling protective over Kourtney since I did not recognize the guy standing so close to him. I stopped at the room entrance, just to make sure it was him I guess. I knew instantly. This is my son! It is 1st Born! "Oh my...Kourtney," I whisper. Slowly and deliberately, I approach his lifeless body, which was covered with the brightest and cleanest white sheet I had ever seen. It's pulled up to his shoulders. "Okay, he does not look dead–just sleep," I said to myself. There is broken glass in his hair, along with little traces of blood. I attempt to touch his curly hair, but the doctors tell me not to because it's evidence. His eyelids are cracked, just enough to see the bottoms of his eyes...they are lifeless. Wow, this is my first time seeing eyes with no life. My head drops, and the floodgates of tears do, too. My initial thoughts (while staring at him and holding his hand through the sheet) were, "Who hates Kourtney? He has an enemy, huh?" I'm puzzled. But this still makes no sense. He was alive and full of life six or seven hours ago at Jazmyn's birthday dinner at my mom's (Honey) house. Hours ago, he had asked me to cut him a slice of cake...he was okay then... he was laughing and talking and walking...HELL, HE WAS BREATHING! Now, he's not. Just like that, he's dead? Yes. All I've ever had to deal with were sick, older folk being dead. Tell me again. How's it that he is dead because Kourtney can't die, can he? Death took on a whole new meaning in my life ever since that moment.

Within minutes, friends and family showed up at the hospital, crowding the room to the point that hospital staff had to move us to a much larger space. I see my cousin Lacey saying a prayer of peace and laying hands on my dear son. He is getting colder and stiffer by the minute. I can feel it. And now his stomach and thigh are puffing up. He's changing - going through what happens when dead bodies shut down completely - forever. People are touching him and crying and screaming. I witness my mother falling out on the floor, my sister Kim throwing up. Jazmyn is standing on the opposite side of me. She says over and over "this some bullshit!" We hold each of his hands and rub his arms. We feel around his body, searching for the bullet hole that ended his young life; we can't find it. He looks so clean and close to perfect. He is at peace. The hospital staff cleaned him up so well; there was no blood on him-just a tiny bit in his hair. This experience is powerful...overwhelming...surreal. I look around the room in a dazed dreamlike state, crying. It's hard to see my face because I have a baseball cap pulled tightly over my head — yeah the one from the Hard Rock Cafe. While people are hugging me, I'm still stuck on "I just talked to him about a slice of cake." I'm fixated on that point in time. Like most people faced with this type of tragedy, I need things to make sense of something that defied logic to me. But I guess it makes sense with respect to the plain fact that someone pointed a gun at my son, my beloved Kourtney, pulled the trigger nine times, with three of the nine bullets striking him. These life-ending projectiles hit his chest, penetrated his heart, and shut down his diaphragm. He could no longer breathe so, yes, the result was death. He died. My Kourtney died.

We stayed at the hospital about three or four hours before the Wayne County Medical Examiner's van arrives to pick him up and to conduct that horrific autopsy. I knew they were going to cut him up and sew him back together. I didn't want them to take him. I'm very grateful that I was able to identify him at the hospital versus doing so at the morgue, where it would have been done by video! That's so scary to think about the "What ifs?" under those circumstances. At the hospital, we could sit next to him, touch him, cry over him, and, above all, pray for him. As they take my son out of the room, I try to look. A lady is holding me close and tight, trying to keep me from losing control and seeing him leave. The harder I try to pull away from her—the tighter her embrace. But, I wanted to break free from her and follow that white sheet that covered Kourtney. Defeated, I gave up because sadly I knew to... "let him go—he has go". And, I stopped resisting her. I remember seeing the pristine white sheet moving towards the door - now he's gone. This means the next time I see my Kourtney he will be in a casket. Jesus Christ! I don't want him to be dead! "I want him back," I say over and over. Please...don't let this be happening. I'm looking at everyone in the room - as if they could change this for me. "Don't let him be dead!" I cry out. I say this over and over, but no one has a response for me, really...just hugs and kisses and prayers. At one point, my mother begs the doctors to take him back to surgery because she can see his eyes. Yeah, the lids were slightly open. But, had she examined his eyes as closely as I had, she would have seen those big, brown – and *lifeless* – eyes. And poor Jazmyn - she saw his eyes the way they were before he died – open. Like "eyes wide shut." No life at all. That bothered her for a long time. His soul had exited his physical shell.

Understanding death, and breaking it down to get into what happens, became important to me. I have never thought about death in the same way since then. I had to explain it to myself over and over. The fact that he had been fatally injured – and there was nothing that could be done – was something that I had to deal with and accept. Finally, I get it. Still, there are those days when I have to remind myself of my revised definition of the word death and what it means when someone dies.

I've learned a few lessons since Kourt's death. One, death is not negotiable. Once someone has entered the realm of death, they totally cross over, they are gone. That lesson has been the most difficult for me to accept. For the first time, I was unable to help Kourtney with a problem. There was no phone call I could make – nothing I could do for him. I felt like I had failed him. I was not there to protect him. Letting myself off the hook, I embraced the position that I would have not been with him at that time of night (or morning), anyway. Additional comfort was found in the belief that I had no way of knowing what was to come. Or did I? I'll return to that point shortly. Two, life is very precious, and we are extremely vulnerable to lose it. That is to say, anything can happen at anytime. Life is not to be taken for granted. It is a gift from God. No one has the right to send this gift back to Him. Three, as parents and potential parents, we should try to make the best decisions in our lives so that those benefits are bestowed upon our children. When interacting with potential mates, you should ask yourself two questions: "Is this the best mom or dad for my child?" and "Is this the person I want my child to say "Hey, this is my mother (or father)?'" I really mean that. It's a very serious way to look at it. Children deserve the love and support of their mothers and fathers. I mean, there is no way to tell if someone is going to change, but, at least before getting too deep into the relationship, and especially before you bring another life into the world, have the best possible life established for yourself and your child(ren). As a result, their choices and opportunities will be made better and easier. They will have a foundation. I made that mistake and, for that, I apologize to my dearest, 1st Born. Unfortunately, throughout Kourtney's life, his father was not there for him, though he traveled from California to attend the funeral. Wow... thanks.... Now you show up. Amazing! Nonetheless, with each passing day, I have tried to atone for the mistakes that *I have made* with my son – even when he was alive – to pay him back for being the great young man he turned out to be, a young man with a giving heart and solid family values.

Now, back to the question I asked earlier: Did I know something was going to happen to my son? Kourtney was killed on Monday, June 11, 2007. I had a horrible dream in the wee hours of the Friday morning that preceded that fateful date. It was chilling, and I never told Kourtney about it. It frightened me so much, leaving me with an ugly and cold feeling. I dreamed of him and another young man, their backs to me. They were in this vividly green field, surrounded by tall trees and bold green grass. I watched the horrifying scene as they both lifted guns to each other's heads and shot one another. I woke up immediately, heart pounding and racing. I've often asked myself, "Had I told him, would that have changed the outcome?" Thereafter, the entire weekend was weird. I had visions and tried to forget about the dream. But I couldn't. My cousin Eric had a fish fry that Friday night and I went with a friend. Out of the blue, I started talking about Kourtney as a baby and how very cute he was (and he truly was). I could not stop thinking about him and talking about him. Honestly, I felt strange. It was unsettling.

That Sunday, June 10th, was Jazmyn's 20th birthday dinner at my mom's home. Earlier that day, Kourtney was straight up raising hell! He had been aggravating to me and my mom, fussing about Jazmyn and a guy she had been dating. He did not approve. After my mother had informed me about his behavior, I called him on the phone in an effort to calm him down. He only got stirred up again. Now, Kourtney was always respectful towards me. If he let a curse word come out of his mouth, he would be right on top of it. "Oops my bad, Mama...I'm sorry," he would quickly implore. But this day was different. He cursed and raised his voice in anger as he expressed himself. I kept waiting for the apology, but it never came. I asked him, "Kourt why are you being so evil to Jaz it's her birthday?" In essence, he told me that he didn't give a damn about it being her birthday because he had to "make something understood!" So I let him vent. About three or four hours later, he showed up at my mom's house. He was smiling, under control and appeared very calm to me. (None of us were even thinking that this boy's life is on a count down to zero within hours.) As usual, he greeted me with a kiss. And, I felt okay about him for once since the bad dream. The ugly thoughts were gone.

I love to take pictures, and I do so all the time. (I may have over 800 of Kourtney!) I remember looking at him with his big framed, round Cartier glasses on. I thought to myself I should take a picture of him. He did not like taking pictures too much as a young man. When he was younger, he had no choice (smile). I second-guessed myself and decided against it. I did not want to upset him. Kourtney could be rude sometimes, and I did not want him being smart assed with me because I tried to take a picture of him in front of everyone. So I just peeked at him from living room window as he sat on my mom's porch talking and laughing. As the day went on, so many people – many more than I had expected – showed up to say happy birthday to Jaz and eat dinner with us. When I think back on it now, her party was the opportunity for everyone to spend sometime with Kourtney, too, in the last hours of his young life.

This raises the question: Do I believe in fate? I'm not sure, but I do believe that *something* was in the works since the dream. His demeanor and demands and being uncharacteristically unapologetic for using bad language with me, as well as the way the party turned out, were signs that something was governing the most recent events. Did *he* know something? I always wonder about that. To be frank, he and Jaz were not speaking on her birthday. They had fallen out over that guy. Did Kourtney sense something and was now turning the fight over to me to help her to move on with her life? It seems like it to me. What follows is one of my "mystifying" experiences. Not long after my son died, and life was slowing down a bit, that guy Jaz was dating came over to our home. Prior to his death, Kourtney did not allow him in or around the house. Nevertheless, I have a Betty Boop coffee mug in my private bathroom. Kourt used to put money inside of it. If I was not home, he would call and say "Hey Mama, I put some money in your favorite cup." The day this guy was visiting I went in my bathroom and the mug was on the floor. "It's glass. Why isn't it broken?" I said to myself. More importantly, *how (or why) did it fall*? I did not recall hearing anything. I just stood in the bathroom for a moment, puzzled, picked it up, and placed it back where it should be. I looked around and examined the area to see how this could happen. "This mug has been there for a long time," I think to myself, and it has never been close to being knocked over. Anyway, I left out for a while. When I returned to the bathroom – the mug was back on the floor. I took a deep breath. Okay. Who's been in here? No one, I answer back to myself. No one ever comes in my bathroom. Once again, I picked it up. I'm feeling strange, but I refuse to say anything to Jaz until her friend leaves. I stayed in kitchen for a while, went into my bedroom, where my bathroom is located – the damn mug was on the floor yet again!!! Now, I'm freaked out. A light goes on in my head. A series of thoughts scream in my head, "This is Kourtney! It has to be! He's here and he's upset that this guy is over! He wants to let me know this by moving my favorite mug to the floor to get my attention." It worked. So, I acknowledged him. I said to him out loud, "I know you're here. I'm happy your soul is free." I told him that I was sorry that he was upset about the guy being at the house, but that we weren't betraying him. Soon after, Jazmyn ended that relationship. And my mug remains in the exact same place and has never moved again. That's just *one* of my "mystifying encounters". I will describe more of them throughout the book.

The party over...the phone call...the nervous drive alone to the hospital...three days of funeral services...the return to funeral home to pick up my son's remains in an urn...crazy ass days and the many sleepless nights...and here I am. Here I am to face it all over again, the raw and unknown. I've made a decision to take my journal notes and turn them into what I hope to be a source of comfort and hope for others in my position. The purpose of this book is to turn an unbelievable life event into a source of inspiration, to show others that we have the ability to cope with the unimaginable: the murder of a son or daughter. In these pages I reveal myself, the hurt and broke-down-to-nothing me in the months that followed this tragedy. I also make clear my reconnection with Jesus...Our Lord and Savior, which contributes to a breakthrough to the new me.

Journaling is 'healthy grieving" my therapist once told me. I found that I liked journaling more than any private or group session, primarily because it's available to me 24/7. I talk as long as I want and say whatever I want. There are no rules to follow, and there are no limits when you journal. It's your world. But I never seriously thought my notes had the potential to help others. I can only hope and pray that they will....

Today is Sunday, January 18, 2009, 4:16pm

I'm writing the introduction to my book, *Metamorphosis: Diary of a Grieving Mother*. (I'm not 100% sure of the title.) I find it easy to sit here and harness my hurt and emotions with the expectation of helping someone else. I feel a lift in my spirit; so, this project is helpful for me as well.

This downward spiral I'm experiencing is all negative. I've been going downhill for a few months now. I don't know if I can get much lower than this. I see myself slipping away. Can anyone see that — can they help me? I'm trapped in a place; I cannot free *me*! I see it...I feel it...I just know what I know! What can I do? There is an urgent calling on my life right now...on my very survival. I must change today. I have to. It's on me. I have the inner power to do whatever I want. I hear that in the worst of times, character is developed. So, in the words of "Red", the character played by Morgan Freeman in the movie *The Shawshank Redemption*, "GET BUSY LIVING OR GET BUSY DYING!" That's damn right!

So, let's get started. I'll take you back to my very first journal entry, dated July 14, 2007, six days before Kourtney's 23rd birthday and just a little over one month after his death. Here we go....

Saturday, July 14, 2007, 5:13pm

Oh my, I had to type this. I'm home alone, which is not uncommon, and I fell asleep for about the third time this afternoon watching *Roots: The Next Generations*. BET is running a marathon. I know I'm depressed. My heart is so broken that I can feel the pieces fall to my stomach! I just woke up from a nap where I dreamed of Kourtney! I first heard a whisper "Mama, Mama" very softly in my ear. Maybe, just maybe, it was for real. I heard him loud and clear - I say it was for real. I feel so cozy right now, crying as I write this because *I feel it was real.* I had spoken to Kourtney earlier today, telling him that I'm feeling so down and sad that maybe he could send me a sign or something so that I could smile and lift my head up (literally) some , just like he has done in previous days since his departure to the other side. Nevertheless, the dream reflected him as a little boy in this blue and yellow outfit he wore on a rainy Easter holiday when he was about 3 or 4-years-old. In the dream, he was with a bunch of kids (Kourt loved the kids) and two adults. He was skipping along and happy. I could not get close to him. We were in a shopping mall and there was a giant screen TV above the escalator. He was on the screen smiling the biggest smile, just like in the actual pictures I have of him. I'm so happy to see him and call out to him. The closer he gets to the TV screen the larger his face becomes. I scream his name, "Kooouuurrrtttnnnneeeeyyyyy!!!", but he skips away with the kids and the two adults. I could actually feel the warmth and happiness radiate from inside of me, just to see him walking and smiling (and not in that casket). I say to myself, "That must be his new family." He seems so happy and, in the dream, I just stand there in tears and watch him fade away. Hearing Jazmyn and our cousin Brittany come in, I wake up. I try to hide my tears, which I find I'm getting good at these days. I decide that I need to locate those Easter pictures, and I do. Scattered about in the middle of my living room floor are literally hundreds of pictures of Kourtney. When I see the pictures from that Easter Sunday, I just break down. Jaz is very concerned and I assure her that I will be okay. Now, I decide to work more on his scrapbook, determined to have it completed by his 23rd birthday celebration coming up on July 20th. I'm planning a big party for him.

Here is a picture of Kourtney as I dreamed of him in his Easter outfit

Sunday, July 15, 2007, 6:45pm

Well, today is an emotionally-improved day! Got some more scrap-booking done, and Jazmyn and I got more T-shirts made to wear for Kourt's 23rd birthday coming up next weekend. Jazmyn and John John have several clothing items with Kourtney's pictures all over them. I got one made but have not been able to wear it. Today, I bought John John a necklace with Kourt's picture inside it, which he will be wearing with all black and red, Kourtney's favorite colors. In terms of weather, it's a very nice day. We went to a classic car show at a trade center/flea market, where we got the t-shirts printed. Jaz and I talked about Kourtney and what we thought about his life and his future had he lived. We agree on a lot of things because we know him so well. The conversation with my daughter just makes me angrier that my son was murdered by this low life, an individual with no ambition to be better in life, the complete opposite of Kourtney. I know this demon seed, this menace to society, hated on my son. The way I hear it, he was envious of Kourtney. Kourtney was a unique young man; he was different, reserved and calm. He may not have made all the best or socially-correct decisions, and was he was quite familiar with the street life, but I, as his mother, I knew his heart. Further, I'm not worried because God knows all of our hearts. His heart dictated to him that he be giving and have concern for others. And we all fall short of the grace of God. But, at the end of the day, as far as I'm concerned, it comes down to what you are about inside. Kourtney believed in a higher source, and he had faith in God. He wanted something better for his life. He was not satisfied with his day-to-day existence. I took notice of his conversations and the plans he laid out for himself. He knew that there was more to life than hustling. He was not a person to brag or even desired to be noticed. He just wanted to keep his head above water and be independent. And he did just that. He asked no one for anything. He left this earth not owing anyone anything! I'm so proud of him. For those qualities – and so much more – I yearn to mother him again. I want to be his mother again in the sense that he calls and asks me to look stuff up on the Internet for him regarding cars or how much utilities costs every month or how much it may cost for a trip to Miami. Now I see that even with the most mundane of things, the requests that I took for granted, I truly miss. No lie, sometimes he drove me crazy! But what I wouldn't give for him to drive me crazy today...right this very second. At this very moment, if only he could call me and ask me to do any of these tasks, I'd jump to it before my next heartbeat. I just miss my 1st Born. My love for him, like any real mother, is strong and infinite. There are no boundaries in time or space. I think about my plans for him and how I envisioned his future. You know, when your son or daughter dies, a part of your hopes and dreams die, too. To most parents, the death of your child seems to be a gross mistake; it's backwards. It wasn't normal to have a funeral for my son. He should have attended *my* funeral and been there for his brother and sister. My hope now is that when I do transition to see my beloved 1st Born, Jaz and John John will be married and have their own families. But I know Kourtney will always be hanging around somewhere in our midst. In the scrapbook, I dedicated an entire page to that dream I had yesterday.

I ended up finding about 10 pictures of him on that particular Easter Sunday. I will always remember yesterday and cannot wait for my next dreams...anything just to feel and stay close to him, to talk to him – and he talk back.

Now, I know that dreams are the way we stay connected. That's the best part of going to sleep. I'm always looking for Kourtney and waiting for him to visit. "He must be pretty busy when he does not show up," I say to myself. To date, however, I have had countless dreams of him and "mysterious encounters". I'll get back to that shortly. Now back to the journal.

Monday, July 16, 2007, 9:52pm

Well, went to work today and it was not so bad. My spirits are lifted a bit higher. How about this: I actually experienced a few "for real" smiles. I don't feel so low and heavy-hearted. On the way home, I stopped by the scrapbook store for more supplies. There are some good developments from the detective. I feel it's time to post that lowlife demon's picture as "Wanted". They are processing the information that they've received. His photo should run on the local news, again, next week. Based on information that they have received from street sources, they feel he is getting tired of running. I had some visitors for a while today. That was cool. In preparation for the party, I need to get a picture of Kourt blown up to 4ft and framed. The marble table that will hold his urn has arrived and has to be assembled. I asked my cousin Lennie to do it. There is so much to be done. I start counseling next Wednesday. I'm really tired tonight - already took shower and ready for bed. I'm trying to stay up to watch Martin at 11pm; and more episodes of *Roots*. Also, I received a very uplifting phone call from a close family friend. Unfortunately, her daughter was a homicide victim 22 years ago. We talked for about an hour. I hope she will also make the party, along with my God mother. I have decided that we will celebrate his birthday every year. Well, I'm headed to the bedroom, but, not before I make a pit stop in the kitchen for vodka and cranberry and some spicy pumpkin seeds. Kourt loved vodka, too. He really could not drink, though. He would get sick to his stomach all the time! He was funny for that. I used to tell him "Boy you can't drink!" He'd just smile that bashful smile. Wow. He's the one who was killed, huh?

The individual responsible for taking my son's life became a fugitive immediately after the murder. Eventually, he was captured. While he was on the run, he murdered another man in July of 2007. When captured, my son's killer was found crying like a baby in an attic of an abandoned crack house on Detroit's east side. The home was without electricity or running water. There was a real coordinated effort between the River Rouge and Detroit SWAT, along with the US Marshals Service and Michigan State Police, to capture this fool.

My son's murder was caught on videotape at a gas station in River Rouge, Michigan. And there were witnesses, too! Most were afraid to testify, but there were four young men who were not! They hung in there, despite the death threats and living in the same neighborhood as my son's killer. They stood up for what was right. I prayed for their safety often. I was simply terrified for them. It was a crazy-ass time for real for everyone involved. Six months prior to June 11th, this punk (the murderer) had pulled a gun on my son in the barber shop as he sat in the chair getting a hair cut. He told my son that he would not make it through the summer...and he didn't. No one from the barbershop wanted to get involved, and I understood why. They were dropping out like two days before trial was to start, and my stress level was beyond the stars in the sky! My biggest fear...he would not be convicted. Losing this case was a constant fear and contributed to my anxiety. Journal time....

Tuesday, July 17, 2007, 6:38pm

Today, better. I think about Kourtney every other second, no matter what I'm doing. I'm still working on the plans for his party. I finished the giant poster and new collages that display his entire life! It's even amazing to me.... Thank goodness for pictures. My pictures are what I have left. Maybe, if I live to be an old woman and my memory does not serve me so well, I will always have my priceless pictures to keep me close to him. Damn! Anyway, I got the new Carl Thomas CD and I'm listening to a song called "Home". I like it. All the while wishing I could get my boy back home with me. How my heart and mind ache for him all the time. Just got off the phone with a friend and they just had death in family. My prayers go out to them. I'm so glad my therapy/counseling starts tomorrow. I'm thinking about starting my own support group right here in my home. Maybe I'll put out some flyers and see what kind of response I get. I know a lot of social workers and licensed therapists that I could get to get to facilitate the group. I'm not working Friday as that is 1st Born's birthday and the party is the next day, the 21st.

9:50pm

My head hurts so bad! It's pounding. I just got a call from Joseph's girlfriend. He's adding me to his visiting list. Kourtney was going to testify for Joseph's brother T. Joseph and Terrence are brothers. They are in jail, charged with murder! Many people believe that my son's murder was in retaliation for what the brothers are accused of. Sort of like "Okay, you killed my friend, so I will kill your friend!" Senseless, huh? I do know this: Kourtney believed in their innocence. This seems to be the reason why Kourt was killed. So, to me, HE WAS KILLED FOR NOTHING!!!! He was killed *just because.* I cannot say it enough. So I'll fuckin' say it again – HE WAS KILLED FOR NOTHING! I'm sick to my stomach and my head hurts. This is just too much. I'm going to bed. Jazmyn is trying to talk to me, but I just want to go to bed. Maybe Kourtney will come tell me what the hell has happened! I'm confused. There are all kinds of rumors floating all over the place. All I know and believe is that my son should be here and he is not.

Wednesday, July 18, 2007, 4:32pm

Today I started my first day of counseling. Much needed counseling. It went okay. I'm not sure how I was supposed to feel, but I will be seeing her regularly in the coming weeks (my insurance only pays for so many sessions though). I've been busy working today, getting things ready for Kourtney's party. Doing things like buying food, ordering the cake, and mailing out last minute invitations. I think the turnout should be nice, and the weather is going to be gorgeous this weekend.

Friday, July 20, 2007, 11:16pm

Happy Birthday 1st Born!!! You are 23 years old! I'm so sorry we are not with you or you with us to celebrate today and tomorrow, but I know you are around in spirit! Thank you, Kourtney. Today has been an emotional day. I found myself actually trying to encourage others. My niece broke down crying so hard, and I had to just let her know that our Kourtney is at peace. He had an "early calling," as the old folk say. Some of us die young and some old and that Kourtney...well, he went young. I'm sorry all this happened and it hurts so badly. I watched Jaz and John John bring in their big bro's birthday at midnight and it was nothing short of electrifying to watch! The two of them were singing and playing his favorite rap songs and Jazmyn.... Oh my...she just got so into the whole thing. She loves Kourt so much, and she just wanted to show her love for him and try to feel good. When all I could do was feel bad. I just walked away to my bathroom – flopped down on toilet seat like a chair – in total darkness to ask Kourtney "Why?" and cried. I could hardly stand to see them trying to be happy and have fun and honor their brother in this way. It was painful for me to watch, but I know they had to do it. I've been out at my mom's house for most of the day, getting ready for his party tomorrow. My niece came home from Atlanta to be here. My sister-in-law Rhonda was there about to clean and season the ribs. Kourtney's friends Mercedes and Heather came over. Mercedes gave me the sweetest birthday card for Kourt. They stayed a long time and we swapped stories about Kourtney. His high school girlfriend, Alicia, called and wanted to know if she could bring something tomorrow. He was – and still is – loved. I miss Kourtney, and this hurts all the time. He should be here. This is all I know....

A detective called to say that they are feeling very confident about where they are with the investigation. Honestly, I hope that sub-human animal is tortured and killed. Jail time is too good for him. He needs to suffer, as he has no idea of what he took away from me and our family. What is this all about? This is so outrageous to me. Sometimes I can't even catch my breath behind the thoughts of this mess!! I think this wild animal was jealous of my son. He hated on him. Everyone has been saying it – and I believe it. Man, fuck him! I think he is lacking in so many ways. He is ignorant, a coward, and all he knows is how to hate and be dysfunctional in his life. Really, he hates *himself*. He needs to deal with that. Why did Kourtney – and, subsequently, why do I – have to deal with what this animal was/is lacking in his life? That's what it really comes down to. Kourtney and I have been affected in a tragic way due to the unresolved issues in this idiot's life! And that is NOT fair...but it is life. (Deep ass sigh — I have to take several deep breaths right about now!) If he was loved, he would have shown others respect and not this viciousness. But, you know, God will make him pay. He will know far worse before it's all over. So, I'm going to end this journal entry the best way by saying: I love you Kourtney...I love you so much 1st Born, and Happy Birthday. We got a few bottles of champagne and Grey Goose in honor of Kourt, too!

Saturday, July 21, 2007, 11:53pm

Kourt's party was an absolute success! So many people showed up and stayed all day and well into the night. We had a balloon release. That was very emotional. Of course, I have pictures! The balloons were all red and black, his favorite colors. As we watched the balloons fly away into the sun, many of us were moved to tears. Only a few weeks after his murder and our first birthday party for him was without him. Incredible! It was emotional, an awesome day for us. I'm so glad we did it! Kourtney asked for this party when we were planning Jazmyn's party. Our last guest left at 11pm. It was Kourt's friend Mercedes. She had been pretty emotional throughout the party. We all took pictures; everything was so nice! I brought over all the collages and pictures I had blown up. Everyone was taking pictures, using all his pictures as the backdrop. It's a good feeling to know that he was loved so much. Not just by family, but also by his many, many friends. But that nagging thought is back: Why isn't he here? He should be here. But that's questioning God, right? "God don't make mistakes" is what I've heard all my life. I just hate the fact that my son is not with me. I think about all the things he will miss out on. Like being a husband a father, traveling, and just enjoying life in general. But who's to say that he did not have a full life? He did so many things and had many life experiences before he died.

Wow, our first birthday celebration and the guest of honor is not present. It was the strangest feeling. It was even stranger realizing that he will never be here again – no matter what we do. How do I deal with that? I think keeping his spirit alive has helped me tremendously. Talking about him and keeping his pictures out and handy, makes me feel better (sometimes). Everyone grieves in different ways. So, we all have to find those ways and do the things that work best for us individually. And that's exactly what I do. I do the things that work best for me. I can't help, nor do I care about, what others think. It's essential to me to work it out...sometimes day-to-day...other times minute-to-minute!

"Happy 23rd Birthday Kourtney", July 2007

During the course of the police investigation, I stayed abreast of the progress that was being made by them and kept close contact with the officers involved. I wanted to help. I did television and newspaper interviews. I wanted this guy – this murdering fugitive- caught, and I wanted to contribute to his apprehension in any way that I could. I remember one night when the police were chasing him. My phone starts ringing off the hook. People calling to say that he was spotted in the area and that the police were on him. Jazmyn and I jumped in my car and drove right out to the neighborhood. And believe me when I say that I was prepared to run his ass down and over myself had I seen him! Although many of us and the police were out combing the neighborhood, he was not caught that night. Little did I know that the day was soon approaching when I would get that call from the police saying "We got him!" I never felt discouraged about the work of the police. I felt anxious because he had been evading them, partly because he had help from others to stay hidden. Personally, I think that's real low down. I understand that some of the people that were hiding him were, suppose to be very religious, God-fearing people. So, I'll rename them: fake ass hypocrites that go to church. Better yet, "thieves in the temple!" You can sing and dance in church all you want. But when you help up hold evil and encourage wrong-doing, God will not reward you. On the other hand, when you do what's right, even in the face of wrong-doing and evil, that's when God promotes you. God says that vengeance is His. So, my decision was to let God handle this and let the police do their job. I did not want anyone trying to get back at these people or involve people that did not pull the trigger. I wanted the trigger guy. He's the one responsible, and that's why he was on the run. Obviously, he was not running far, which I'm sure due to the fact that he had no money. Things got very interesting, too. Information started coming in from surprising sources. Turns out, my son was well liked by some unlikely associates - more than anyone knew. The sources were associates of the murderer. They felt that what he had done to my son was really wrong, and that this freak was "just on some hater-type bullshit." Wow, this is coming from his friends. But, you know, the truth is the truth. Sometimes you take the side of what's right. That's being an individual. That's also being a leader, not a follower. So, some reward money was offered and his ass got caught! Let's get back to the journal.

Tuesday, July 23, 2007, 11:11pm

Well, the past couple days have been rough. But what's new, huh? Most times, I just don't know how or what to feel. Most times I just want to scream. I miss Kourtney more and more. I heard on the radio today a song by Teddy Pendergrass: *Love TKO*. It's an old school jam, but Kourtney liked it. I had just asked him for a sign, to let me know that he was around when the song came on. I think he knows his passing is hard on us; yet maybe he is doing all he can to help us out.

And I know God is doing all He can, too. Question is: Am I doing all I can? As I told Kourtney earlier this year: "If you take one step towards God, He will take two steps towards you!" I believe my son did just that. I can't help but feel sad for Kourtney, the tragic way he left, and it's been eating at me for days now. Typically, yes, I'm sad. But I find a light and hang on to that. In past several days, however, there has been NO LIGHT. It's been all dark, and I cannot find an outlet. I go back to counseling tomorrow. I considered not going because I just don't want to talk about Kourt in a therapeutic manner, or I'm just too scared to proceed that way. It's hard to talk about him sometimes, you know. Also, I have to change the subject when talking with others sometimes. I'm Kourtney's mother, and it's just too hard for me at any given time. People coming to me with gossip-type shit. Man, I don't want to hear it.... It gets on my nerves! This and that about the case, what someone has said about Kourtney, or just about anything surrounding the investigation. I'm his mother! Is anyone listening? Does anyone care? Spoke with the detective this evening. He called to let me know what's going on, a basic update. Not sure how this lowlife punk continues to evade the police. The U. S. Marshal's Service, the Michigan State Police, the Detroit Fugitive Squad.... With all these agencies involved, I just don't understand why it's so hard to catch him. This is very frustrating. They now have enough evidence for an arrest warrant; it will be signed tomorrow by the Wayne County Prosecutor's Office. They also have been given the authority to proceed with force to take the murderer down – and I hope they shoot to kill his black ass, too! Kourtney was too nice of a guy; he no where near deserved this. I'm outraged! I'm about ready to hire a bounty hunter to catch this fool. I was contacted today by a guy who says he can put together a team that will hunt him down and catch him. I declined. Let the police agencies handle this. They are on it. They will get him. The police tell me they feel this creepy snake is running out of time and his chances are better than ever for getting caught. I try to be patient, but it's so difficult. I can hardly sit still. I missed work today. The day started off very stressful. Kourtney remains a constant in my thoughts, no matter what I do. I think the longest I can go without thinking about him is about 5 seconds – or less. I miss you Kourtney.... I want to talk to you, 1st Born. Please come see me in my dreams tonight so we can talk about *anything*. Don't have to be about the tragedy, okay? Well, I hear Jaz pulling up. So, I'll talk to her for a minute and then get ready for bed. I am going into the office tomorrow. I can only pray for an arrest overnight. I await for that phone call 24/7 now.

Wednesday, July 25, 2007, 11:16pm

Today, better physically and emotionally. But I know the "bad days" will return, and that's okay because I do understand that is the process. I thought about Kourtney a lot today, but I thought about him in a different way. In a way, the thoughts did not stress me out; things did not feel so bad. I attended a therapy session today; I showed her (the therapist) the scrapbook. That scrapbook was a true labor of love. But, hey, *anything* for my 1st Born! I have to show him off. The detective called to let me know that the "Murder in the first degree" arrest warrant is official! Man, I hope we get good news overnight. Good news being that they arrested or killed that lowdown bastard.

I miss Kourtney, though. Life is just weird and, all so suddenly, a change is forced upon me. I try to resist, but I cannot. It's so unfair. I feel guilty sometimes... like I let Kourtney go too fast. Meaning, perhaps, I let him grow up too soon. He got on the wrong path. He wanted that quick money. But he had other dreams, too. Yet he was caught up in the street life. What I know is this, though: I tried to work with him, tried to talk to him...right up to his passing. I was so worried about him. I prayed for him all the time. As loving parents do, I was always hoping for the best for him. I know he had plans and desires to do things for his future, such as owning a heating and cooling business. Unfortunately, time ran out for 1st Born. What I saw in Kourtney was a frustrated and sometimes hurt young man. He carried a burden, always trying to help others and never complaining, really. Never asking anyone for anything, nor expecting anything...like a father. He was always giving, always trying to give his friends advice about family and raising their kids. This was a burden he needed to carry for himself, to fulfill something deep inside of him. The foundation of his character was clear. What I saw is others depending on him, and him trying to help in some way. He was always trying to help others but could not help himself in the end. I feel bad for him, being a young person taking on so much. Frustrated with life, he was always trying to find the meaning of life and the answers that would propel his life forward in a positive way. Becoming a man and standing on his own was of great importance to Kourtney. Robbing and stealing? NO!! Disrespecting women—no way! But selling drugs? Yeah, he did that. He kept saying, "Just a little more money, Mama, and I'll have enough to stop and get my business going"..."buy a house "...or something.

He came across like an old man when he talked, but my son was *so young*. He seemed advanced for his years. To me, he resembled a man who had lived a much longer life. He did not talk much, but, when he did, he usually had something insightful to say. He wanted to engage in deeper conversation, not just make a bunch of dumb-ass or stupid statements. He had low tolerance for certain things. He liked to watch the local and world news. He was more current on world events than me. Plenty of times, he would ask me what I thought about something that happened and I would have no idea what he was talking about. I say "good for him." Some young Black men didn't possess those qualities nor cared about what was going on in the world or their community. I miss Kourtney. He should be here. That's been today's theme: He should be here. The harsh reality, though, he *is no*t here. I have all the pictures and mental notes which make me proud of Kourtney. He was not with us as long as we thought he might have been, but it's about what he did with his years he was with us. He impacted others in a positive way – I heard all the stories. Someone hated Kourtney for what he represented – and his character. Yeah, he was a street guy and not making good choices in every way. But, still, there was something very unique about him and the way he carried himself. He was reserved. He'd rather observe than run his mouth. He'd rather not be noticed. I think he knew the loudest person in the room is the most insecure person, the one who has something to prove to everyone else and can't even prove it to themselves. Kourtney did not need that. He knew exactly what he was about, both in heart and character. (The term "heart" is not used in terms of street life bravado. It was deeper meaning than that for him.)

Someone hated Kourtney for who he was - simple as that. That's so sad. Now this individual has made his own life worse! I'm certain he will come to realize that. It may be 10 or 20 years from now, but he will know that he made a horrific mistake. I think he knows that *now*. He's on the run. There is no kind of peace in that day-to-day surviving (not living). He is running low on resources, and folks are tired of supporting this cold-blooded murderer. That's what we are hearing on the streets. They don't want their doors busted down and homes torn apart because of his wrong-doing. So, it's just a matter of time before either the streets give him up or the police catch him. Either way – I REPEAT, EITHER WAY – his life is over as he knew it. It will never be the same. And, even after this is all said and done, he must pay in terms of "Divine Justice". He can spend the next 40 years in prison, repent, be born again – and anything else holy he thinks will help him. Although God forgives, you will still pay for what you did! He will pay for what he did to MY FIRST BORN – MR. KOURTNEY E. DUFFIE – on June 11, 2007!!! And that's that! He will see the error of his ways. I know Divine Justice is coming his way, and that in itself is comforting to me. But a more immediate concern for me is that I want to know that he has been apprehended or killed in the process of his arrest. This sick individual has made it known that he is willing to take out a police officer when they come after him. So, he should be prepared to take a few bullets – and I hope they shoot to kill his ass! So, every night I pray for the safety of the Fugitive Teams as the go out and hunt down this bottom-dwelling animal!

Thursday, July 26, 8:02am

I'm headed out to work, but there is this deep physical pain in my chest because I just miss my son—simple as that! I can't believe he is not here. Is there anywhere in the world he could be? No, not when his ashes are in my dining room. However, I keep wondering where he might be, despite knowing the truth? Reality check.... He is dead!! Let's see.... He was not sick, or even in a car accident. So, how is it he is dead? I am in deep anguish, coupled with depression, grief, heartbreak, confusion, and miserable frustration. I hate the person who did this. I will feel better when he is dead, and I hope that's sooner than later.

4:55pm

Right now, I'm upset with Kourtney. Did he not take seriously his actions when agreeing to testify for Terrence at his trial? I hope he was not going to be lying for T. I find it hard to believe that he would put his life on the line like this. Did he even think about me or his family? I don't know.... Kourtney loved them and they loved him. They had been friends since they were little boys. Maybe they would have done the same thing for Kourtney. Kourtney loved them to his death! This is very upsetting to me. Jaz said to me earlier today that I need to realize that Kourtney was fully aware of what he was doing. It's just hard to accept this. I've been talking to Kourtney and asking him to explain himself to me! He has to!!! I wish I knew everything there is to know. All I can do is pray for my own sanity at this point.

5:22pm

The detective just called to tell me they have passed out flyers with the full name of the murderer (LRJ) – Oh, that's the initials of my son's murderer. They are planning a TV press conference. He will also be profiled on America's Most Wanted as well as on all the local news channels. So, I continue to pray for an arrest anytime now.

Saturday, July 28, 12:53pm

Oh my, Kourtney and I were on the news last night. Since we now have an arrest warrant, I gave an interview with the press. The interview went well, and I feel like I'm helping. I feel so empowered now. My youngest son, John John, or "3rd Born," asked me if I was scared. I was, like, "NO!" Kourtney was right there with me. He wanted me to do that. Now there is a $5,000 reward for information leading to the arrest of this animal. I do expect that one of the murderer's so-called "friends" will be giving him up! If I were him, I would not trust anyone right now. Oh, I'm glad he is scared and paranoid! Believe me, someone wants that money, and the fact that the tip can be called in anonymously will make it even more inviting to the tipster. It's so fuckin' over! Many people called me to say the interview was powerful and presented well. I'm just waiting on that call to say we got him! Dead or alive – don't matter much to me! John John said the interview was beautiful, and that he is proud of me. Hey, I'm still and always a mother to my end!

2:29pm

I just got done talking with one of my neighbors. We were talking about how handsome Kourtney is! Even during the days of his funeral, he was so handsome. He looked like a doll. That's all I kept saying during the funeral. I was kissing on him, rubbing his curly hair, and saying how beautiful he is. I said to myself, "How absolutely beautiful you are!" His hair was so soft and curly, just the way *I liked it*. He had not gotten the haircut he intended to get. Sometimes, I do wish that he had a kid of his own. But then I say "No!" That would be more heartbreak. That kid would never know what a wonderful father they missed out on. So, NO THANK YOU. I'm glad he did not have any kids. Just a passing thought. Death is no longer scary to me. I tell him that most nights that when I die, he better come get me. That will be a happy day!

Sunday, July 29, 2007 11:11pm

OK, the police local and State have chased the murderer and even blocked off some streets. I'm going back to the neighborhood and if I see his ass he will be ran over. He's certainly crazy *and* mistaken if he think I won't do it!

Monday, July 30, 2007, 6:59am

Woke up today and prepared for work. Ummm, I feel alright I guess. Been praying and talking to Kourt...as usual. My bottom line feeling this morning is that Kourtney was good to a fault. He wanted to help others so much that it was he who got hurt in the end. He was a true friend to the end. I believe that Kourtney was very unconcerned about that nigga. I think that bothered him (my son's killer). So, any reason in his mind to justify killing Kourtney would do. Poor Kourtney...putting his life on the line this way. I don't know if he fully thought it out. I know him, and there is no way he would have ever wanted me involved in this kind of mess. He just wanted to help his friend. It's not his fault. He just wanted to help.... Oh well.

Tuesday, July 31, 2007, 7:34am

Well, they chased him again yesterday afternoon. So we thought -- turned out to be a look alike. The SWAT team and several police officers were there, not to mention a large crowd had assembled. A news helicopter was circling the area, a couple other news cameras were on the ground, and undercover police officers blended in with the crowd. I did another TV interview on the spot. The lead detective asked me not to go near any more chase/arrest scenes - just to be safe. Today, I feel okay far as emotions go, but I'm anxious and hopeful – always. We stayed over my mom's for a long time. All of us sat on the porch and had some drinks and talked and cried about Kourtney. This is so hard and unfair, but it's my life now. I hate my life.

12:35pm

I came home from work early today. I don't feel well. Emotionally, I'm down and it's hard to focus. I'm headed to the park; I just want to be near some water. I plan to take some of Kourt's ashes with me to spread around. I decided on Lake Erie Metro Park. They have a wave pool. When my kids were younger, I used to take them there all the time. When I got there today, I saw some kids splashing around in the water. The sight immediately took me back to hot summer days and Kourtney swimming at this park. It's been a hard day. I need someone to talk to. Everyone is busy. And I do understand that others have their lives. But, still, I feel alone. I'm doing all I can to stay positive, but I hate my life. Opened my mail.... Got a big bill from the car rental company for $8, 620!!! And they sent me them fucked up pictures of the car that had Kourtney died in, showing the bullet holes and blood. I can't believe them! How insensitive. This has not helped my day. I cannot afford this. I hope the Violent Crimes Compensation Fund will allow me to add this to my claim. I have no money for this, and I have no insurance. I find that I keep getting mad at Kourtney, but I know he never intended to leave any kind of burden on me. I know it's not his fault. He was the best friend to the end, putting the lives of others before his own. Well, that's just who he was. Always thinking of others and placing his welfare next or even last sometimes. He paid the ultimate price for it, too. Gone too soon....

4:08pm

Just came home from the park. Trying to regroup and find some peace. But there is no peace for me. I just don't know. I tried to read this book that I had bought earlier this month. I can only get through two or three pages at a time. I just can't focus or concentrate. I mean, my surroundings were pretty and calm; the lake was pretty relaxing, but I can't get my mind together now. As I looked around, I noticed something awfully familiar to me. It was the scene from my dream. You know the dream I had about Kourtney a few nights before he was killed. The tall trees are very green, and there was bold green grass. It was exactly like my dream! I walked to that area and took pictures with my camera phone. I had to leave. It was way too much for me to see this in a "real-like" state. I cannot handle this. My therapist says it's "wishful thinking" on my part to feel like I could have saved Kourtney had I told him about the dream. I did talk to Kourtney at the park. I talked to him about me being mad at him and stuff like that. But, again, I knew that he would never ever do anything to bring hurt, harm, or burden to his family. That's just not the kind of guy he was, not even close.... I realize that I must figure out how to handle things that have come to me as a result of his death. At this point, I'm not doing that good of a job. I received a letter from The Wayne County Prosecutor's Office. The letter listed the formal charges, condolences, information about my victim's rights advocate, and how to contact her and what her role will be during this process once there is an arrest. Also, it touched on the victim's impact statement. Yes, I will be making a statement – better believe that!!! Actually, I hope they kill him. Then we don't even have to go to trial. Maybe all the pressure will get to him and he will just kill himself – since he likes guns so much. The reward money has been increased. Hopefully someone will call in! What kind of person murders and run and hide? Must be a chaotic and hopeless existence. In my opinion there are some things worse than being dead. One example is going to prison for the rest of your life and having sex with men when you're not gay!

At this point, I'm tired and exhausted. There is much going on in my life. I'm looking for normalcy, but my brain doesn't know anything about what is "normal" any more. I don't fully understand that I'm changing. *My life will never be the same.* Furthermore, if I admitted that around the time of my son's death, I would have had no idea of the changes I would encounter during this process. With all the police chases, TV interviews, the waiting, wondering, and crying, I knew deep down that justice was coming for Kourtney. That's the only thing that made sense to me. The so-called *reason* or *justification* for killing him seemed so bizarre to me....

Fast forward to courtroom activity - one of the lead Michigan State Police troopers came and talked to me during the trial. We were waiting on the jury verdict; they had been in second day of deliberations. That morning, the officer approached me and said, "I just wanted to let you know that your son was a good guy." He talked about the fact that they had interviewed literally "hundreds of people" yet they could not find one person that had anything negative to say about Kourtney. He said that made them look even harder at Kourtney. "In our line of work," he noted, "you don't find a murder like what happened to Kourtney and the victim didn't do *something.*" Thus, when they just could not find anything on Kourtney, they became more determined to bring the murderer to justice. We were all nervous and hoped for the best, of course. Most people thought he would receive the 20-year or second degree murder life sentence, which would have made him eligible for parole. Some believed that even with the video and four eyewitnesses, it was possible that the jury would not convict on the first degree premeditated murder charge, which would confine him to prison for the rest of his natural life. It can be hard to convince a jury that someone thought it out. So, the lead investigators, as well as my victims' rights advocate, were preparing me for that possibility, the possibility that my son's murderer might be released one day. But I kept saying to myself, "We will get the murder in the first and he will NEVER come home – EVER! I want his life, a natural life sentence without the possibility of parole.

We were in court less than one hour when the prosecutor came to get me in the hallway, and with a serious tone, stated, "They have a verdict!" Many of my family and friends were there. When the prosecutor came out to tell me, my girlfriend and I were looking through a magazine and talking. There were others there for the murderer who heard this as well. I started shaking. "This is it," I said to myself. We gathered up our things, but the judge did not allow everyone into the courtroom. Due to previous fights and other conflicts that arose when we attended the district court in River Rouge, the trial judge in circuit court was not having it! So, some people, of course, waited in the

hallway. In the courtroom with me were Jaz, my sister Angie, Toya, and my cousins Lennie and Eric. I started to cry. I looked at Jaz; she had her head down. Eric and Lennie were steady and kept their heads up. I could not see my sister that well. My legs were literally jumping by themselves. I could not stop shaking. They called several deputies into the courtroom. They realized that there was a lot of tension between the families, and that the scene had the potential to explode either way, from either family. It was scary. Then I heard, "Please rise for the jury." They came in. I know from TV to try and look at them, to see if they will make eye contact with me; that way, I will know their decision. But a large monitor was in my way, so I could not see them or even maintain eye contact with them. After they sat down, we sat down. I swear, I'm going to jump out my skin.... "Is this not the day," I ask to myself over and over.... "Is this not the day I've been waiting for?" It is.... The jury foreperson begins to read their verdict. Now, I'm bouncing up and down to the point that my butt comes up off the seat! I'm only thinking of Kourtney – I have his bashful smile right in front me. "This *is* justice," I say to my first born over and over. Then they say it - they say he is "Guilty"!!! And he is not only guilty of murder, he is guilty of murder in the first degree!!! He's not ever going home! YES!!! I'm crying so much. I nearly loose control of myself. A female deputy comes over to us. She nicely says and gestures to us keep as quiet as we can because there is more information to be related in the courtroom. I'm trying... I'm trying... I try to restrain myself, but I am so overwhelmed. It's more powerful when each juror is polled, when each one stands and says that this is their decision. With each "Yes," we cry harder. Some of the jurors are crying, too. I touch the small urn around my neck. It contains his ashes.... This is the best (and only) way to get Kourtney in this courtroom, yet HE IS HERE! He is here.... I heard someone crying from the other side. While it wasn't all of them, the family of my son's killer had been acting up with us since the first court day in August of 2007 – as if we had done something to *them*. However, all of their time and energy should have been focused on him. It was a sad thing to witness. He was defeated. Finally, he knew it. There was nothing that could be done for him. He knew it, and his family knew it. It was completely over for him. Just like for Kourtney.... I could not help him. Now it's their turn... they can't help him. When court was over, my family and friends hugged one another other and cried. His family left out immediately. I hugged and thanked the prosecutor; that made *her* cry. This was her first case! She worked so hard. The lead detective was there; I hugged him as well. The state trooper came over to me; he looked to have tears in *his* eyes; I also hugged him. It was so emotional. We left the courtroom with the victory! Feeling hurt all over again for Kourtney, but knowing that, hey, we got the best we could get under such horrible circumstances.

Everyone went to my house and we celebrated all day long! Even the police officers came over. It was great. I sent out text messages, providing my usual email update to friends and family outside the state. Wow!!! February 21, 2008 – that was a good day! "Kourtney, you are so free now!!!" I say that all day long! Just writing about that day broke me down to tears. While it brought it all back, it's all good! Another good day was March 12, 2008, when I got to confront this murderer! We will get to that later, though. In the meantime, let's get back to the journal....

Tuesday, July 31, 2007, 9:14pm

To say the least, it's tough. I'm having disagreements with people, and it feels sort of like certain people don't give a damn about me. So, I say fuck them, too! I try to forget about certain people who obviously are not my friends, anyway. Further, I'm going to visit some old friends, and I need to gather up all of Kourtney's pictures. We have not seen each other since Kourtney was like 5-years-old. We lost touch. Lisa used to often baby sit for Kourtney, I named her one of his Godmothers. She found out what happened to him when she caught a news broadcast about the incident. She located my mother's number. That's how we reconnected. I first met her back in the day, when Kourt was a baby and I dated her brother, who was a male exotic dancer. They fell in love with Kourtney...their whole family. He was a very fat, and adorable baby.

Wednesday, August 1, 2007, 9:36pm

The visit with the Lucas family went really good. No surprise we were all emotional. I told them all about Kourtney, about the years they had missed. I stayed a long time. Sorry to see the Mrs. Lucas' health is failing. She used to pick Kourtney up all the time and keep him for the weekend. She called him "my baby". On the way home, I stopped in the hood and visited with my sister Kim. She bought me a butterfly for my yard. We have a thing about butterflies now. They seem to get very aggressive with us. So, you know what I think? Yep, it's Kourtney! Also made a stop at Honey's house. Honey is the nickname we have for my mother. The lead detective ended up coming over as well; he talked to us for a while. He gave us some "Wanted" handouts, and there is an article about the incident in today's newspaper. My spirits are good, but I'm always missing 1st Born. I had a good talk with him today; I felt better afterwards. But, that weird pain always returns in my heart and chest area, the area when he was fatally wounded. It's just that deep hurt in me. I wonder is this the brief pain Kourtney felt before he died? With me, it hurts so deep that it has become physical pain! Amazing when you love someone, huh? Indeed. Yesterday, I thought of a title for a book: *What's Wrong with Dying?* My dad and I talked about the fact he likes the way I write and my ability to communicate on paper. So, I'm thinking of including some of my journal notes as part of the book. Maybe I'll write a book of my journey and the healing process? I wonder....

I decided not to attend my counseling session this week. I just didn't feel like going. I feel that I am my best counselor...me and my journal. And since I already understand that I will go through waves of emotions, then that's okay. I can get through this without the close monitoring of a therapist. Since I know to expect these waves, these ups and downs, I can be better prepared to recognize the changing of moods. The mood swings are like from sad to mad to okay to depressed. I just ride the wave, opting out on medication. I spoke with Kourt's best friend Ed. He sounds a little better. He has been so sad. We gave him Kourtney's dog, Ruby. Ed has Ruby's brother. Well, I continue to pray for an arrest and the safety of all the officers involved. I think I'm going to turn in early. It's been a long day, and I'm tired. I love you, Kourtney – but you know that....

Thursday, August 2, 2007, 6:53am

More often than not, when you see a person, you have no idea it will be the last time you will see that person, or it will be the last time he/she will see you. Wow.... It makes me think about June 10, 2007, the last time I saw Kourt - alive. I was trying to get out of the house with the cake from Jazmyn's birthday dinner. Ms. Jazmyn had requested that I bring her cake home. But people starting bugging me about the cake, mostly Kourtney. I just turned around and went back in the house with it. Life can be really strange. Jaz never got any of her birthday cake – but Kourt did. The cake never made it from Honey's house. Sadly, at Kourt's birthday gathering the following month, Kourtney never got any of *his* cake – but Jaz did. Ummm.... When I woke up this morning, I heard the distinct voice of Stevie Wonder. I sleep with the TV on most nights. I'm always waiting to see Kourtney. This way, I can still have a room with some light while I get some sleep – or try to, anyway. Nevertheless, I hear this song called *Stay Gold*, which is part of the soundtrack to the movie *The Outsiders*. The song was touching and made me miss him so much that I had to turn it off. That's how you handle this kind of grief: through AVOIDANCE! If something becomes too much... AVOID IT!! Change the subject, or be direct and say you can't talk about right now. I do what I have to do to ensure that I get through the next minute, hour, and day. Everyone doesn't understand that. It is only the people in THE CLUB, that special club that no one wants to join, understand this. I have brothers and sisters all around the world now. We are connected through a horrible tragedy: to our son or daughter. That's how you get in the club: you are forced in. But we're there for each other. We seek each other out, especially our new members. We know all too well the first weeks and early months can be especially difficult. I have to go back to Kinkos. More requests for his obituary. I don't mind because that just shows me how much he is loved. That makes me feel good and warms my soul. It firms my resolve to ensure that he's not forgotten.

Damn, I think about the last time Kourtney seen me! The last time I saw him, we weren't looking back at each other. It had been years since I had bought a suit for him. My dad and I were in the men's suit department, shopping for my son's funeral clothes. I was distraught during that shopping trip, but I had to do it.... I was the only one who could it. So, there I am, crying and trying to guess what size he wears in a suit and shirt. My dad and I were pondering different looks. Someone said to me that a popular thing for young guys were to dress them in their every day clothes. I considered that, but then changed my mind. I wanted to see him in a suit. I knew he would be handsome...all grown up now. I was having it my way. My dad chose a classy brown suit and tie and shirt hookup. But I knew better. Kourtney was low key and did not like to be noticed. All black would be the color for him. So, in the end, there it was: His attire would be triple black, and his tie must be in the "Windsor knot". It's a trendy fashion statement. I demanded that the funeral home dressers get it right.

I remember when they called from the funeral home and said "Mr. Kourtney Duffie is dressed"! I leaped from my bed (once again I had been trying to get any kind of rest as I had been up for 2 ½ days, no sleep/same clothes); like I had springs on my legs, I bounced out of bed, called my friend Maria, and hit the shower. I was dressed so fast. I was anxious; I wanted to see him. When I entered the funeral home, it occurred to me that he may not look like himself. How many times have I seen someone in that state and they looked totally different? Oh shit! My heart is pounding now. They had him in a room on the second floor. I'm getting so dizzy that I grab the handrail. I see him. I go over to him and start to cry. There were two men in the room with me and Maria. One did Kourtney's make up; the other dressed him. One of them said to me, "it's only a shell". I'm sure they could see me begin to hyperventilate. Kourtney's lips are really stretched and his cheeks are swollen. Why? I almost lie in the casket with him. Then I see it...."Fix the tie, please!" I turn around, stand straight up, and look at them with a mean glare. "I told you guys make sure his tie is the Windsor knot!" I admonish. "And what's wrong with his neck?" I ask them. "Why does he look like that?" Maria walks closer to me because I'm about to got from zero to 60 in 2 seconds! I hated the way his lips looked. Sure he had fat lips, but they had pulled them. His lips had also become stiff from those chemicals. But nothing could be changed at that point. He was hard as a wall of steel and cold as ice. Yet, the more I looked at him, the better he looked. I kissed him so much. His hair, goatee and beard were cut with precision. Of course I took pictures. A few of us posed in the pictures with Kourtney. My feeling was that this is part of his life too...at the end, but, nonetheless, a part of his life. My friend Yolanda's mother is a master barber and prefers to work on the deceased. As a gift to me, she did the work free of charge. She made Kourtney look so good. She washed and conditioned his hair. His hair was so soft...like cotton. Kourtney had really

nice hair. It would get curly if he did not get a hair cut. Two days before he was killed, I asked him when he was getting his hair cut and beard trimmed. He was like, "I'm going to take care of it, Mama." But he didn't.... I thought about that when looking at him at the hospital. A slight smile came across my face when it became apparent to me that he did not get his hair cut; now I could do what I wanted. I used to beg Kourt not to get all his curls cut, but he would do it every time. For a deceased guy, he sure looked good. I think we kissed him and rubbed him so much that by the final day of services, he looked exactly like himself. We had kissed and rubbed all of the makeup off of him! I will never forget the smell when being close to him. That brings to mind me preparing for my big birthday party on November 1, 2008, and I wanted to look my absolute best. I decided to let MAC do my make up. I went in for a trial make up session. As she applied the foundation, I could smell that now - familiar smell. It was how Kourtney smelled. It was all those chemicals and formaldehyde in him. At the make-up counter that day, it does not help that someone walks up to me to express their condolences.... Now I'm crying! Damn! When a death occurs, there is not much time to plan. I think back so much now about what I could have done better, chastising myself on why didn't I remember to do this, that, or the other. At the end of the day, though, Kourtney looked good and had three beautiful days of service, with a very unique obituary. He was cremated, and I brought him home with me. I also had to work on letting some things go that had happened; that were truly not of any significance. For example, such things as what I could have included in the service or songs I could have played or changes on the obituary. It's seems so stupid to me, but, back then, I used to get upset over the smallest details while still focusing on his death. Maybe that was my brains way of protecting me from having the nervous breakdown I seemed to be gearing up for.

My ways out (of the insanity) have always been praying, journaling, and talking out loud to Kourtney. Another way of coping has proved to be unusual. Whatever this psychological phenomenon is called, with me at this very moment, it's in full effect. It's like my brain splits into two, with one half constantly asking questions about Kourtney and the other half always reasoning and answering. The half that constantly questions is the half that is most difficult to deal with, particularly if it's not checked by the other half. It is then that the WHOLE ME goes off the fuckin' edge! So, in my mind there is this constant back and forth. It's like there is the half that keeps asking "So where is Kourtney?" and the other half responding "You know where...." As the moderator, I'm like, "Come on other half – keep it together!" Then the reasoning half states, "You know you had a funeral service – and don't forget you have the urn in the dining room to prove it!" It continues, "If you called him, will he answer – if he is still around?" I accept the side of reason for a little while. What is this madness? This ongoing,

bugging me. Makes me frown when I don't even realize that I'm wearing a frown on my face! Oh, I forgot – Kourtney *is* dead. He was murdered, I reason yet again within myself. Did you say murdered? Now the other half of my brain kicks in. Yep, the two sides of my brain are communicating. One side of my brain asks, "How could you forget?" I just do. I do – and I don't – at the same time. That's how it goes. It makes sense...then again, it doesn't. It's real...then it isn't. On any given day, I live this life that I call "Organized Chaos". I have learned how to function in the midst of my new life, too. There are only a few choices when you live life on the edge. One is easy: suicide! Yeah, I have thought of it many times – too many times. But, then, where does that leave Jaz and John John and the rest of my family? Further, I take too huge of a chance not seeing Kourtney again. Two, I must accept this new life. Yeah, yeah, yeah...it's being forced on me. I hate this new life most of the times. I want my old life back. Kourtney exists in my old life. I want Kourtney back. But what's my answer? What's the question? Am I going to get busy living or get busy dying? Which is it? (BIG SMILE) Well, I'm writing this book, and I'm alive!!! (Duh, right!) Journal time....

Thursday, August 2, 2007, 3:36pm continues

Just got in from work and having manicure/pedicure. I've been praying all day, even as I was driving home. Always thinking about Kourtney and talking about him to anyone that will listen. I just miss him. Sometimes I wonder if I get on folk's nerves. I hope not, because I cannot help it. Kourtney is deeply loved and is MISSING! It must be horrible on another level for parents of missing children: the *not* knowing. That's how I feel right about now, like he is missing. I really don't know where he is. Even with spreading his ashes all over the city, and even the places I've traveled. Still, that does not always answer the question, and it does not ease my mind on his whereabouts. It seems like he vanished...and disappeared. Will I ever stop looking for him?

10:15pm

I walk into my house and there are Kourtney's shoes and clothes. I keep three pair of his shoes at the front door in the foyer. I kept a lot of his clothes. Some are in the house; some are in the garage. All of the funeral flowers are still in the garage. I can't throw them out right now, maybe never. Jaz hates going to the garage. She says Kourtney's funeral is going on still. We laugh a little, but I know it's somewhat strange. I moved most things from Kourt's apartment to my house. I sent his futon over to Honey's house. I look at his things all the time. I don't want to see them, but I know they are there. I was just outside and asked myself, "Why are Kourtney's clothes here when he never lived here?" (I just purchased a new house about seven months before he was killed.) And here we go...I have to reason with myself. Damn, for real, he was killed, I think to myself. Indeed.

Friday, August 3, 2007, 5:26pm

Today has been long and I'm like "Whatever." I walked out of my office talking to Kourtney. I bought this heart-shaped necklace/urn in white gold. I got it engraved too. I have to pour a small portion of his remains inside of it. The manufacturer sends you the kit and instructions. One side reads "Kourtney"; the other side it reads "Always Loved 1984-2007." I like it a lot. I'm sure I'll like it much more once I get his ashes poured into it.

Saturday, August 4, 2007, 10:14am

Woke up today feeling more and more like Kourtney really is gone. He is dead. He is gone so far from me I cannot begin to imagine. I hate that word - dead. I try very hard not to use it. Most times, I say he has "passed" or "transitioned" or "he's deceased." Yeah, that feels better. I have to do and say what works for me, right? Sure I do. I made breakfast this morning for myself and thought about how I will never have to cook for him again. There are so many components to this whole thing, like the things he will miss out on and the things in which he will not be a part, such as too many life events and celebrations. I hate this...I really do. That must be nice when parent's become older and their kids come over for a visit and bring the grandkids. I won't ever share that with Kourtney. So unfair.... I do realize that when his young life dangled in the balance, it was God's choice to put an end to it. God wanted to take Kourtney home with Him. I believe that God is Almighty, and He could have spared Kourtney's life. What if he had? Maybe, just maybe, Kourtney would have been paralyzed! Imagine that. He would have been miserable. God knows best. I have tried not to question God or even be mad. Sometimes I am, though. Here is my affirmation for this day: "Do not put a question mark where God has put a period." Hello.... Need I say more? I don't think so. My plans today are to attend a jazz concert with some friends. It's an outdoor concert called "Jazz on the River at Elizabeth Park". I'm looking forward to it. It's really nice outside today. The concert has been going on for a couple of days. I'll head to the park around 5 or 6pm.

9:08pm

I attended the concert and am back home. It was nice. I cried on my drive back home just thinking about the current state of my life. What's new with me, huh? Shit, *my life* is new. I'm rejecting it like a body rejects an organ transplant. As if to say, "This ain't gonna work!" I'm trying to jump to Step #5 in the grief process. Step #5 is the "acceptance" phase. I want to accept this so that I can settle down and figure out my life. I just want so badly to feel better. Even if I could get a day off from the heartache that would be so helpful. But I'm fighting something bigger than me. I'm losing, too. No one knows this little fact. Everyone comments on how well I'm doing. Yeah, I've gotten pretty good at hiding behind a big smile with pink lip gloss! This is some sad shit, I swear it is. And why is it that I'm gaining weight? I'm stressed the hell out. Shouldn't I be *losing weight*? My body and mind are working against me. What's up with this? But, still, I'm functioning within this state of "organized chaos". I don't know how. Humbly, I do know...its God. He is showing me how to be a survivor. I just pray for the parent's around the world who have loss a son or daughter to homicide. Right now, I just worry that Kourtney will be forgotten. That scares me so much. I got to make sure he is not. I've been walking through the house tonight cutting my eye at his urn. Yeah, I know it's there, but I don't want to acknowledge it. Sometimes when I force myself to face his pictures or his urn, my breath is taken from me. I seriously lose my air and I struggle to breathe (it's like holding my breath) for a few seconds and my heart races. His things around the house just sit there. They never move unless I move them. He doesn't need these things anymore. So, they just sit there...day after day, collecting dust and spider webs until I finally see that I need to dust his things off. And the reason he doesn't need his things anymore is because DEAD people don't need earthly things. That punk-ass nigga who stole my son's life is out running around and making a mockery of this. But I know his ass will pay! He will pay, and – as my grandma Duffie would say – "I just pray day-in and day-out" that he is arrested soon. I could care less if he is killed in the process, just as long as he realizes that his life is now over, which can amount to either prison or the funeral home for him. Man, I'm so sick of this shit. He's on the run now. He's running because he guilty. The fact that he is wanted has been not only been in the local newspapers, but also on TV! When will this end? What if he is never caught? No justice for Kourtney? That can't be! Kourtney did not deserve this. God knows we're right. Yes, he knows our hearts. Kourtney had been reading the Bible and praying; he told me that. I told Kourtney that if he took one step towards God, God will take two towards him. I know this has to count for something in God's book. Please let me be correct. Please. Justice and Peace for my son. Well, I'm closing out for this day.

Sunday, August 5, 2007, 2:02am!!!

The murderer has been ARRESTED!!!!!! YES! I got the call about 11:30pm last night (8/4/07) from Detective "H". Jazmyn and I cried as we called, texted, and emailed our family and friends. It was so overwhelming...and bittersweet. My heart just feels so low because although this is a good thing – and I've been waiting for it – no matter what, this does not bring my son back. NOTHING will bring Kourtney back. All I have now are ashes, pictures, mental notes and memories. I've been on the phone with many people since I got off the phone with Detective "H". I just hung up with Kim. I feel like just driving to the police station and blowing my horn and screaming out "Kourtney!!!" Not sure if I can go back to sleep. We have company at the house now. We are having what you might call a "That ass got caught!" celebration with the Moet champagne. We did a toast for Kourt. All I could do was cry, but, hey, that's real.

Yeah, I'm told that *he* cried like a baby when they found him in the attic of that abandoned crack house. I visualize him sobbing and telling the police to get the guns out of his face because he is afraid of guns. Yeah, I guess so, punk-ass motherfucker. You might be dumb, but you do know that guns kill. So that's what he gets.... "How's it feel to have the gun pointed at you!" I say to myself. Man, fuck him. He had no problem waving one in my son's face. I bet his ass is thinking right now and realizes what a huge mistake he made. Now he will have the rest of his life to think about it - or don't think about it.... I could care less. He is caught, and I know he is never coming home. I got what I wanted for the most part. Yeah, I know we got to go through a trial, yet I'm feeling pretty optimistic. But this first hurdle has been crossed. Earlier this evening, I flashed back to the funeral to getting through all the ups and downs of the investigation to obtaining the proper arrest warrant, and finally, just a few hours ago to - CAPTURED!

Life is quite amazing and altering. I take nothing for granted now. I look at everything differently. It's almost 2:30am and we've been drinking and crying. I start to feel that unreal feeling again, as if I'm a bad dream.... It's a real bad dream, and I swear that I'm trying to wake up. Our phones won't stop ringing. As I sip this champagne, I think to myself, this could very well be Kourtney, hanging out at some club downtown, buying him a bottle, as he was known to do. I just noticed someone placed a glass of champagne next to his urn.... Thank you! I tell you, life just ain't right without Kourtney. But we have to deal with life as it comes....

All those weeks I had been waiting and praying for that moment: The phone call to report he has been arrested or killed. I believe that I expected something else, too, other than knowing the murderer was behind bars. I thought Kourtney would be back - as if by magic. Knowing full well I've never heard of anything like that before (smile), that's how desperate I had become. I really thought he could be brought back to life or that Kourtney's part in this nightmare was not over. This is why I say the celebration was "bittersweet". The bitter part hit me because I felt the void once again. And I clearly see that nothing changes for Kourtney. No matter what, since June 11, 2007, he is dead. Oh, my God! No, not dead. Yes, dead. I was so broke down trying to talk on the phone to people and received so many text messages coming through, I could not keep up. I was crying so hard that the tears not only flow from the corners of my eyes, my entire eyes shed tears. It was like a bucket of water dumped on my head and the water just crashed down. I guess my body was producing tears so rapidly, my tears felt like warm water washing down my face. As fast as I could wipe them away, even more are back to replace those tears. And my chin was wet and my shirt was soaked with tears. There was so much celebrating going on in my house that when it was time to talk to my dad, I had to go out side and sit in

my car. We talked for a long time. We knew what was next. The legal business: Going to court. All I can think is that we've never dealt with anything like this before. Not knowing what to expect gave me butterflies in my stomach. But, we would soon find out that going to court was not an easy thing to do; yet we must represent for Kourtney! We did just that! I found a scripture from the Bible late one night as I was reading out loud to Kourtney. It is Chapter 7 of Ecclesiastes. I just turned the page to it. It was like I was supposed to read this. It basically starts off by saying that a good name is better than good oil, and that the day of death better than the day of one's being born, and so on. Wow, how comforting and just a nice thing to read that was for me...and so relevant. Kourtney's name means "From the Court and Justice" (in part). Kourtney has a good name, and he was named appropriately, especially now when I factor in what happened to him. I knew then that we are getting a solid conviction and not some crappy one.... We are going to get a life for a life! Sure, from time to time, I would get nervous and worry about the possibility of losing the case. But I just continued to pray, stay focused, and be positive. I continued trying to enjoy my life and take care of myself, Jaz and John John, doing the normal daily activities as we awaited the start of court. We had our first court date in River Rouge, MI on August 10, 2007. I'll get more into that within the upcoming journal pages.... So, with that being said, let's get back to the journal.

Saturday, August 5, 2007, 2:57pm continued

Well, the TV news crew will be here to do a "captured" follow-up on the story. My cousin Lennie is over putting together the black marble table which will hold Kourt's urn, a nice picture of him, and other special items. I expect the reporter to be here by 4pm and story should air tonight on 6 O'clock news. Wow, Kourt's table looks nice.... Lennie just got done. I am pleased.

Kourtney's table and urn at home

9:55pm

The TV news interview and broadcast turned out good! I think I looked good. Not tired and worn down. If I just give in to how I feel most days, I bet I'd look pretty bad, as if I've aged 50 years. I really need to try and hold it together for all intents and purposes.

Monday, August 6, 2007 (no time documented)

Today has been an interesting day. First Born is always on my mind. However, today I'm not feeling so down when thoughts of him flood my mind. I did a telephone interview today with a local newspaper. I did some real venting and, hey, whatever he decides to print will be what he prints. Oh well. That murdering bastard is being held without bond. River Rouge took his ass downtown today. The first court date will be this Friday at 9am in the River Rouge courthouse. I expect a large crowd. Detective "H" feels it will be adjourned because his court appointed attorney will not have time to prepare. So, for now, he can sit his ass right there with no phone calls or visits. I hear someone has been trying to visit him, but they have denied visits. And that's good! Man, Kourtney has three phone numbers! I can call each one of them until I die and he will NEVER answer any of those phones—EVER AGAIN! So, exactly, deny his visits and phone privileges for as long as possible! Fuck that. What about Kourtney? Did he ever think about Kourtney? Hell no! So, I am Kourtney's voice now – and to hell with him! I just came from the mall, looking for something to wear to a wedding next month. Man, life just moves right on, huh? Yep. Soon as I walk in the house, I see Kourt's three pair of shoes in the foyer. I quickly adjust my eyes sharply to the left so that I can pretend they are not there. I get a strange sensation every now and again when I see his things, even his school book. There is one item that I don't see too often and rather not see: his Cartier eye-glasses. Even if those glasses are sitting on the counter – they look just like him. Jaz has his glasses now. And when she puts them on...I only see Kourtney. I tried them on one day, looked in the mirror, and still I see Kourtney. He had those glasses with him when he was killed. Yeah, and people were asking me about his glasses. You know, "Did you get them?" and "Do you want to sell them?" Those glasses would never be for sale. Sorry. I mean people were even asking me the night he was killed "Did you get his glasses?" Not long after I arrived at the hospital, a nurse informed me that a pair of glasses had been found on him. I bet he was wearing them. I was able to retrieve from the police the Cartier glasses; $330 in cash; his wallet, which, of course, held his driver's license; a condom (good thing, Kourt!); and some business cards and a few pictures. I have displayed all those things in his scrap book. I planned a gathering at my house today because my mother and a few other friends were not able to see the TV interviews. So, I invited about 15 people over to eat and watch the interviews. I also have a video of Kourtney that I'm afraid to watch. I don't know how I will respond to it. It was recorded earlier this year at my "Sweetheart House Warming" in February around Valentine's Day. This particular night, Mr. Kourtney decided he would try to get all up in my business and demand that everyone – including a male friend of mine – leave when HE felt it was late enough. He made himself so clear that my friend did leave. Kourtney was so embarrassing that night. I could not believe him. But that's how he was...very protective. He had his way of making you feel uncomfortable sometimes without many words – or with a few "right" words. He was a trip. He used to say to me that I'm "the only honest woman on earth." I just have to laugh at him (and that's a good thing when I can smile). Did he overstep his boundaries sometimes? Yes. But, you know, it was all out of L. O. V. E. - Love.

7:58pm

Wow...I got over the fear of watching the video of Kourtney. It made me happy to see him. He was talking, too. Wow! I watched another one when he was about 6 or 7 years-old. I held up well and could not stop smiling. See, there is more proof that he had a life.... He was alive before. Maybe not today–or any longer–*but he was here*. It's so good to see him moving around–in motion. Yeah, the still frame pictures are priceless, but I wish I had more movies of him. Speaking of still frame pictures, I found a roll of undeveloped film in his room. It's shocking because he usually did not like pictures. So, for a guy who would try to block pictures, I'm kind of hesitant to find out what's on the film. I don't know what to expect. I hope the pictures are decent.

Tuesday, August 7, 2007, 3:55pm

Gee, the mystery film is not developed yet! Now I've become that more intrigued. What's on this film? *Who* is on this film? I turned in a few other rolls of film that I took and they have been returned. I've been emailing pictures out to family and friends. These are pictures of Kourtney throughout his life. I have funeral pictures, too, but have never shared them with anyone. Wow, look at me, always at work for Kourtney...I really stay busy with things related to him.

5:00pm

Not sure why or how, but my stress level has gone up and I'm having crazy thoughts. Like I feel like giving up. I've started writing my victim's impact statement. Not sure when I'll be delivering it, but I just feel it's time to start putting my feelings on paper and get prepared. I often fantasize about that day and what I will say. I think, too, will I try to jump on his ass? Ummm. I want to say some things that I know Kourt would want to say to this lowlife. I want to come across very strong and make a powerful statement. I just keep praying that God will help me be articulate, that my passion comes out, and the love I have for Kourtney is reflected in every word I speak! I'm so sick of this mess already. We go to court on this Friday. Jesus.... I'm just tired. I'm so tired. How do I keep going? I just do.

Wednesday, August 8, 2007, 4:48am

This whole grief thing is so difficult! I miss Kourtney so much. It's so irritating to know that he is not around. No matter where I look, I will not find him. I get panic attacks and shortness of breath if I think about it too much. So, I try to catch myself before I go too far. I can sense when "too far" is upon me. It's scary. I hate this happened to him...and to me, too. John John just asked me if he could see the video of Kourtney. I let him and he cried so hard. I turned it right off! To John John, his big bro was untouchable and he looked up to him. John is only 13-years-old as of July 9th. All of us miss Kourtney; we are devastated. Kourtney meant a lot to us. He was a primary male figure in our family. He was young, strong, street smart, and family-oriented. He looked after his lil sister, Jaz, and lil bro, John John. It's hard for me to see about Jaz and John these days. I know they need me, too. I'm so fucked up, I can only focus on *my needs*. And, barely doing that! I don't know how to handle it all. I know they need attention, too. I'm trying, though. Yesterday, very quickly, my stress level skyrocketed, like someone set off a firecracker of inside me. The stress just came out of nowhere. I never know what's going to trigger a wave of emotions, nor do I know what emotion will manifest itself. I started having bad thoughts, though, like ending my own life. After all, I've tried to live a decent and quiet life...then my son is murdered! Why? Again, I don't mean to question God, but this is one of those days the spiritual side escapes me and I can barley hold on. How about this: No one really knows how serious or low I am. I'm in this struggle alone. My sleep pattern is unpredictable. Who knows when I'll get another good night's sleep. I hate the fact that there is absolutely NOTHING I can do to change the outcome of this! Nothing. Am I being punished, I wonder? My life has been so disappointing...for as long as I can remember. Sure, there have been some good times and good things in my life, but a lot of hurt has come my way. Maybe others feel like this, too. I don't know. Even if I deserve a sad life, Kourtney did not. He did not really get a chance to live. OK, here we go.... My spiritual side kicks in and requires me to believe that the 22.9 years he got was his life. God made the ultimate decision. Kourtney is actually God's son. Sometimes I just don't understand, and I don't feel like trying to understand this. I wish my grandma Duffie was here to talk to me. She loss a son, my uncle Chris, when he was 17-years-old. He was sick. Well, it's 5am. I hope that today, with the rise of the sun, my mood improves. I'm only working ½ day today; I'm not going to counseling; I just don't feel like it. But I do need to update my therapist on a few things; so I'll try to make it in.

12:19pm

Kourtney made the front page of a local newspaper. The reporter printed a lot of the derogatory comments I made, which is just fine with me! What the hell do I care about whose feelings I might hurt or whom I offend or, for that matter, who I might piss off! What the hell, I've been pissed on! That individual had no regard for Kourt's life and, obviously, his own life, either. So sad for him....

11:20pm

I'm ready for bed, and I hope that I dream about Kourtney tonight. I've had two dreams about him this week already. It's cool because that is how we visit now. So, this is how it's done? This is how I heal or move on? Moving on does not mean that we forget about our beloved. I say moving on and healing is what we do when we take care of ourselves and still honor and cherish the memories. I think it's normal to feel that he will be forgotten. You know, so young at the time of his death and not sure what impact he made on others. Is it enough to remain over the years to come? I know the love in my heart is. A mother's love is eternal....

Thursday, August 9, 2007, 1:31pm

I changed my counseling session to today instead of yesterday. I told my therapist my feelings about Kourtney and the type of young man he was. I said he was a loyal friend to the end. The way he put his life on the line for others proves that in my opinion. And now I get mad at Kourtney sometimes. Like, damn boy, did you even think about me or your brother or your sister? However, I did not tell my therapist about my thoughts of suicide. In all sincerity, I don't believe Kourtney thought things would get as bad as they did. Today is a PMS day for me. So, I'm going to try and chill and get ready for our first day in court. For the first time, I get to see the person the individual who took my son's life. I have an idea how he looks from pictures in the newspapers, but I've never seen him in person. Tomorrow is that day.

6:45pm

Okay, finally, the mystery film is ready. I had been upset, because I was informed that the film could not be located and somehow the film was lost. I went off on the clerk! I was like, "Look, my son was just killed and I must have this film! You better find it! *Somebody* better find it!" (Deep sigh) They called and told me that they had found it! I rushed right over to Meijer to pick it up, which is not far from my house. I nervously open the envelope. To my relief...they are all pictures of Kourtney and his friends! Whew.... Okay. And there are some good pictures, too. I really like them. Of the pictures, it's easy to see that he took one of himself. Funny. I'll post some of these up on his Myspace page. A big reason I moved earlier than

I expected was because Kourtney wanted me out of the "hood". I moved further away from everyone and closer to my job, which was good. But one thing that also changed is how often Kourt and I saw each other. We still talked on the phone every day, but it was not so convenient to visit daily like we used to do. I used to see Kourtney every day, unless I was out of town or something. Other than that, he always came over. Our in-person visits had gotten to be about once per week on average. In our old neighborhood, sometimes we would see each a few times a day and out and about see one another in passing. Many times he would catch up with me and pull me over or follow me home.

Here is a picture from that roll of film. Based on the position of his arm (not holding the money) he was holding the camera and snapped this picture of himself!

Friday, August 10, 2007, 6:21am

Okay, today is the court date...the examination...start time is 9am. I'm up early, making a light breakfast. I'm a little nervous, but I'm constantly praying. I guess I just don't know what to expect when I see this bastard. I packed Kourtney's picture and his Bible in my purse, ready to take them with me. My co-worker Beth gave me a prayer coin, and I've got that with me, too, in my purse. So, let's see how this goes...I'm being told it will be brief, suggesting that I don't come. I'm like, "No way." At this point, NO WAY! The murderer needs to see Kourtney's family! Even if the proceeding last for only five minutes, he will know we are there. Don't matter. We are there in full support of Kourtney – and each other!

4:07pm

DRAMA! That's all I can say. The court hearing...I can't even get into it. I have to come back to my journal when I have the mental strength! I was overcome with emotion when he was escorted in. He was in chains from every possible angle of his body...his neck, his waist, his wrists, his ankles! It was a pitiful sight. He looked dirty and evil. It angered me more with each passing second to see him. A lot of people on both sides started to loose it and things escalated. But I will write again later tonight. We have to go back to court on Friday, August 24th.

10:26pm

Exhausted is what I am this evening! Jesus! I'm emotionally drained. I've been home alone, crying so hard and missing Kourtney without let-up!!!! I've been talking to him and looking at his pictures. Death is final. There is nothing I can say or do to change this. Isn't that true? That is true. Damn, how long am I going to live and have to miss my 1st Born this way? This is torture? I have no answer for that question. I'm so miserable. This is like the worse heartbreak. The worst breakup. Only thing is, I'll never get over this one. I keep thinking about what happened in the courtroom today. I've told the story to a few people over the phone, like my dad, who lives in Las Vegas, and Ray, who is Kourtney's Godfather, and a couple others. As I said to them: I did not care about anyone else in the courtroom, with their distractions. My eyes were on the mutherfucker in the chains! I was there to handle Kourtney's business, and I don't give a fuck about the smart comments or trying to intimidate us – believe that! They (his family) were making smart-ass comments. But there were some in my family who were more than willing to go back and forth with them. My cousin Lacey was trying her hardest to cast a spell on them. Before court started, and before they separated the families, she was walking around chanting in low pitch. She was walking close to them. I tried to talk to her, but she was in a zone or something. She was red and in another level of concentration. But I was not fazed by any of them. I wanted to choke the life out of his ass, and I had a mean ass glare on him. Talk about "if looks could kill," that nigga would have dropped right there on the spot! Just to know that this fool killed my first born son. He got no fuckin' idea what he did! He just don't know who he took from me...from our family. But now he has messed up his own life, too, because he did not get away with it. So now it's on him!

I could not believe it when this punk turned around and said "I didn't do it." He said it twice. Everyone had seen it! Amazing. Okay, so now *he's* the victim? That's how people in his family were treating us – as if we did something to them or him. "What kind of ignorance is this?" I say to myself. I didn't know what to expect, but this certainly was not even within the realm of what I thought would ever take place. Now, someone from the murderer's family (an older female) made an attempt at an apology. But that seemed to anger people in my family and, with what was already going on, all hell broke loose! My sister Kim shouted out "Fuck that!" and it was out of control at that point. At the start of court they separated us; you could feel the tension in the air. When exiting the courtroom, fights broke out and I could hear Jazmyn yelling and arguing with some guy; I found out later who the guy was! I was crying so hard and felt in a daze. People are running all over the courthouse and outside. I can't figure out what or why this is happening. I just stand there crying and Detective "H" yells at me to get inside his office right now. My sister Angie grabs me by the hand takes me to his office. Now the police are chasing people outside. People are being arrested and zapped with the taser gun! What the fuck! Damn! I'm in Detective "H's" office feeling crazy as hell and in need of tissue. His secretary checks on me and goes to get some tissue for me. I feel so bad and helpless. It was quite enough having to see the individual, who killed my son, and now to be even more disrespected and encouraged to argue with his family. Wow.... At this point, I am convinced that this bastard has killed before and after Kourtney – with no problem. I am further convinced they are mad because he got caught and is being brought to justice to pay the price for his capital crime! He and his family probably thought this was going to be another case where the police could not get enough evidence to arrest him and he would just be free on the streets bringing about more devastation to the lives of others.

Wow! I narrowly survived the first court hearing. Yeah, it was hard, too. I don't claim to be perfect, but, I know this: I've never been a troublemaker. I keep to myself for the most part. That's how Kourtney was – anyone will tell you that. My kids are a lot like me. But that shit on August 10, 2007, was off the hook! Even thinking back on it now evokes anger and sadness. You know, I expected his family to show up to support him or whatever, but going so far as to try and start physical fights and arguments? Are you serious? Yes, they were. And that's how things were when we met up in court. Well, not nearly as much drama took place when the case was transferred to Wayne County Circuit Court in downtown Detroit. The county courthouse is where the actual jury trial would be taking place. Now, they did not play that mess downtown. River Rouge, a small city where the district court was located, is not the same as criminal trial court. I'll get more into that later.

I sit here tonight typing away (today's date is January 23, 2009, 11:35pm) and I think about all this. I'm actually reliving my hell on earth days, a period in my life that was so ugly, a period in my life when I could not get enough air to breathe. I still struggle now, but nothing like that first year! With all my suicidal thoughts – even planning it all out – and still God saved me. It's my responsibility to try and help someone else. I pray this book reaches some heartbroken-in-grief mother or father. When someone dies, that is quite enough. But, when it's a murder, that adds another element to the whole thing. It's an additional tragedy to deal with, along with the death. A murder is an unexpected event. If someone dies because they had been sick for a while, you have an explanation for and time to prepare. If someone dies as a result of some kind of freak or car accident, you have an explanation for it. And,

sure, some of those circumstances are unexpected, too. But, with murder, it's intentional. Someone wanted to do it. They may have thought about it, if only for two seconds, and carried it out. Had it not been for that person and their evil thoughts, our loved one would still be here with us, isn't that true? Now we have someone to blame for this senseless act, a murderous act with a gun can be carried out within seconds. My son was shot at 9 times. As I mentioned earlier, three bullets penetrated my son's skin and ended his life. That life-altering decision only took a matter of seconds to execute. That was it. As the gas station video shows, Kourtney goes in one direction and the murderer goes in the opposite direction. Both their lives end in one way or another. Kourtney life ends across the street next to a utility pole he managed to pull next to. He knew he was in trouble and felt the best thing to do was pull over. He could have tried to drive further and innocent people could have been hurt in his efforts to get help for himself. His true character showed in his final moments of life. He got away from his attacker.... Talk about courage under fire. And he did all that he could do. What more can I say or ask? He showed me that he fought and that we fight and fight to the end – until there is no more.... That's exactly what he did. For me, these are lessons he left behind. I'm proud of him. The murderer...yep, his life is over, too. I mean, unless you *like* being in jail. I got my opportunity to ask him just that.... But I tell you more about that day much later because it's journal time...

Saturday, August 11, 2007, 5:44am

Gee, I hope some of this missing Kourtney syndrome is PMS. I feel crazy as hell. I literally feel like I need to be out walking or driving around looking for him, because there is no way he is dead. You know, I think he is hiding somewhere. I think I'm going to see that big smile, like, "Hey Mama" and then he will ask me to look up something on the Internet. I hope he does so soon (that is, come out of hiding) because I'm close to something weird and dark. These feelings are becoming familiar to me. With PMS symptoms alone, I can make a mountain out of a molehill. Now, factoring in the tragedy...I'm catching it mentally. This ain't nice. What can I do? Keep praying...please. I have to keep reminding myself that Kourtney only wants what's best for me. I think that if he knew how I really feel, he would be troubled. What an adjustment to life!

Sunday, August 12, 2007, 1:00am

P.M.S. Only three letters, but a BIG deal! I'm increasingly emotional the past few days, and I know why. Can I please jump right out of my own skin? All this constant thinking about Kourtney...and the very very specific details of how his life ended. Sometimes, just thinking about his life, period. Him being funny, being serious, trying, falling down and getting back up, eating, laughing, the cologne he liked. Jesus Christ! Come on! How can I ever get a break? Does a break ever come for me? I need some relief. With each passing hour, I'm worse off than the previous hour! But, you know, functioning in the world of "Organized Chaos," I got other things done today rather than being consumed by thoughts of the tragedy. I went to a bridal shower. I felt okay when I left. I genuinely had a nice time. That can happen, you know: having a good time. And I have had some fun times, despite of what's going on. Just got to get through this one day at a time. Time does march on. On the way home from far east side of Detroit, I'm contacted by a friend who asks me to meet him downtown. So I do. We hang out for drinks and good conversation. It was nice and warm out tonight. We carried our good conversation outside. He asked me some deep questions; we talked a little while longer and called it a night. I think I need to call my doctor because my grieving process is too intense and seems to be magnified! Maybe I need to take medication. I really don't want to start with that type of stuff. You know, taking anti-depressants, etc. No thanks.

7:58am

Very interesting and unexpected at the bridal shower yesterday; Christine was there. Christine was Kourtney's funeral director at James H. Cole Funeral Home. Small world, huh? We hugged. She moved her seat and sat with me. I showed her my heart shaped urn. I told her about the court hearing the other day. We all know and agree that he (the murderer) will suffer in prison in various ways. There is so much going on...it's difficult to try and comprehend it all at one time. It's never-ending I'm realizing more and more.

Monday, August 13, 2007, 7:21am

All I can say is that my nerves are so bad! I'm very jittery this morning. Everything is eating away at me, and I can't handle it...or can I? Does not help that my hormones are raging out of control. My eyes are still puffy since the court hearing on Friday, and I have a headache already today. Let's see how the day goes.

8:17pm

This day just whipped right on by. I'm having panic attacks as the thoughts fill my mind and crush my heart. It's over and over, like a car at a junk yard being smashed to nothing. I'm so tired. Does not help that this one guy is pressuring me for something more than friendship. Why don't he get it? I just ended a relationship. Yeah, it was only a few months. But now is not the time. I hate to get rude with people, but seems I need to go there. I just hung up on him because he is not listening. Life is hard enough right now; I don't feel like dating, especially after dealing with that last stupid-ass situation. Straight up! Where the real men at!?! Damn! Back to the real issue at hand: It occurs to me that I will have no new memories of Kourtney. All that I have is all that I will get. Now, that's deep! That's that!

Tuesday, August 14, 2007, 2:50am

I can't sleep. I'm tired and stressed to the max. My eyes are puffy and I think look much older. There is so much on my mind. It seems like no matter how I think things are okay in my life, something shows up to prove me wrong. I keep going back to thinking that perhaps I'm being punished for something. But what? I'm not perfect, yet I have no malice in my heart. So, why then?

My son, now a statistic: He got caught up in the fast money game. There are only two real ways out. One is prison and the other is death. But let me keep this fact clear: Kourtney was not killed because of some drug deal gone bad or during a robbery or gang-related incident (as I'm often asked). This was a *personal attack* on him. But, I must add, due to his lifestyle, he got the attention of what you call a "hater". There is a third way out of "the game". That way is through being fortunate enough to leave it alone. But the guys need something to turn to. I know a few guys who used to deal and they are totally straight now, with legal jobs and legitimate businesses. So, it can happen that way, too. I know my son wanted that third option...to get out of the game. I want so bad now to have a "do-over" in my life. But *no one* gets a life do-over. All I can DO is *do better*. That's all any of us can do when we feel that we've failed.

Life is 10% of what happens to you and 90% of how you respond to it. It's not long ago that I've tried to adopt this philosophy in my daily thinking, you know, because bad things and rude people enter our lives all the time. I can argue with them, lend my energy to it, and lose my focus to that madness, or I can exercise my right to ignore them. I'm refusing to give away my power and my peace. I know this will take some practice. I have a situation right now in my life that is challenging this philosophy. And I'm not doing too badly. Life is so short. So why be offended and upset all the time – especially over small things? Now, I reserve the right to be outraged over what happened to my son – oh, and I am! At the same time, I decided to harness all of those feelings and turn it around. I needed to help myself, and I realized I was in my own way. How could I ever help another mom or dad in the club? I wouldn't be able to if I was still messed up and making no real progress. Smiling so much on the outside but tormented inside and in a downward spiral. I started praying a different kind of prayer. My prayer theme changed. I asked God to change my approach to MY life. I asked God for clarity in MY life. I asked for these things so that I can see just how to move on. Realizing that was *then* and THIS IS NOW! Instead of harboring resentment and trying to figure out ways to get back at people that have disrespected me – and who dealt the ultimate disrespect to my son – I decided it was best for me to take the high road. I don't have to respond to

everything – every time. I think I knew that already looking back on the early days in court. Yeah, the other side was showing their ass, but, to me, they were not worthy of even a glance – not from me, anyway. I believe we know many things, but never use what we have. Why is that? Maybe we're too scared to believe more in ourselves. That's one of my biggest complaints, if you will, with Kourtney: He never realized his full potential. I used to tell him that all the time. And you know what? Me either.... I know that I asked God to clear the path for me, so that I can receive what's coming to me: Peace and understanding. Finally, I'm on my way.

Tuesday, August 14, 2007, continues, 7:15pm

Okay – long day. I'm tired and cooking dinner. I had a date last night, but I cancelled. He is asking me about tonight. I might go out. It's a gorgeous summer night. I love warm summer nights. Earlier this afternoon, I stopped by my mom's house. I planned to clean up Kourtney's room. Although he had moved to an apartment, he kept a room at Honey's house (he left my house and went to grandma Honey's about 1 year before he was killed). I did not have the mental energy to enter his room. It feels so strange being in there and he is not. My heart just skipped a beat. Wow. That room that he had was the same room I brought him home to as a newborn baby....almost 23 years ago. How about that....

Wednesday, August 15, 2007, 3:25am

What I've realized since he died is how vulnerable all of us are. Anything can happen at any time. All it takes is a stupid decision of another person and your life can be over – just like that. I know – it happened to my son. I never in a million years EVER thought he would be shot and killed. I frown up just typing that sentence.

Wednesday, August 15, 2007, 3:25am is hard to get into. I'm really having a hard time in the middle of the night. Can't sleep. Can't breathe. Can't focus. My mind is going 100 miles per hour is the best I can do to describe how I'm feeling. Visions of his life from beginning to end would speed and soar through my mind, causing me to feel sick and moments where I know I stopped breathing! All I can say is that it was a bad night for me.

3:10pm

I'm so tired today. Hardly any sleep overnight. I'm going to take a nap and go out later today and do a little socializing. John John called and he is going to see his therapist today. That makes me happy for him. He needs it, too.

10:28pm

Just came back home from Honey's. We chilled over there for a while. Kim came over, too. I gave Honey $50 out of Kourtney's money. I'm sure by now he would have given her a little bit so she can go over to MGM (the casino). I can't do all that Kourt used to do, and I hope people understand that. I dropped Kim off on my way back home. We were talking about the stupidity of that guy—the murderer. He fucked up his own life being overly concerned about Kourtney. Kourtney still beat him. Kourtney won. Kourtney beat his ass in life and death. What the murderer don't get is this: When he shot Kourtney, God granted peace to Kourtney, but, in return, gave Mr. Murderer a harder and more miserable life. Sometimes God will use another person to bless someone else. Hello!!!! I plan to include in my victim's impact statement that "Kourtney may be dead, but he has peace. But YOU (cold blooded murderer) are the walking dead and YOU will never have peace!" I'm not going to get wound up too much tonight. Instead I'll try to get some sleep.

Thursday, August 16, 2007, 10:22pm

Today is a good day. I've been downtown hanging out with a friend. Had a good time. I used to date him in 2005. I typically don't go back, not even for friendly date. But what the heck.... He asked. He's sexy, too. I know he was hoping I went back to his house.... I don't think so buddy! Not tonight. Ha, ha, ha, ha!!! Plus, I just want to come home so I can talk to Kourtney and write in my journal. I can take only so much of a good time (that was a joke—so smile!).

10:51pm

I have a new obsession. I count down the days, weeks, and minutes of Kourtney's life. I look at a picture, and, based on his age, I say to myself how much time he was going to be alive. It's a horrible thing for me to do to myself, but I do it anyway. I just want to thank Kourtney for everything. My emotions are running high, so I will stop for the night. I love you, Kourtney.... Good night.

Friday, August 17, 2007, 12:59pm

Today, my pain has become physical again and it's very deep inside me. However, I still find the strength to talk about other things going on in my life that are funny or business-related. I mean, life does go on, right? Funny how I can be on a whole other subject and thoughts of Kourtney are ever-present. It's almost like I love him more now in death. What's that all about? I would imagine it's because I can't have him here and I'm trying to hang on. I have to watch myself, though.... I can go down hill quickly. I get scared sometimes and think I may go too far. So far so good, I guess. I'm still here. But when I get scared, I try to rescue myself by engaging in what my therapist refers to as "healthy grieving". I call it "my journal". Others may say "diary". I think talking about him; reflecting on his life has helped me, too. Often times, I can speak of him without the emotion. That's when I feel like his spirit is soaring over me, and I like it when I function that way. It shows strength and I can only hope that this helps other people when they are feeling down about Kourt.

Saturday, August 18, 2007, 1:23am

Okay, just getting home from a night of dinner, drinks, and talking. In the midst of my night out, my friend sent me a few text messages. She was saying that Kourtney was the perfect gentlemen and other things like I "raised him right." I appreciated that, you know. And she is right. He could be charming and grown up. I texted her back and said "Yes, he is a very special young man." And that is the absolute TRUTH! Matter of fact, my next T shirt will say "The Truth" with his picture. I'll wear that to the court hearing next Friday. Well, I'm going to bed. "Hey, Kourtney...where you been? No dreams the past couple nights.... Will you come see me tonight or what?"

7:38pm

Today...uncertain about life and everything. I miss Kourtney every second. But I notice one thing...I'm trying. Went to Meijer to scan some pictures of Kourtney that John John wants. Today is one of those days when I'm handling his pictures and I actually try not to notice them too much. The recent photos are more problematic today. Sometimes it's his baby pictures and sometimes it's his middle school-aged pictures. When other people are present, I try to put on a smile, but, on the inside, my heart is so crumbled. Well, I'm about to go out for a while and need to get dressed. It's a cool day for summer...and it's gloomy, too. That does not help my mood.

Sunday, August 19, 2007, 9:51am

Lazy morning.... It continues to rain. Yesterday was not warm...and no sunshine. It rained all night, and I slept all night. That's good. Really good, because I have not been sleeping since the arrest of that person. Why my peace is interrupted now, I just don't know. Probably all this court stuff. That's enough to give anyone anxiety. Being face-to-face with the person who killed my son.... Yeah, I think that would do it! I'm now this grieving mother. What's wrong with dying? Everything when you're only 22-years-old.

What's wrong with being dead? I've been trying to understand death and what happens to our soul. Is being dead just a state of being unconscious? How does our soul detach and live on? So many questions and so few answers for me. I asked a question: What's wrong with dying? We all know we are going to die one day, right? I would have to say, then, it's the manner in which one

dies. Was the person murdered, died peacefully, or were they sick? My son was murdered. His life was stolen from him at only 22-years-old, and that makes a huge difference. My grandmothers Duffie and Taylor died after being sick. It felt very different to me. Kourtney's death was tragic and unexpected. I use to think that due to his young age, he did not get to fully experience life. Then, I had to take a step back and re-examine his life.

I was able to do it through over 800 pictures of him mostly and the mental notes I had taken throughout the course of his life. As for the pictures, I started looking at them and noticed "Wow, this is when he was in a wedding..." and "Oh, this was him on vacation..." and "Oh, this was him playing with our dog, Max..." and so on. It occurred to me that many of the things that I had complained that he didn't do, he did! See, for whatever reason, I had to break his life down if only to make it okay for me. It's hard to come to grips sometimes, to see a smiling face when the next thought is that smiling face is no more. According to the facts of his life, he has been in a wedding; had graduations; had pets; had lots of birthday parties; had numerous family vacations; traveled by train and airplane; been on road trips, had jobs, dreams, highs, lows, disappointments, victories, served on jury duty twice, registered voter and voted, lived away from home in Job Corps in Grand Rapids, had to opportunity to drive all makes of cars, paid bills, been to court to pay tickets and sometimes won his case, stepped up like a daddy in many cases (no kids of his own), went camping and fishing, was on wrestling team, ran cross country in high school, he learned how to tap dance and acrobatics and so much more. I see now that he did have a life. And, who am I to say what a "full life" really is? Obviously, to God, that was enough for Kourtney...since those circumstances came to him on June 11, 2007. Like I said earlier – and I'll say it again – I no longer place a question mark where God has placed a period! At least I try not to. (I'm guilty of drifting from time to time.) I'm getting better all the time, though.

My New Year's resolution for 2009 is to fully accept what has happened and appreciate – and be grateful for – the time he was here, and just deal with this in a way that promotes well-being for me, as well as do the things that would make Kourtney proud and glorify God. Kourtney had been praying and studying the Bible in 2007 (the year he was killed). I often wonder what his prayers were about? I think that maybe he got what he asked for: Peace. I know he was hurt by some things lacking in his life, things I could not fulfill for him. I tried – I really did. But that's not on me. Deep down, Kourtney was a tender-hearted young man. The streets were turning him a little cold and harder I noticed. Maybe a couple of months before the tragedy, I asked him about it. His response to my inquiry was "Mama, I'm trying. You don't understand." And he was right – I didn't really understand – then. But *now* I understand much better. With that in mind, I say to my Kourtney: I'm so sorry.

Sunday, August 19, 2007 continues, 2:05pm

Just came from getting more "Kourtney" T shirts made. I got a really nice one. I had the guy transfer his actual driver's license onto a shirt. It's cool. The words say "The Truth". I will be wearing it to court next Friday.

10:09pm

Finally, I got his ashes poured in the urn necklace. I've been wearing the urn/ necklace but had not attempted to fill it. As I filled the tiny opening of the urn, his ashes sprinkled all over my hands and my fingernails. When I was done, I did not want to wash my hands. I liked it. Like, wow, this is Kourtney.... What a warm feeling it gave me. I decided to release more of his ashes off my balcony. The wind just swept him right up...and off he goes to fertilize the earth. How does it feel to be totally free Kourtney? This is what I was thinking. How does it feel to be free? I just felt that I needed to journal that. Maybe, one day someone will read all this and find some comfort during a rough time in their life. I feel empty, and it's ever-present that someone is missing from my life. I know just who it is. It's 1st Born. Damn. I've been looking through his belongings. Some of this stuff he had just bought for himself. That's so sad. Things with tags on them; his new futon, not even one month old. He has a lot of nice things. He has/had good taste. All of this evidence that he is not here. Sometimes I'm in denial, as if I'm going to go pick him up from some distant place, like a deserted gas station. Or maybe he will be at the front door waiting for me. Ummm... I better change the subject.

Monday, August 20, 2007, 11:03am

Had to come home for a house repair. It's still cold and raining. They say effects from Hurricane Dean. Had an interesting conversation with a friend who is an ex-Detroit police officer. He seemed to know a lot about recent local murders. He knew a lot about our case, too! I just listened and tried to take it all in. It's hard to listen, you know. I try to keep my "game face" on. You know, be tough, stick it out, and look for a way to break in and end this conversation or change the subject. But he was on a roll and telling me about people I've never heard of. Oh, and another reminder of the reason my son was murdered. JESUS CHRIST!!!!!! I got it. Killed for nothing.... I want to say "Please leave me alone and don't talk to me," but part of me wants to know – do I need to know all this I wonder? I stick it out until he is done. I just hold the phone... I don't know what to say. I just get into the facts that I know about, that we are due in court again this Friday. When I got off the phone with him; I feel ugly inside and so bad for Kourtney. The streets have no rules. Who you gonna call when the shit goes down? I'm so angry right now. My life is altered so much. Do I know how much? I don't. But there is something different about me.

5:47pm

I wish this rain would go away. It's having a negative effect on my spirit. Am I depressed? I guess so. I know I'm more on edge and worried. I think it's because this court shit is coming up again later this week. It's just added stress. I really don't want to be there. Don't think I have a choice. This is Kourtney's final business, and I will be there. I'm praying for the right attitude. I'm struggling today.

Tuesday, August 21, 2007, 10:05pm

Ahhhh, today – so much better. I think the good weather helped. I was like "Thank you, God, for letting the sun shine!" I went out to dinner with a friend. He loss a daughter. Although not a homicide - we still can relate. Trying to get prepared for court Friday. I'm nervous. I'm busy at work, trying to get things in order since I will be out of the office. Just got off the phone with a friend of mine who loss his brother, along with a friend, to gun violence in 2000. What are our young men thinking about? Simply killing each other – for what? What does it prove? And, then, look at what a mess they make of their own lives and their families. My friend and I talked about violence in the Black community for most of the evening. A very serious discussion, too. I told him that I've been trying to think of something positive to help troubled at-risk young men and others. I hope and pray for guidance and courage from God.

Thursday, August 23, 2007, 9:11pm

Okay, trying to get emotionally prepared for court tomorrow. Actually, I've been trying to do this all week. But it's tomorrow, and I expect more of the same ignorance that was displayed a couple weeks ago. Just being around them does not make my fuckin' day. I've been looking at Kourt's funeral pictures to keep my focus right where it should be! These pictures remind me of just what I'm doing this for and WHO I'm there for. I look at these pictures, and all I can see is my very handsome son who is gone too soon! Why? Please, somebody tell me why? Help me, God. I need to pull all my resources to handle this. I will not be weak in the presence of anyone. I keep my game face on no matter what. I will look right through everyone. They are all transparent to me. From now on, breakdown time is when I'm at home in my bedroom ONLY!!! "Keep it together," I tell myself. I remind myself of the "courage under fire" that Kourtney endured in his last minutes of life. Oh, I'm getting there.... I'm tougher by the second. I get all the things I need ready for court. Make sure I have a picture of Kourtney in the car to ride with me. I have my urn necklace and clothes ready. I'm striving to accept this ordeal, but all this other stuff is in the way, like this court hearing tomorrow. But I know this is part of the process – and it's how we get Justice for Kourtney! This is the only road. I know that in the end, I will be okay. I'm just tired. Maybe I should go out to Vegas and chill with my dad for a week or so after this hearing. I don't know. What I want right now is some good sleep. I want to look refreshed and not worried tomorrow. If things get too graphic in court, I will walk out. I don't want to hear the details. No way. Not right now...maybe not ever. I'll be there proudly wearing my "The Truth" T shirt. I'm ready. Here's the deal: I'm Kourtney's voice now.

Sunday, August 26, 2007, 10:30am

Courtroom aftermath: All I can say is, ignorance breeds ignorance. The judge closed the hearing because of what happened on August 10th and threats to the witnesses. We sat there for over two hours and, eventually, were told we had to leave and could not listen to the testimony. But there was much going on for the two hours we sat there. Lot's of gesturing and rolling eyes and stupid shit! It was just crazy. Actually, I'm glad the hearing was closed. How about one of the murderer's close family members got arrested right in the courtroom for an outstanding felony warrant! Wow. Now they have cells right next to each other! Upon leaving the courthouse, for extra security, they had us leave separately. They let us go first, then they made sure we were all gone before they let them go! I made a call to Detective "O" this morning, basically, telling him that I'm sick of their behavior, the threats, the grim looks at my mother, and so much more. I was advised by The Prosecutor's Office that in the event of threats, I should alert police immediately. So that's what I did. I feel there is no reasoning with these people. They like this kind of nonsense and drama.

Well, September 7, 2007, we will start going to court hearings at The Wayne County Circuit Court (downtown Detroit). The judge in River Rouge bound the case over, which meant he says, yes, there is enough evidence against this person for a trial. I'm told the hearing on September 7th will be brief and, thus, there's no need to come to it. I probably won't attend. It's not like I'm going to see my son. So, what the hell.... "Whatever" – for now. I'm sick of the bullshit in the courtroom and just being around those people. My stress level is so high. I have not calmed down since Friday – and with good reason. After we left the courthouse in River Rouge, I was told by the police that they had found knives and razors hidden in bathrooms. I guess they were preparing for a war – and, what, cut us up? Wowwwwww!!! These people. River Rouge tried to be more prepared. They had Michigan State Troopers there, who had metal detectors. But they were only at courtroom entrance. They (the family) needed to be searched as soon as they walked in because they got all the way in with weapons. All I know, this is some crazy mess. And why are they so mad at *me* and *my family? My son* is the person who was killed. Kourtney is the victim! I'm so mad. I'm hurt. I keep seeing his things around the house, and I just ignore them. Yep, I know exactly where his things, including all of the pictures, are located. It just makes me mad to look at them right now. Fuck this shit, I swear. Wow... he's dead. Incredible.

So, that was our second time in court. And it was much more intense and drama-filled. You would have to have been there to fully understand that mess! I will never understand the anger and hostile attitudes shown towards us. You know, trying to incite us to physical fights, as well as trying to intimidate us. Seriously, I was not there seeking new friends. My family or friends did not initiate that madness. But they would respond to them. We are all fully aware of who killed Kourtney. What's wrong with people, I wonder? What's really on their minds? Not much, huh? I just accepted the fact that these people do not want to be at peace with me. And you know what? That is their choice. I also have a choice. My choice: I don't have to respond to everything – or anything – that they do. Just that damn simple. But, still, all of the courtroom drama certainly did not help me to relax. I knew for certain that these courtroom encounters were not going to be easy. I also knew, too, that I would not be poisoned by anyone. I exercised my inner calm and kept my mind on what I needed to think about. I left the fighting and arguing to whomever wanted to do it. Don't get me wrong, there were times when I wanted to indulge in that insanity. But I would get my day. And my day of VENGEANCE was coming! So why get upset or give them the pleasure of knowing they got to me? I would just laugh or smirk at them if I happened to make eye contact with them. You know, just shake my head, as if to say that this is such a shame and a disgrace. So, what I'm saying is, for the most part, I overlooked them and waited for my day when all ears and eyes would be on me. I was even more determined to write the most powerful and stinging Impact Statement I could write.

4:15pm

We've been out school shopping for John John. That was hard. He shops in the men section at Macy's, same as Kourtney. Everything in there reminds me of Kourtney. I wanted out of there. But I have to stay and get John ready.

10:41pm

Today has been weird all day. Dead means gone forever. Yep. So, what happened? Kourtney's death is like a bad breakup, only thing is that there is no chance we will get back together. I have no way to contact him. So that makes it even worse. He does not need me anymore. His being gone is a tremendous loss. Now I'm accepted into the club. Don't need to fill out application or pay dues to join, just surrender your heart and soul for the rest of your life – without negotiation or prior consent. May as well give in unless you plan on dying soon. I don't, so I'm in. And I'm learning how to live my life without him. Talking about him and making jokes about him...yeah...that's how I do it. That's how I heal and live my life without my Kourtney.

My "brain split" (reality and fantasy) is in full effect that night. It's a bad episode too. I go back and forth for like an hour. I go over everything. Literally, from the phone call from Kim to the funeral – and I mean EVERY single detail in between! For the first time, I felt sorry for myself. Based on my notes, I'm angry and demanding some answers. But from who? There is no one to give me any assistance. I'm alone to ponder, and I'm able to reel myself back in before I go too far. I see in my notes that I start to read some favorite scriptures. I read out loud from Kourtney's Bible. I recognize that I'm in spiritual trouble. My mind is wandering out of control. Kourtney's Bible has special meaning to me.

Later in the morning, the day he was killed – like 11:30am. – I had not paid attention to the weather report, but it was scorching hot. My cousins Lennie and Brittany, Jaz, and I went over to Kourtney's apartment to remove his belongings. I just felt this strong urge to go over there. I wanted his things with me immediately. I started to feel protective over his belongings – and paranoid. It was so emotional for all of us...including the apartment manager. To prove I was his mother, I had his birth certificate, my driver's license, my birth certificate, my social security card, and other documents I felt were relevant. (At the time, I had not gotten his wallet from the police, so I did not have his driver's license or social security card.) As I began to introduce myself, I felt the lump in my throat. I had to tell her why we were there. I started pulling out our birth certificates and fumbling for the other proof of our (Kourtney and I) identity. She started crying, too, and saying I did not have to show her all that paperwork. I could hardly hold it together talking to the apartment manager, whose name was Diane. She walked us to his apartment and used her key to open the door. We walked in his apartment and all of us cried instantly. Diane never came in. She stood at the door crying; she just asked Me to stop by the office when we were done. I went to his bedroom first. He had not long moved in. Actually, he was still in the process of moving in. What I noticed first was his Bible. I'm crying so hard now, after seeing his Bible and I cannot control any body functions, like my mouth, lips, saliva, my nose running, my tears, or my breathing. I immediately rush over to it (the Bible) and flop down on his new futon. I held his Bible close to me, knowing for sure his hands had touched it. And once again – like a ton of bricks – it hits me! Something very serious has happened! I just can't believe it! I put his Bible in my purse and started packing his things. I felt that of all the things he could have brought over, he felt his Bible was something of high importance that he needed. He told me he had been studying and praying. Not that I ever doubted him. To this day, that Bible stays either in my bed with his picture or on the chaise in my bedroom. When that Bible is not in my bedroom, it is with me...such as when I travel or go to church. We packed up as much as we could. We boxed up his clothes, shoes, underwear, video game system, sheets, cologne, CDs, movies, even his

toothbrush (which is in his scrap book). His best friend Ed would be coming with a moving truck to get his big screen TV and futon. As we left, the apartment manager pulled me aside and told me that she knows how I feel. I just look at her with my bloodshot red, swollen, and teary eyes and, in a weak and broken-spirited voice, say "How?" She told me her son was also murdered about 9 years ago! We just hugged each other right in the hallway. She had to hold me up because my knees buckled. The others were loading up the truck. As we stood there, a guy was in the hallway; he asked if we were okay. I told him what happened. He said he knew Kourtney, and that he lives in apartment a couple doors down from Kourtney's apartment. He said Kourtney was a nice young man and that he always spoke to him. I said, "Yes, he was a nice person." We got everything loaded up....and I never returned to that apartment. Eventually, though, I met a new friend and their apartment was the same route. As I pass Kourtney's old apartment building, I either blow my car horn or look over and smile at his picture that I keep in my car as I breeze by... Journal time....

Monday, August 27, 2007, 8:01am

Finally, I'm up and dressed for work. It was a long night for me. I was sleep, then awake, sleep again, then back up again. My eyes are puffy today. No need trying to do anything about it. What do I care what people think about my red and puffy eyes. Actually, I do care. I guess I know that there is nothing I can do to make the swelling go down. I know people may look at my eyes and feel sorry for me. I'm not looking for pity. I'm just tired. I don't know. I just miss my son. Being in denial, then back to acceptance, then back again, is driving me insane. I know that we were not that far apart in age, but parents die before their kids, right? Suppose to be. My mind is weary, but I know I hate what happened to my son – and I hate the person responsible for it. I hope he's having fun in jail. That nigga ain't ever coming home and I'm going to work!

8:35pm

Today...so-so. Got that cloud following me around no matter what I do. I had to stop by the car dealer – thinking about Kourtney. I had to go shopping for a dress to wear to a wedding next week – thinking about Kourtney. It never ends. I give up. I love my son, but I need a break. This whole grief thing is taking over and I'm barely alive myself. I've been keeping my thoughts and feelings inside. I really don't want to talk to anyone. I know I'm alone. I just better keep praying that's all I know, or it will be lights out for me—by me! Spoke with my victim's advocate this afternoon. She advised me that my son's murderer will be in court this afternoon. He is due for a preliminary exam and evidence hearing on the second murder he committed while on the run. He killed a 30-year-old father. I sent text and email to all my family and friends to pray that the judge will bound that case over for trial as well. Then he will be facing not one but *two* murder trials! I hope he realizes that he has no more control over his life and what happens now. If he doesn't, he will. Just like Kourtney on the morning of June 11, 2007. He could not make any more decisions about *his life*. It was in the hands of the police, medical personnel, funeral home staff...and me. He could not tell me what he wanted for his final service – it was all up to me. Since he was such a private guy, I thought about just having a simple and by-invite-only memorial without his body on display. Poor Kourtney. He left Honey's house, telling her he would be right back to help her with the chairs. And that just did not happen. How could he have ever known that he was driving to his death? I often wonder did he feel out of sorts? Was he relaxed, not expecting anything? I think about as he pulled away from Honeys. It's a nice, warm summer night. He probably had the music playing and windows down a little bit...maybe. Probably leaned back in the seat some. And alone – that we know for sure. He drove straight to the fight of his life, and he loss his life within minutes. I think about that all the time. I catch myself daydreaming about it. I really want to know what happened – I think. They say there is a video from the gas station, but I don't want to see that. I guess the police have it as evidence now. There is a guy running around the city right now that hated my son and robbed him of his life. I'm willing to bet that whatever the issue was between my son and the murderer, it was not that deep to Kourtney. Kourtney was the type of person who would rather "do him" and found it easy to avoid someone who was a source of irritation. I know him. He was that way all his life. I wish I would get it through my head that Kourtney is really gone. I wish I would get it through my head that he does not need anything else from me. I wish I would get it through my head that he's not calling me today or any other day. I wish I would get it through my head that he is not pulling up in driveway today or any other day. I wish. What is getting through my head is this: Death is final. You can't take it back. The police are developing a new program to help families of murder victims. They are using Kourtney's case as a test. This program will address every step immediately after the murder. That makes me feel good that, even in his death, he is still helping. That's the theme of his life, really. I will make sure my son is never forgotten.... That is a promise!

Wednesday, August 29, 2007, 7:18pm

Here is something I want to say to the murderer: **You don't have to put out someone's light for yours to shine!** Today, I'm rolling with what God has promised us. That promise is that if we live right and believe in Him, we will see our loved ones who have preceded us in death. So, I know what I need to do so that I can see my son again. When you get down to it, we have not much to fret about, according to what God says. We will meet again. So that means that our entire family and friends will all be together in the end.

I've had errands to run today. Had to stop over at Kinkos to make copies of pictures to mail off to Joseph and his brother T. They are friends of Kourtney's; they are in jail. They have been (in jail) since before he was killed. I stopped by and visited with their mom today, too. Funny thing is that I get letters from many Michigan prisoners, expressing their condolences. Most of the guys I don't even know. Some of these guys knew Kourtney, though, and they all say the same thing: "Kourtney was a cool dude...did not mess with nobody...and kept to himself." It's painful to read what others thought about him – especially when all the comments are nice. I wonder, if Kourtney was this horrible person, would it be easier for me to cope with his death? You know, like, he was hurting others, disrespecting women, known to be an idiot on the streets, a troublemaker, and people just did not like him. Kourtney was just the opposite of that. Not saying he was perfect. However, I can speak on the very core of his character. Just got phone call; the murderer will face first degree murder charges on the second murder he committed in July of 2007. Wow.

Today is gorgeous outside. Yesterday was hot; there was a heavy rain storm, too. I wonder what Kourtney would be doing today? My plans tonight are to attend a birthday dinner for Mercedes' mother. Kim is going with me. I received more letters today from guys in prison. I have tried really hard to acknowledge each and every act of kindness shown to me. If I have the person's address, whether in prison or at home, I send a "thank you" card, which includes a picture of me and Kourtney together. That picture was taken on Thanksgiving 2005. I wonder how much I've spent on postage? It don't matter...just wondering.

Friday, August 31, 2007, 1:24pm

Another beautiful and warm day. It's a holiday weekend. Another one of those days when I avoid his pictures. Yesterday, I called his cell phone just to hear his voice. He only says "Leave a message." But that's Okay...good enough.

I have a regret. That regret is not lifting his voice off his cell phone voicemail. That way I could always hear him say something. That phone number does not belong to Kourtney any more. If I call it today, some other guy answers. Now, it's too late to get his voice onto a permanent file. Joseph or T had a cell phone movie of Kourtney. They were teasing him and trying to wake him up. Their mother showed it to me one night. I kept saying that I would figure out a way to get that movie to my phone or my computer, but never did. I regret that as well. Then, one day, she called me to say the phone was broken or something. I do have a couple movies of him. I encourage everyone to take the pictures and make the movie clips, then store them so that you will always have more than just the mental notes and pictures. I had so many pictures to chose from that could be used for his obituary. The one I used for his cover was a picture that I had to be sneaky just to take of him. I got him smiling, too. It was on Memorial

Day 2006, and he was in a red Jeep Cherokee. That was the best picture to use. Kourtney was known for always being behind the wheel – driving. To me, that picture gave all who cared a clear view of him. The picture is just him and his life...kind of. How would I had ever known that picture would not only serve as a great memory, but would also grace the cover of his obituary – and be used in the courtroom to show the jury the victim.

The prosecutor blew up the picture on a huge TV monitor. Kourt's face just about jumped off the screen! It was so big! I remember looking at his happy smile as I sat on the witness stand about to testify. I had just been sworn in. I just cried and put my head down. Then I looked over at the murderer. He took a quick look at Kourtney and turned away.

This picture was used in court room, taken May 31, 2006

I felt he should have been forced to continue to look at his picture. To my surprise, what I did notice were a couple of the female jurors wiping away tears with tissue. The prosecutor started to ask me questions, like is that my son, how old was he, and was that him I identified at the hospital. With each answer, I locked eyes with murderer, turned my nose up, and rolled my eyes at him. He was something completely disgusting and detestable to me! He uttered his famous words "I did not do it" while constantly playing in his hair. He sat there on trial for a capital crime and unbraided his hair, took off rubber bands, then put them back on, twisted his hair back up, then untwisted his hair again! After Ms. "Z", the prosecutor, completed her questioning, she asked the judge if I

could stay in the courtroom and he approved her request. I stepped down and took my seat with my family. The defense lawyer – I only remember his first name – had no questions for me. I had feared that. Thinking he may try to find something – anything – negative to say about Kourtney to make him look bad. It is no secret that Kourtney was a street guy. He smoked weed – sold drugs. But the lawyer did not go on any kind of attack. In the end, while I think he put up decent defense, the evidence was so convincing against his client. I think he knew the best he could try to get would be 2nd degree murder, because there is no way this guy is walking. I think he knew that coming in. The defense lawyer said to me the next day, when the jury left to deliberate and we were hanging around the courtroom, "I'm real sorry about your son and please don't take any of what I've said personally." "Thank you, and I know you're doing your job" is what I said back to him. We both just kind gave each other that look of *yeah...okay, this is awkward*, but with a mutual respect. And we just kind of floated away from each other. I appreciate him saying that to me.

Since the jury was out, we all just kind of talked about the case, among other things. Cell phones were not allowed in court, so I could not make any calls to let my family and friends at home know that the prosecution and defense had rested. "This was so quick," everyone kept saying. I mean, think about it. Our first day in court was Tuesday, February 19, 2007. We spent the morning sitting around. Then, by lunch time, they called a huge group of potential jurors up to our floor. I made myself noticed. I was dressed in dark brown and caramel colored "houndstooth" pantsuit. I had my hair pulled back in very neat ponytail and accessorized jewelry. The prosecutor insisted that I dress as nicely and professional as I can. "No jeans!" she said. My family and friends were in hallway and we were discussing lunch plans. I had to get permission to leave, as there had been things jumping off in the hallways, threats, just the typical ignorance and drama the other side seemed to enjoy. There had been some arrests and people thrown out of court who were waiting in hallways. As I discussed lunch plans with my family, I made sure I looked around and made eye contact with as many of those men and women as I could. I hoped that they saw me walk in the "witness room," which was clearly labeled "Witness Room," so that they would know that I was connected to this case. Thirteen of them would see me that next morning, taking the witness stand and finding out that, yes, I'm connected – I'm the victim's mother!

Wednesday, February 20, 2008, I'm ready to testify and I'm told days in advance I would be first to go. I was nervous. I chose another nice pantsuit to wear that day. I knew the look I was going for. I put my hair up in high bun. I wore pearl choker necklace, with matching pearl earrings and bracelet. My suit - a very soft wheat, almost pale, yellow. I had matching alligator pumps and handbag! Mom is ready! I only talk about these pant suits because it is

interesting how the purchase of the two suits came to be: I recall walking in the store and talking in my head to Kourtney. I said something like "Okay, boy, Mama don't have too much money for these new clothes. But I must look my best, so I can show them who your mother is and make you proud. So help me out." I kid you not.... I walked directly over to this rack of pantsuits (actually, this rack was not even in clear view, yet I was drawn to it). I picked up the brown one; I went for the price tag first. It said $14.99. Yeah, right! Okay. Next test.... Is it my size? Oh, snap! It's my size, too! I hold on to that! For sure, no way I'm putting it down! Keeping in mind, we could be in court for weeks, maybe months, I'm thinking I'm about to go broke on new suits because Ms. "Z", the prosecutor, said I MUST look professional each and every day! I told her that I don't even dress up for work! She did not care.... So, back to the shopping trip. I see another suit. The color is what gets my attention. It's different, like, almost yellow but not. I take it off the rack. This time, I go for the size first.... Awww shit, it's my size and I think I like it.... Next test.... How much is it? What!! It's marked down to $49.99!! I was so excited. I say to Kourtney, "Good look." For the final and most important test, because I know I can finance them, do they fit well? Go to fitting room.... Hell naw...PERFECT fit, too! I hurried and put my clothes back on and head straight for checkout lane. I had another nice pantsuit at home, one that I had wore only once at the end of last year. I knew I would be good for three days from start of trial. I had a few other suits at home, but I felt they were too old -- No thanks! They just hang in my closet to take up space I suppose. (Smile) I started to plan out my wardrobe with the things I had. I figured, for the first few days, I would wear the pantsuits, then play it down a bit on the following days. If this trial continued past one week I figured that I would wear one pantsuit per week, maybe two, and rest of week just more business casual dress-down. I was prepared to buy at least one or two new suits the next week. I assumed that I would have to. I assumed WRONG! Both sides rested that afternoon at around 3:00pm; and around 3:45pm, the Judge had given the jury their instructions. Based on the evidence, they were told they had three options on which to deliberate: 1) Not guilty; 2) guilty murder in the 2nd degree; and 3) guilty murder in the 1st degree. Among the many things I was thinking at the time, the one thing that I realized was that I did not need anymore suits! My two-suit shopping spree turned out to be exactly what was needed. Thursday, February 21, 2008, I did wear jeans and cute top as we waited for the verdict. We did not have to wait long at all. Most of us arrived to the court between 8 to 8:30am and they told us there was a verdict at 9:05am!

Friday, August 31, 2007 continues, 5:39pm

It's a really painful and panicky situation for me sometimes to think about Kourtney. I think to myself that no matter where I look around the world... high and low... near and far... I will not find him. He is gone. It's mind-blowing. How does a person who is young and healthy, who was just eating and laughing, be dead hours later? Dead, once again, means that he cannot talk, he cannot breathe, he cannot see – he no longer exits. I'm really trying to come to grips with this. I swear I'm trying. This is not going to be easy. I do get that part of it. Death is not all about the victim, either. It is also about the survivors. We are the ones left to deal with the changes and, in cases of homicide, all the legal business. Today feels different, too. I'm doing all I can to stop thinking about Kourtney. Due to an upset stomach, I decided on not going to the jazz festival. I've got the inner conflict (another "brain split" episode) going on yet again... I get sick of that, too! I'm disturbed by the fact Kourt will never have a wife or kids. Now I have to go get in bed. This is all too much to consider, and I know it will never be! I hate the murderer.

Saturday, September 1, 2007, 12:25pm

Today is okay...so far, anyway. Weather-wise, it's better than even yesterday. No more upset stomach. Kourtney's auntie from California called today. We talked for over an hour. We talked about a lot of different things, including things that made us laugh about Kourtney. So, it's not always sad talk about him. This I know, I truly hope to get out today and enjoy the sunshine. I'm ready to go if anyone else is ready! I wish Kourt were here to enjoy this warm day.... But who's to say he is not?

Sunday, September 2, 2007, 10:49am

I've been on the phone most of the morning. A friend of mine asked all sorts of questions about Kourtney. The whole time, I'm in the "wishful thinking" state of mind – I wish he was still here. I don't want to be telling these stories about him because he is *not here*. But this is reality. It doesn't matter what I do or say...he's still gone, right? Yeah, I guess so. I have to use my memory to the fullest now. I sit here and look over at the loveseat where he would sit and fall asleep. I remember, maybe about two or three weeks before he was killed, he was over to visit. I had some leftover food from a Greek restaurant. He asked me, "You ain't cookin' nothing today, Mama?" I said, "No, but I have this really good, spicy chicken and rice I can heat up for you from last night." He was down for that. Before I knew it, he was done with the food and chilling in the family room with the remote. I sat with him for a few minutes and went to my bedroom. I was gone for not even 5 minutes, came back, and he was sound asleep! I just quietly left back out and let him sleep. Those are the times I miss so much. It's just the little things I miss so much. I went to lunch with a friend today. Fearful, again, that I'm going to forget about Kourtney – and determined not to let anyone forget about him – I bring him up into the conversation. I know I must get over that fear. How would it be possible for a mother or father to forget about their son or daughter – no matter where they are? Dead or alive? I'm in un-chartered waters now, and I'm feeling my way through. Most days, just trying to keep my head above water. Some days, feeling like I'm going under...and going fast! I should be confident that I will not forget him. I feel so different now. I look at things in a different way. I'm changing all the time. Welcome to my new life, huh? You know what happened to Kourtney happened to me, too. I mean although, he took the bullets and he died, but part of me died, too. Both of our hearts were destroyed. His shattered by a bullet...and mine shattered by a mother's grief.

That's exactly right. Something happened to Kourtney AND something happened to me, too! I remember seeing the pictures, his blood on the seats of the car in which he was killed. I say to myself, "Hey, that's my blood, too." Another parent told me that's how he felt, too, after going to the location where his son had just been shot and killed. And it's very true. It's our son's or daughter's blood. But is it not also true that it's our blood as well? Well, it is! Our children are from us. They are a part of us – and we are a part of them. So, when my son was in that casket, it was a *part of me in that casket.* And when he went to the crematory, I again said, "A part of me will be cremated, too." Wow...that's deep when you really think about it. When my son was killed, my hope and dreams for him were killed, too. There were no more plans to make. What we do now is cherish the memories and make the mental adjustments as needed.

Sunday, September 2, 2007 continues, 10:49am

I keep thinking why didn't Kourtney and I follow up on that insurance policy? Of course, now I wish everything. We had just talked about it once again a couple weeks before he was killed. It would be helpful to have extra money around so that I can take the time off work and not have to worry about the mortgage and other bills, as well as help Jaz out more. Some days, it's simply too hard to get out of bed and go to work. This is my life now. I have to deal with it right? Yep.

2:48pm

Just came back from Honey's, cleaning Kourt's room. I actually found some things that I could throw away. Believe me, the things I tossed out was trash for real, like used paper towels and candy wrappers. Clearly trash. Still, I can't take the trash bags outside yet. I know I'll get there. I asked Honey to put, and keep, a picture of him in his old room. She agreed. The room is looking better. This will always be his room, but the most important thing will be missing. Him. Well, we can set up the futon now. He had just purchased that futon at Meijer. He was getting a taste of adult life. He could not believe the prices of things and the self-checkout lanes frustrated him. I think he told Jaz that he gotten in the self-checkout lane, but was not aware and was waiting for a clerk. He could be easy to laugh at sometimes. This is still so hard to believe that he was killed, and that he is never coming back. That's what the doctor said: He didn't make it. I'm glad he did not suffer. Based on his injury, he died within a few minutes. And the few minutes that he was alive, he went into shock. The police found him unresponsive. I would imagine Kourt knew he got away. That does provide some comfort for me. According to the ER doctor, he pretty much blanked out. I'm sure Kourt felt himself going out. That's why he pulled over to that utility pole. He knew he was in trouble; he didn't have enough time to make sense of it.

9:54pm

What if I live to be 100-years-old? That could happen, which means that I will have *60 more years* to grieve over him! That is too long. I mean, of course, he was going to die one day... so will I. But that's just the issue here: He was suppose to attend my funeral, not the other way around!!! Kourtney was really just a kid. When he was alive, I saw a mature young man in many ways. Now, however, I see much clearer that being 22-years-old is *still a kid* in many ways. So much more to learn and do. I'm not trying to get into that questioning God thing right now. My hope is that his spirit is really free, and that somehow he is still connected to us. I believe that he is. I go back and forth over the various things I've learned from different religious affiliations. If I died today, that means I get to see Kourtney today. Sometimes, I don't care when I die.... It can be today or tomorrow, because the sooner I get to see Kourtney again, I know that things will be better for me. I'm headed to bed. Good night, Kourtney, and I love you...always loved and never forgotten.

Monday, September 3, 2007, 11:14am

Today is the Labor Day holiday. So far, today is going okay. A friend just left. Just stopped by for a minute. Once again, the weather is gorgeous. I miss life for Kourtney. But back to yesterday's thought about him having a spirit or soul that is aware of life with us. I wonder if my dreams mean anything that I cannot fully explain. I dream about Kourtney all the time. In my dreams, he never realizes that he is dead. Is this confirmation that he is not aware of his state of being? I don't know.... I'm confused once again.

7:53pm

Just came home from a cookout at a friend of the family's home. He is a criminal defense attorney. And, yes, he can get someone off a murder charge! He and I talked for a while. I told him "I don't like you anymore!" I was only kidding with him, but we just kept it real with each other. Everyone at the party showed me lots of love and spoke kind, encouraging words. I appreciated it. But the more time marches forward, I realize that nothing changes for Kourtney. No matter the outcome of anything, he will not be back. I'm sure Kourtney never imagined this would happen. He tried so hard to protect us. Many times, it came out as anger, but it was all love with him. All I can do now is put my head down and stop typing.... Got to go.

Tuesday, September 4, 2007 (no time documented)

Today, I'm fighting back the tears. I keep getting the shocking revelation that he is dead. I hope the murderer is ever so miserable. I mean, how happy can you be, facing what he is facing? And we have evidence, too! So, "Keep enjoying the lowlife," is my message to him today.

I have so much on my mind, Sept 4 and Sept 5, 2007. I wrote so much, and it's difficult to revisit it in such graphic detail that I've written in my journal. My son is deeply missed. And the best way to describe my anger those days is its "extreme and hostile". As I look over my notes, that's how it goes for me over the next couple days that week. I'm having panic attacks and trouble breathing. I can't sleep or be awake! It's easy to think about suicide during this time – and easy to make plans to carry it out. I just want my pain to be gone. How do I turn my brain off? I can't. I was in deep pain and in very serious mental trouble. Probably could not tell from outward appearance, I bet. I had become really good at looking good on the outside. But, inside, I was messed up. During the next few days, I try really hard to reject the fact that he is gone... as if something is really going to change. It's not...it still has not...it won't! My bottom line over these days is that Kourtney's life was his own. He had the God-given right to pursue his dreams and happiness. My mental state is quite questionable, and I have a never-ending headache. I'm constantly overwhelmed with all sorts of thoughts and emotions and plans to kill myself. I have a great degree of internal conflict, and the two sides of my brain are both prominent. My notes go on to say that I really start to believe I'm in a nightmare. "When will I wake up?" is the question of the day. Visits to my mother's house become increasingly difficult, and I hate even looking at his bedroom door. Still, to this day, I cannot describe those feelings in the early days of being at Honey's house. Now, back to the journal.

Thursday, September 6, 2007, 5:38pm

It just occurred to me that each day I live is one day closer to seeing Kourtney again! That is a wonderful thought. I told my cousin Lennie today that we address the murderer by his full name. That would be his first, middle, and last names.

We are not on first name basis with him, as he is no personal friend of ours. I'm going to just continue praying for peace and to be encouraged. And that I get my point across at sentencing. There is so much I want and need to say to him. It's of extreme importance to me that I get a message to the murderer. That's what Kourtney would want.

6:46pm

People tell me all the time how they're amazed by me, at my strength and how good I look and how well I'm holding up. I say to them I know that Kourtney would expect no less. Then I say to myself, "Yeah, inside I'm torn up, though." But I find that I'm trying to keep others' spirits up, too. So, it's like I can never be caught crying. If other people see me down, they will be down, too. Suddenly, I feel the weight of the world on my shoulders. I have no escape. I have no relief. I don't know how to grieve, do I? I say that because I'm not letting things flow. But I can't just break down in public. I just can't. So, I'm pushin' on. Today, I think about how helpful Kourtney has been to me. He helped out with Jaz's college expenses, and he even helped me financially to move. I did not bug him for money, but I knew that if it came down to it, he had my back. He was dependable. We could rely on him. He never asked for anything. Maybe a home-cooked meal.... He took little for himself. When I had my condo built, he and his best friend Ed helped me move in. About a month later, I had an open house to show off my new pad. I themed it a "Sweetheart Open House." It was around Valentine's Day 2007. Kourtney showed up, and I was already feeling good from the champagne that was flowing freely! He brought his friend T. T is currently locked up in the Wayne County Jail charged with murder, he and his brother, Joseph. Kourtney promised me that they had nothing to do with that murder and were in no way responsible for that crime; he was trying his best to help them. I believed my son. Kourt was a good guy. I sit here today and think about all of his plans, plans he had for this year. He wanted to visit my dad in Vegas for his 23rd birthday, or visit Miami. I had looked up so much information for him. I remember laughing at him because he was not sure if he could get back on an airplane. He said that he was not getting on another plane until they give out parachutes! It was good to see him laugh and relax. To me, he was so serious about life and taking on so much. Trying to save the world, he paid the ultimate price. He knew the risks of his decision, you know, trying to help his friends. But, still, he moved on. Unarmed. Unafraid. Unaccompanied. Unconcerned.

Kourtney & T (hat on) at my Sweetheart Open House, February, 2007 (that's me on the side and Kourt's God-father, Ray shaking his hand)

9:10pm

Just had a mini breakdown. I wrote two letters, one to my brother Ken and the other to Kourtney's uncle on his father's side. I decided to read the letters out loud to Kourt. I talked to John John for a little bit. We discussed recent dreams we've had about 1st Born. I actually dreamed that Kourtney came back to life...and I was calling people, telling them that he was back. Wow... I wish that were true.

Friday, September 7, 2007, 4:07pm

I think I survived PMS this month. I don't feel extra sad and it's okay to think about Kourtney. Did I just give myself permission not to be sad? Am I making progress? Ummm. My sister Kim wants to go see the psychic Sylvia Brown. I've seen her on TV before. She's expensive for a personal reading. I checked out her website; she has some books, too. I would love to know what she would say to me. I visited with a physic already, though...

About one month after the tragedy, I was in Florida. This was a trip previously planned and I decided to keep the arrangements. Well, we were at Universal Studios in Orlando, Florida. I noticed this ornamental tent and could smell the incense burning. I told John John that I was going to talk to a physic. A friend asked me was I sure I wanted to do that. I was like, "Hell yeah. Any information I can get, I want it." So, I stepped over and paid $45 for a 15-minute reading. In the back of my mind, I was like "If they're on point, I will pay more." After a brief discussion, I decided to myself that I would not tell her about Kourtney. I want to see how good she really is, right? So, she gets into it. Immediately, she says I have three kids. I told her "Correct." She said two daughters and one son. I was like "No." She stares at me and asks, "What are their names." I told her, "Kourtney, Jazmyn and John." She said she wants to talk about Kourtney. I think based on his name she thought Kourtney was a girl. So I let her off the hook for getting that one wrong. I'm so interested now. I say, "What about him?" She starts to pray to the Archangel Michael. I go along with it. She tells me that she sees my son and asks me about cars speeding off, rubber burning. I'm intrigued. Then she asks, "Something happened to him with cars?" I bite my bottom lip and go ahead and tell her. She has the most puzzling look on her face. And I think, too, my time is ticking away, so I better just tell her. I told her he was killed, and that it was a homicide. He was shot inside a car. She jumped in, "But he did not die right there." I was like, "No, he didn't. He was able to make it across the street and he died in the car along side a utility pole." That explained to her the burning rubber and cars speeding away. And that is what happened. When my 15-minutes were up, she told me some things that were true, such as that Kourtney had some money in a sock. She was right. He did. She insisted that there was a large sum of money in a black bag, but I never found it. I kept looking for that, because I had a dream and Kourt was showing me money in black bag prior to the Florida trip. So, when she told me that, I was like, it's true there is money somewhere in a black bag. I found a black bag in his room, but not the kind of money she was talking about was recovered. True, he had a couple stashes, but, that I already knew about even before he died. Still, though, the physic consultation was interesting and I'm glad I did it. She also told me the guy I was with was NOT the one for me. I

did not even ask her about him. She described a totally different man in my future. When my time was up, she would not let my hands go. But I had heard enough, really. She kept saying, "Pray to Michael, the Archangel. He will help you, Karen." I said "Okay," looked at the guy I was with, and was, like, "Damn, this ain't even the guy I'm supposed to be with!" And, sure enough, when we came home from Florida, like a light switch, he and I were over! It would be several months before I had a real boyfriend again. I just dated from time to time, nothing ever serious. I've never seen another physic, either. There are times when I consider it, though.

Friday, September 7, 2007 continues, 8:25pm

I've been looking through Kourt's scrap book. It's for real, I think to myself. How do I ever get over this? He must be gone, because he has not called in a couple of months. I watched *The Nutty Professor: The Klumps*. He used to laugh so hard at this movie. I would give anything to have him sitting here with me now. We could watch whatever he wanted to watch. I just imagine to myself that he is sitting in his favorite spot in the family room. I'm so conflicted. I want to believe one thing, but other thoughts come up and I just don't know anymore. Our last days on earth together were Wednesday, June 13 to Friday, June 15, 2007, at the funeral home. I decided on three days of service. It was hard to let him go. Wow...those were our last times together. I hope his spirit was there. I hope he saw all the love for him. He had a beautiful service, with so many flowers and plants and cards. He was so clean and handsome. I never thought that the next time I would see him in a suit would be at his funeral. But, as they say, the best planned things don't work out. Speaking of best plans....

The day of final services, a couple things that were planned did not fall into place. We had no obituary. The graphic designer had dropped off the printing job at about 7am that day. As time drew closer to start of final services, I was in panic mode. The graphic designer called and told me the printing machine at Staples had broken down in middle of our print job! Let's see.... Oh, my singer, he was supposed to sing two songs, but he lost his voice overnight. But God bless Tyron! He got up there and did one song; he got that song out as best he could. Tyron is my good friend Maria's son. We had an unexpected singer to sing "Amazing Grace". (I got my two songs, didn't I?) None of us knew who he was. He had been hanging around the funeral home from the start. I thought he was an employee. He had been handing out tissue, comforting everyone as he almost stood guard near Kourt's casket. He was greeting folks – and even showing emotion. On the second day of service, I was at the funeral home from 9am to 9:30pm. I stayed all day, greeting his visitors and getting my last hours in with my son; "the angel" was there with me all day. He was being helpful and trying to comfort everyone. Still, we did not know who he was. And, then, for him to get up and sing at the funeral took me back. All of us started to question his presence when a couple funeral home staff put him out after he had sung! We were, like, "Huh, who is he?" We started calling him "an angel" and "a messenger from Kourtney trying to help us." On the second day of service, "the angel" approached me, gave me a note, and hugged me. (I never read the note and, to this day, I have misplaced it.) He then turned, went over to Kourtney, and touched his hand. He stayed all day; the next day too, until he was asked to leave. Thank you, Kourtney, for sending a messenger...and we got the message! Since the obituary was not in hand, I started realizing all the things that did not make it that should have been in the obituary and wondering about what pictures I should have put in it. I still feel to this day that I did not put enough current pictures of Kourtney in it. But, you know, during those times, it's hard to think of everything. And I was handling all the major and minor details of his final business. Here are a couple of cherished pictures that I've never shared, with anyone outside of a few family members until now:

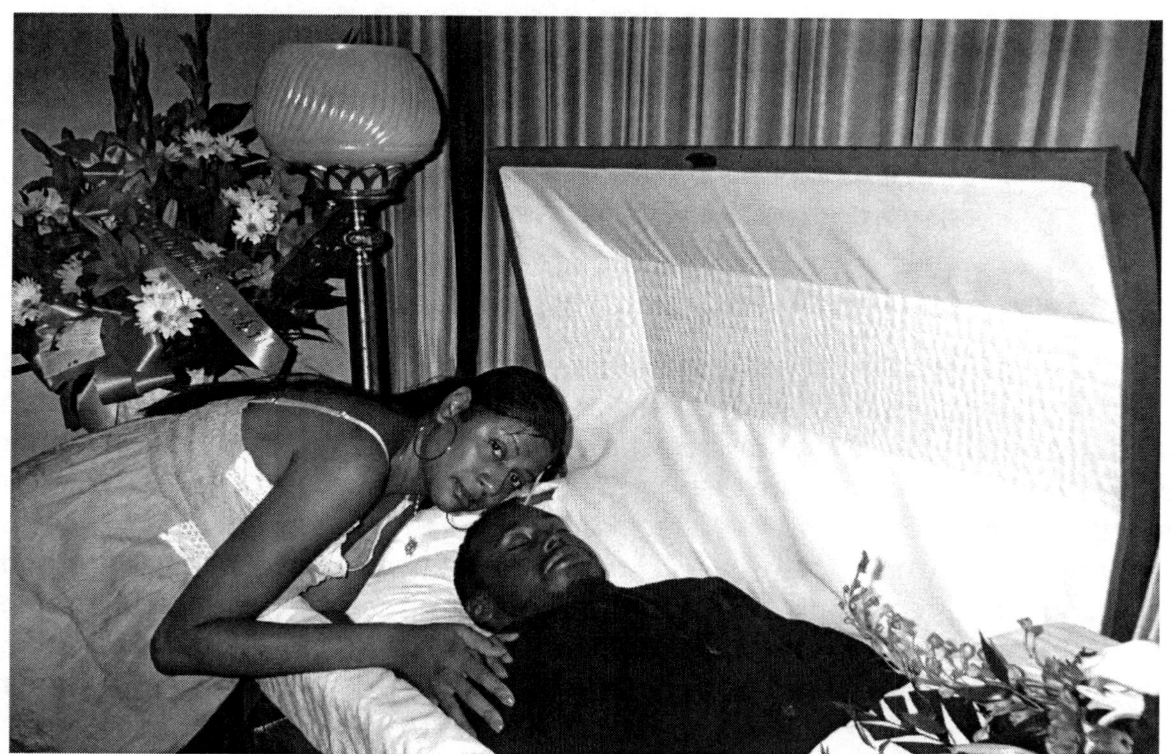

Mom & Son, 6/13/2007. This was the first day of visitation. Visitation was Wednesday, June 13 through Friday, June 15, 2007. The final services were held on June 15, 2007, 3pm

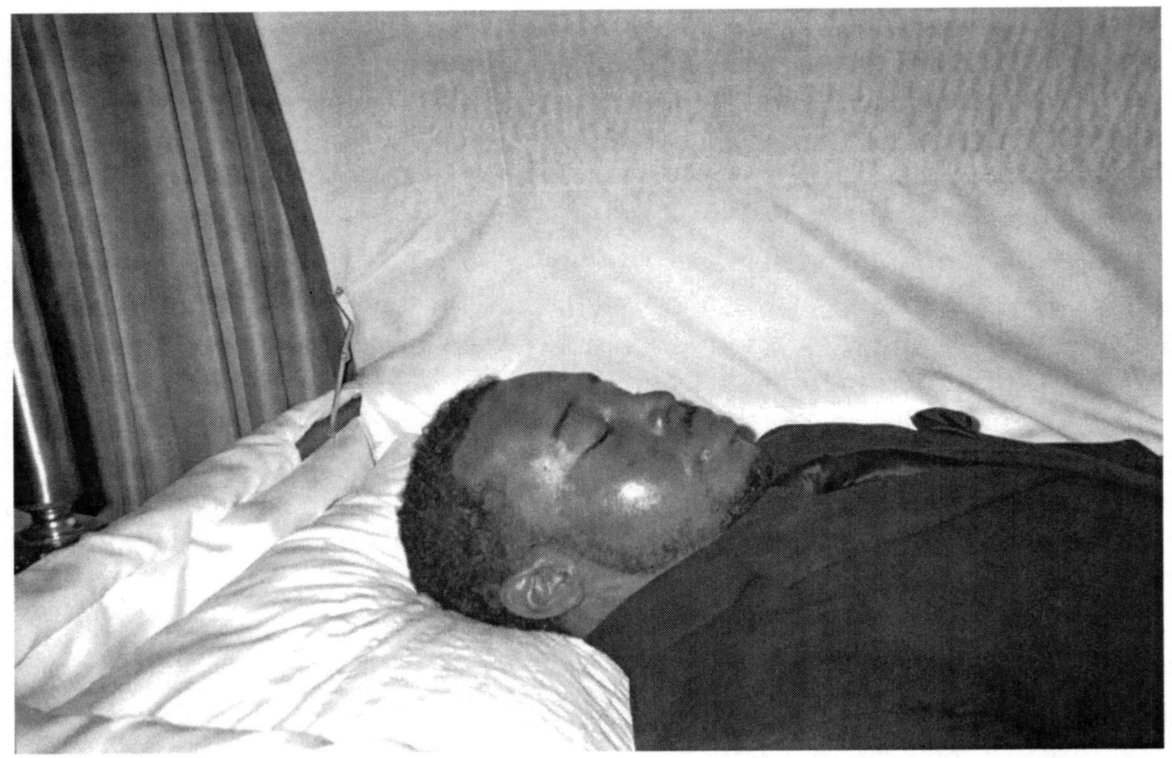

Incredible image as he Rests in Perfect Peace. (I'm not sure why, but his cheeks were swollen—I think from the surgical autopsy.)

Friday, September 7, 2007, continues, at 8:25pm

I have vowed not to let my son's death be for nothing. I know there is something I can do. I'm not sure yet what it is. I promise to take care of all of his pictures and other items. We will always celebrate his birthday, even if it's just me...that is my promise. I made a promise to Kourtney: I will take care of me. I'm really trying...I promise that I am. This is so hard. What a task on my hands. My biggest fear now is that when I die, who will take over his things. I have talked to Jaz and John John, and they know they are to take care of their brother's pictures and urn. They are to find a way to honor him; that's what I hope. He deserves that. I feel that if they have any children, they can tell them from infancy about their "Uncle Kourtney," just like with the movie, *Roots*. Many of us feel like we know Kunta Kente. That's because they kept telling the stories (and they did not even have pictures). Alex Haley immortalized him in the book. To me, it would be the same thing. Not for the world, but just for our family. I feel like I should be doing more. I've been thinking of starting my own support group. I continue to pray on this idea. I'm trying to be patient. Also, I have to keep in mind Kourtney has been gone for only three months.

Sunday, September 9, 2007, Noon

It's been an okay weekend. I attended a wedding; it was nice. I kept thinking about when Kourtney and Jaz were in Tracy's wedding...a long time ago.

11:02pm

Not sure about today, now that today is just about over. Had some good thoughts and wanted to write them down, but that was when my head was clearer early today. I'm sure those thoughts will come back – they always do. I slept with my urn necklace on last night. I find I do anything just to feel or stay close. Like my therapist said "You love them even more when they die." That is so true. I'm trying to hold on to everything that is about Kourtney. I have his mail and clothing receipts, all kinds of miscellaneous receipts. I even kept his hotel receipts. I guess he was just trying to get some peace in the days before he had his own place. He would tell me he got a hotel room for himself and a date. There were times he told me he just wanted time to himself. He had a lot on his mind. Poor baby...he was stressed out I think. He wanted so badly to make things different in his life and go for that "third option" (leave the game), but he was not exactly sure how to do it. I just wish he had talked to me in more depth about his concerns. I know I could have helped. Part of me rejoices for him, because I know he doesn't have to deal with every day life any longer. He wore himself out. I feel so bad for him this way. Once again, I apologize: I'm so sorry Kourtney. I wish I could have made your life better. I wish I could have saved you. I'm so hurt and sad now. Maybe you know that. All I can do is hope to see you in my dreams. Every night would be just fine by me.

Monday, September 10, 2007, 3:21pm

It's almost three months since his death. This is the first time I have paid attention to the 10th or the 11th of the month. I will make an effort to stay away from that. I promised myself not to become fixated on dates and doing countdowns. It's like mental torture. So, it's my resolve not to get into calendar or date recognition. Today, I wrote some letters. I purchased a new frame for a picture that I had enlarged, the picture of me and Kourtney on Thanksgiving 2005. I used this one for the "thank you" cards I sent out to everyone after the funeral. All of my pictures are priceless now. I found some more national organizations that I will be contacting and maybe get involved. I will be going to a support group next week. But it's for all kinds of deaths–not just murder victim survivors. I've been trying to reach someone at the Detroit chapter of Save Our Sons and Daughters, or SOSAD, but I have not received a response yet. I'll keep trying. I keep thinking more and more about starting up my own group, especially if none of these groups work out. I pretty much deal with my grief on my own terms; I wear my broken heart and my suicidal thoughts as a badge of honor. It's all for Kourtney. That's just my life now. I've been explaining this to others. My heart is broken...in a million pieces. I don't think everyone understands. It's hard to relate to this level of grief. I do get it. All too well do I get it. I don't mind because it is what it is. I'm reality-based.... Well, sometimes. (Smile.) Although I do my share of wishing and dreaming, I just roll with it because it's all normal for anyone in this position. There are many of us hurting from this. I tell everyone that we don't have to forget Kourtney. We don't have to leave him behind. We are the ones who can keep him alive. It's just how we handle what we are left with. I can make this whatever I want and need it to be. Then it's all good. That being said, I will continue to send out my courtroom newsletter, where I express myself and give the latest updates. I am the only person who can do this. Plus, it keeps me engaged and constructive. I have to be involved in all aspects of this.

10:42pm

I survived PMS this month. No emotional breakdown. I'm happy that I was not an emotional wreck this month. My day-to-day is quite enough.

Tuesday, September 11, 2007, 12:49pm

Strange thoughts today. I'm getting the physical pains again when I look at Kourt's pictures. I printed one of him and his auntie today. I did not realize how clear and real life the image appeared. This one is particularly hard to look at for more than two seconds. I'm not overly-sad today, I am however on guard...from MYSELF! I have to watch me watching me. I've been telling Kourt all day how sorry I am for this mess and that I wish I could have made things better for him. Oh, there goes that wishful thinking again. I just don't want him to be dead. But he is. As a parent, I did not get a chance to save him that night. I could not do anything for him. I'm hopeless. What can I do? The murderer faces a harsh rebuke.

7:15pm

Went out to lunch today. It was cool. Drove back to Honey's house. I decided to get some more cleaning done in Kourt's room. It's coming along. I'm making progress. Found more interesting items. Some made me laugh. Looking at his shoes. It's something about his shoes and boots that sadden me. I just fight back the tears. My mom keeps saying leave the boots for my brother Ken but I can't leave them all. I keep justifying to her why I can't. Then I say this is my son and I owe no one an explanation for any decision I make with regard to him or his things. Far as I'm concerned, his things can sit for the next 50 years without any use and, if that's what I want, so be it. My mom doesn't trip with me.... Well, at least not out loud to me. I'm sure I bug out some people. Oh well! Everything that belonged to Kourtney belongs to me now. And that's it. I will decide what is okay to give away. The pains in my chest, wrist, and thumb are back. I literally get sharp pains in the same areas where he was shot. It's so strange. Had Kourtney known a decision he made to testify in that case would have left his family involved, I know he would have took a different course. Him potentially testifying for T was another "reason" for his murder. Kourtney was a protector. He tried to protect everyone, and, ultimately, he could not protect himself. I just feel so bad for him sometimes. That had to be horrifying, no matter if it was only for less than one minute. To go through being shot at, glass crashing and breaking all around you, and just hearing the shots being fired – horrifying. According to the actual video, it happened very fast. I wish so many things all day and night, even in my sleep. That don't matter, and nothing changes for Kourtney. Was his life's mission really complete, as I stated in his obituary? I guess I have to keep on praying and finding new ways to cope with this tragedy, even if it's something to believe in for one day. It's just how it is for me now. I want to run from this. But where am I going? I said I wanted to live. But I'm afraid. Afraid of what I wonder? I believe I know...I'm afraid of me. So, I'm here. There is nowhere to hide, especially since I'm going to keep living. I may as well welcome ME to my new life. Pull up a chair and try to get comfortable. There are no changes going backwards. Everything.... Everything moves forward. (Deep breath.)

Based on my notes, over the next couple of days, I'm in an angry frame of mind. I go over and over in my mind how I know my son was set up...called out to his death. What cowards! Would not even face my son. Instead, they hide behind "private phone numbers" and shot him when he least expected it. I often wonder about the person who called my son out (of the house). Was this a person whom he trusted and thought was his friend? There is no loyalty, huh, Kourt? I believe him now. He used to say that all the time. He knew what he was talking about. These little details add more agony to what happened. You know, my mom heard his phone ring and he told her he would be right back. This was well after Jaz's birthday dinner was over. He was helping my mom with chairs and stuff like that. According to Honey, when she got back from Meijer and MGM, Kourt was relaxing and watching TV. She asked him to help her with the bags and put the chairs up. His phone rang.... He told Honey he would be right back. She was like, "Don't forget about the chairs." He promised to return shortly. That did not happen. He drove off to his death. Police reports indicated Kourtney was shot about 12:47am. He was pronounced dead at 1:12am. I arrived at the hospital about 1:30am. I drove to the hospital alone. I called my sister Angie. I also called my dad in Las Vegas. Henry Ford Wyandotte Hospital is not that far from me, but, damn, it took me a long time to get there. I met up with my cousin Eric at the emergency room entrance. We waited for our escort. I knew it was not good. The male nurse that came to get us would not look up. He kept his head down. I thought *not good* more than likely meant he

was injured or worse, like on, life support, but never "DEAD"! He was, though. Still, today, that is hard to comprehend. I have self-trained so much through these months that I can say the "D" word and not get that creepy feeling all over. I've come along way. Here is what I do know: There are good days and bad days. I imagine it will always be like that. It's how you chose to deal with your life going forward. With a tragedy such as this, any mother or father has to have that time to really grieve. At some point, decisions must be made. How do I carry on now? Someone once said to me when I was younger, "Plan your work and work your plan."

Friday, September 14, 2007, 9:05pm

A court trial date has been set! Trial is scheduled to start Monday, December 10, 2007. My spirits were dampened after I hung up the phone. I should be happy right? I don't know. Hopefully it will be over before the year ends. I thought we wouldn't be doing this until, like, spring 2008. I start a new 6-week group session next week. It's highly recommended. I'm looking forward to it. I've been receiving spiritually-based letters from friends to encourage me. I do write back. It's good to know that I'm still on the mind of others and they want to help. Keep having dizzy spells and allergy symptoms today. I just took two Benadryl pills. I just cancelled a date. I just want to be alone and talk to Kourtney, look at his pictures and write in my journal while listening to my favorite music. That feels much better to me. I don't want some guy trying so hard to get close to me. I'm not in the mood for that. Not right now.

Saturday, September 15, 2007, 10:52am

Not feeling good. I dreamed about Kourtney all night. I'm happy about that. My head hurt, and I still have the dizzy spells. Just got out of the shower. I think I should go to the E.R., but not the one where Kourt was taken. I don't think I can handle that.

8:42pm

The harsh reality is on my back! I'm angry, and I want to take it out on someone. The person I want is not within my reach! I can't believe this nigga killed my son! What! Let me get a hold of myself in order to keep my sanity intact.

Sunday, September 16, 2007, 6:28am

The panic attacks are back. The more I think about Kourtney, the worse the attacks become. I get shortness of breath, too. Damn, what to do with myself? How do I hold on? This is personal! This is crazy as hell, and I hate going through this every day! I want my son back. This is not fair; it's cruel. I need help. I start the support group this week. I bet I'll be the only one there with a murdered son.

It's just general grief support. I need more tailored assistance, a group where your son/daughter was murdered. I was up watching the Suzi Orman show. She was talking about how AVON is awarding $5,000 to women trying to start a business or help the community. I went ahead and applied so that I can get my women's empowerment group started. I hope they pick me. I can run the group from my home. "See, I'm trying to fight back, Kourtney.... I'm trying not to let your death be for nothing."

8:30am

I went back to sleep for half hour or so. I had the best dream about Kourtney. I'm so happy – and I needed it! Kourtney walked over to me. He had been waiting for me on a sofa at Honey's house. I was in his room cleaning up. I walked out the room and there he was. I said to him "Kourtney." I could feel the warmth and love for real. He got up slowly, we hugged, and I said "I miss you, Kourtney," still hugging him. He said "I know and I miss you, too." We stopped hugging each other and I said "I love you." He smiled. That amazing smile...the amazing smile that he gave you that's almost a blush! I said to him "See, beautiful. That's what I mean." (I was speaking of his smile as being beautiful.) And I woke up immediately and was smiling. With my eyes closed, I said "Thank you, Kourtney" out loud. I opened my eyes. I closed them again and these powerful sunrays (I think) just beamed over me. It was almost blinding. I never felt it before, or saw anything like it. I think it was his spirit still over me in the bedroom. Oh my God...thank you! I needed this. God knew...He knew I needed a little more, and He provided that. Thank you, Jesus for always the peace and blessing when I needed it the most. I'm crying so hard as I type this. I'm not sure how I'm getting through this to see the computer screen. But I know what it is! Thank you, God.... Thank you, Kourtney.... I love you, boy, and I know you know that. Still, always, forever. Kourtney will be always loved and never forgotten. The past few hours have been so enlightening for me. First, I woke up around 5:30am and saw The Suzi Orman show, got that information, and applied to AVON. I wrote about that in my journal earlier this morning. Then I went back to bed and came up with a name for my support group. What a morning. I had been praying and trying to figure out a name for my group, a name that made sense and was relevant. I will continue to pray to God for guidance and assistance. Thank you, God.

10:30pm

I just came back from dinner and drinks with a friend. He let me know he wants to be there for me. I appreciate that. I really do. Everyone's trying to help. But, truly, there is little anyone can say or do that will make me feel better. This is on me in some ways. It's between me, God, and Kourtney. That's my healing circle, when it's 3:30am and I think I'm alone. I'm not. Today has changed some, though.

I was riding high this morning after the beautiful dream, but it did not prove to be enough to last through the day. I've been fighting with myself all day. It seems best to just let the wave of emotions flow and roll, and I'll pick up when it's safe. Trying to fight this grief thing back only makes it worse for me. My panic attacks are out of control and thoughts of Kourtney eat away at my very soul. I just can't take this. Or can I? How about I just don't want to take this. I'm so tired. Mentally, I'm exhausted. I hate these kinds of days. It's never-ending torture!

Wednesday, September 19, 2007, 4:14am

I miss Kourtney. I'm drained. I attended the support group's first night called "Journey Through Grief". It's at a church in Dearborn, MI, and sponsored by Howe-Peterson Funeral Home. I'm glad I went. Jaz went, too. (She doesn't feel it's for her and I doubt she will go back.) Our facilitator is a world-renowned speaker, Mr. Peter Wolfe – and he is amazing. I liked him instantly. After he spoke for about 45 minutes, we broke off into smaller groups. Groups designated according to our loss. If you lost a child or grandchild you're in the same group. Even with such a large group, I was the only one there for a homicide victim, the youngest parent, and Kourtney was the youngest deceased person. I feel the next 6 weeks will be empowering and helpful. The focus is to learn how to handle our emotions better. I see now that I can get my group started right from the people who are here. My personal therapist agreed with me.... She feels that I'll get my initial members from other groups. Just yesterday, I heard on the news that four people were shot and killed in Detroit. This makes me want to reach out, not sure how to. I need the funding to make it what it should be. I don't want a group just thrown together, you know. The mother of a suicide victim was in the group last night, a mother whose son died on motor cycle accident. Though not murdered, they are just as devastated as I am. We go around the room, introduce ourselves, and, of course, tell our stories. I go last and tell his tragic story. Everyone was interested. I felt their eyes pierce me. I figure it must be pretty shocking to hear "My son was murdered." It's not the thing you expect to hear. I started to get sad again then I remind myself of what someone told me recently: Kourtney learned his life lessons and it was time to move on. They went on to say that all of us learn our life lessons at a different pace, then move on to the next lesson...as God has planned for us. Not that it takes away the pain. But making an attempt to understand the "other side" does help me find some solace. I'm so desperate that I'm willing to listen to anyone these days.

8:35am

Decided that I'm not going into the office today. Not sure how I'm feeling but motivated is not an emotion I can claim at this time. However, I do feel motivated to visit one of Kourtney's favorite places: Downtown Detroit's Belle Isle Park. The weather is nice today, too. Yeah, that's what I will do. I'm taking his ashes to spread in the Detroit River and around the park.

9:27pm

Today turned out to be not so bad. I did take Kourt's ashes to the park and stayed downtown for a while. I released a lot of his ashes around the park and in the river. I met a cool guy. We just talked and stood near the water. We could not get over how the butterflies seems to attack me. It was almost funny. They were chasing me around and getting in my face. He was like "Wow, they like you!" I had to go ahead and tell him that since my son's death, butterflies have taken a strong liking to me and a few others in my family. The butterflies have been so friendly, and none of us have ever experienced anything like it before. He and I ended up having lunch at Kourt's favorite place "Southern Fires". We bid each other a good day and I headed back to the waterfront to sit and think near the GM Building. Then I hit I-75, stopped over my sister Kim's house, then over to Angie's house for a while, then back home. It was a day good for my soul, and I'm glad the day turned out the way it did.

Thursday, September 20, 2007, 9:44pm

Yep, here we go again. I'm back on the "downside". Incredible. But I'm hanging in there. I leave for NYC tomorrow to visit with a friend for a few days. I'm hoping this trip provides an opportunity for me to get a break, relax, and have fun!

Monday, September 24, 2007, 7:28am

I'm so glad to be back home! I actually changed my flight and came back one day early. I sprinkled Kourt's ashes at "Ground Zero," among other places. Where the hell is my son I ask myself all the time because I miss him so much. I cannot believe he is no where to be found. I'm told that I must let him continue his journey, that I cannot keep calling him back to me. I'm told he understands my pain and will try to hang around to help me. So, for me to help him, I have to get stronger - and smarter - about this situation. Kourtney still needs me they say - and that makes me smile. Well, I'm about to get ready for work. I hope this week is better than last week. I love you, Kourt...but you already know that!

Tuesday, September 25, 2007, 4:02pm

I read some good letters today from a couple brothers in prison. Kourt's uncle liked the obituary very much. He thought it to be more of a celebration. And I would say that it was. "Kourtney's earthly work is complete," he said to me. He had to move on, just like that physic in Florida told me Kourtney said to tell me. He told the physic to tell me that I would understand everything when I "transition" (die). It's hard right now to see how I will get through the remainder of my life, but I know that I must. There is a way for me to make it. And, although I lose my way sometimes, I know that I'm not alone. I've been spending some time on Kourt's website; but I want to also make sure I make time for my journal, which is therapeutic for me. I have grief support group tonight, and we are asked to bring in a picture or something of our loved ones to share. Of course, I'm taking pictures.

11:42pm

Grief support was good tonight. I passed around pictures of Kourtney and made him a card for the memorial wall. I took some good notes, too. I'm a little depressed tonight, but I'll just go ahead and try to get some sleep and it will be gone. I'm tired.

Wednesday, September 27, 2007, 10:48pm

Constant thoughts of Kourtney. I think about him as if it's a surprise to me that the young man that was killed is my son. Weird but true. My brain tries to tell me that it's my son that was killed. "Oh, I guess it is," I say back to myself. I refer to all the reminders around the house as proof that he is dead. I think about his personality, his smile, and that way he laughs. And, still, *I can't believe he is dead.* I got a letter today from Kourtney's uncle, who is in prison. I'm very anxious to respond to it. Apparently, he has written a letter to his mother and brother confronting them about their lack of involvement in Kourt's life, as well as their lack of support and concern in the aftermath. He wanted to know if his brother would be coming home to Michigan from California to attend the trial. I can't wait to find out how they respond to his uncle. I bet they will be mad to find out that he and I are corresponding. Oh-fucking-well.... They will just have to deal with it – and themselves. They know they are wrong and if they don't.... Then they just don't give a damn. And that could be the case. I think that *is* the case. Over the years, his auntie and I have managed to stay in contact. And, in all fairness, Kourtney and his Grandma had a level of communication. But that happened a few years back for the most part. When she would come here to visit from California, he would go over to her best friend's house to visit with her. I told his uncle that whatever was going on in recent years, it did not make up for the years when he was a hurt little boy and when he needed his father's love and guidance. No one is off the hook with me! Kourtney was really hurt by them. Kourtney referred to his father as "the sperm donor".

I smile right now to stop from crying for my son when I think about "the sperm donor". Whatever transpired over the 22.9 years of Kourtney's life was of *his* (the sperm donor's) choice. I never tried to keep Kourtney from him – and he never tried to see him. Moreover, Kourtney wanted, needed, and DESERVED a relationship with and financial support from that individual, yet he did not get it! I do recall an argument when Kourt was young – maybe 9- or 10-years-

old. What I said to "the sperm donor" was something, like if, he can only hurt Kourtney, then stay away from him. My justification for even going there with him was because, once again, he was in town and ignored Kourtney, giving him false hope as he brushed him off. I dare to imagine all trips he made to Michigan to see his family and friends – you know, the people he loved and cared about – and we never even knew he was here. And right in the same neighborhood! The visit in question was when his mother had gotten married and we were attending the reception. I expected that Kourtney would be going with his father back to his mom's house; Kourtney *wanted* this. Wrong. Kourtney was so hurt. I remember us preparing to leave the reception. I tried to make a last-minute pitch to "the sperm donor" about his decision (without making a bad scene). The answer was still "No." I had to break the news to Kourtney, of course, right at the reception. He had watched me go over to his "dad". I think he knew I was pleading his case. I mean, after all, he really wanted to go with his "dad" and be with his people. He was so happy to see that man–had not seen him in years. But that man had no time or interest in his son. We (Kourtney, my mom, and I) left quietly. I dropped my mother, Honey, off at home – and in the car complete silence! When we got home, and started to undress to get ready for bed, I looked in on Kourtney. As he removed his clip on tie, I asked him was he okay, knowing full-well he was not because he seemed so subdued, he looked up at me with huge not-yet-fallen tears and tried *not* to cry. But he could not hold them back and burst into tears. He asked me – and I will never EVER forget this – "Mama, why my daddy don't care about me?" I hugged him, cried with him, and told him that I did not know why. Truly, I did not have an answer for his father's lack of love and concern for Kourt. It was so pitiful to see him that way. Everyone at my house cried that night with Kourtney. From that moment on I hated the "sperm donor"! I guess, all the years of him staying away was his way of saying he could only hurt Kourt...and that he did— more than he can ever know. "Bullshit!" I say to that attitude, though! If that is true, that's all the more reason not to attend his funeral. Was it just for show? I think so. But that is no excuse, either. How do you have a son – your first born – and just let him be?

The "sperm donor" and I did not have a one night stand. I was not a "hoe" (whore) to him. And, he was not just "any guy" to me! We had plans to be married. Kourtney was a result of our young love for each other. When Kourtney arrived into this world on July 20, 1984, he had young parents who loved each other *and* him. We had plans to join that man in Germany. He had been in the military ever since Kourt was three weeks old. That was to be our life. Then, to just forget about him like he never existed.... Kourtney never understood that, and I will never understand it either. Kourtney used to say, in these exact words, "He erased me." He said that when he was, like, 20- and 21-years-old,

still hurt and angry – and rightfully so. The damage was done. The hurt of it was still with that boy. We can't even count the number of days that went by when this man had nothing to say to his own son. He had no concern for him. I would have NEVER gotten in the way had he made an attempt to see or talk to Kourtney. That man knows me better than that. We had no address, no phone number, and no financial support. I asked his ass, after the army checks stopped coming, just to send $25 per week so that Kourtney knows his dad cared about him and is thinking about him. Something...anything. But he would not even do that. And I never got the court involved. Although I tried, he avoided everything and would not sign and/or accept the papers I had sent out to him. Big mistake on my part not to pursue it all the way!

Around that time, Kourtney – at the age 8- or 9-years-old – did go out to California for about 1 month to be with his "dad". I cut short what turned out to be a big disappointing visit, because it was more of the same with this guy: Kourtney would call home and report that his "dad's" objective was all about being with various women and never spending time with *him*. He was alone all the time – or made to be quiet – while his dad spent time behind closed doors with different women every day. So, a month later, I purchased my son an airline ticket and he came back home. We had big welcome home party for him, too! When Kourt was about 16- or 17-years-old, I recall when he asked his "Dad" for $200 dollars to help him buy a car. And he actually agreed. The $200 never showed up in the mail. I remember him always checking the mail or asking me. Wow... Kourtney was hurt and let down once again. He responded with pent-up anger towards his "dad". He felt he was old enough now to confront the man that was not acting as his "dad". I remember him being kind of sad after that. "Let down once again," I say to myself. It had been years – literally, years – and we never asked for anything, with ME never making sure he got anything more (something I will always regret). How dare he not follow through?!? Kourtney, obviously being the bigger man, called his "dad" back a few days later and tried to make amends. I knew then he wanted more than just the $200 and was still reaching out – still trying. The "sperm donor's" response to the son he abandoned was: "I'll give you the money when you get your high school diploma." I was outraged!!! So, now Kourtney owed this nigga something! Are you serious?? Bottom line, he had no intentions on doing it from the start. After that, there was some phone time between them, but just here and there. Soon, even that no longer existed. After that time period had passed, the next time either of us would hear anything from that man would be on June 11, 2007, or roughly 7 to 8 years later – without contact. Yeah, when Kourt was dead and gone!

He called when he got the news about Kourt. I had sent one of his family members an email. I remember thinking to myself, I hope this is a current email

address, because I have no other way to reach any of them in California. When he called, I was crying yet spoke calmly to him. I gave him the details that I knew. Now he says, "Here is my personal phone number." Funny. I have to chuckle even thinking about it today. Had we asked just a week ago (prior to Kourt's death), there would have been no way Kourt or I would have been able to reach him. Amazing, some people, huh? And to this date, February 1, 2009, this "man" has never called me directly to ask what happened in court. "Was the guy arrested?" "Did we get a conviction?" Yeah, I'm sure he knows through other sources, but still.... Right down to the bitter end, Kourtney still can't get any love from this man. Shame on him. The last time I spoke directly to the "sperm donor" was on June 15, 2007, the day of the funeral. Yep, he and a few of his family members attended the funeral and came back to Honey's for dinner. It was a huge dinner prepared by all my mother's neighbors and other friends. Due to the obituary printing problem, the graphic designer came over; but she only had 14 good copies. He approved of it. He said that he liked it. He never knew that I was trying to leave his name out of it! I was told I could not do that. My decision was based on hurt feelings for my son and me, as well as what Kourt would have wanted. I know him. Well, anyway, I knew that they were headed back to California in a few days. So I went ahead and gave them a copy. I may have given a few to others in his family. I really don't remember now.

He and his family showed up to the funeral home on Thursday, June 14, 2007, in the morning – and they were there maybe less than one hour. (However, one of his family members did come back by herself later that day; that was cool.) The "sperm donor" and I had a brief moment together when we stood over Kourtney. He showed no emotion at all. The first room they had Kourtney laid out in was on the second floor, which was a nice and roomy, with space outside the door and a sofa. It was a room to move around in and socialize...to comfort one another. However, I paid for the much larger room downstairs. The funeral home staff came to move Kourt downstairs. While we waited for the new room to be set up, he asked me if everything was paid for. I told him yes (thinking to myself, fine time ask that question). Then I told him the obituary was not paid for in full, only because it's not been delivered. I left a deposit with the graphic designer at my house a few nights ago, though. He said he would take care of the balance. I replied, "Sure." Well, due to all the technical glitches, I was given a refund on funeral day (June 15, 2007). For some stupid-ass reason after the funeral, I gave the money back to him at Honey's house. I don't know, maybe because he had just given her (the graphic designer) the rest of the money a few hours prior. And you know what? His ass took it! That hit me a few days later. It was not about the money, truly. I'm sure it was to him, though. I'm sure he was hoping I said everything was paid for so, once again, he didn't have to be responsible for this young man – not even in his death!

I feel like this, "sperm donor" if your heart was really in the right place, when you called me on June 11, 2007, to confirm the death of your son, you would have said then what you were contributing to his final arrangements. You know, step up and take some responsibility! Don't say "Let me know what you need." I needed a lot. That should have been obvious. Plus, we needed for you to contribute from the start! Plenty of people were giving me money – *hours after he was killed.* They did so without me having to ask for it or let them know what I needed! Dude, it's a big fuckin' need whenever *anyone dies*! Why should I have to ask my son's father for anything at that time? You should have been leaving money with me for whatever bills or expenses that were coming up. Oh, and the bills did come, too!

The "sperm donor" left Honey's house (after the funeral)...never to be seen again. He and I did have an email exchange in November of 2007, and he did offer a phone conversation with me; I declined. It was because of his brother and I corresponding by mail. After his brother called him out on his behavior – before and after the tragedy to Kourtney – the "sperm donor" had the nerve to make a judgment call on Kourtney, or, perhaps, his lifestyle. He never figured his brother would forward that letter to me! I had to set some things straight with his black ass! There was so much he did not know about Kourtney, and I was highly offended. I think he wanted to believe Kourtney was this horrible person, this thug-ass-nigga on the corner selling drugs and being a menace-so he could make it okay in his mind not to deal with him. Based on that letter he wrote his brother–one that *he thought* was between the two of them (he and his brother) I had no question in my mind how he really felt about Kourtney. He basically compared Kourtney to a common criminal that he was trying to protect the streets from! Really? My response to him was pretty raw and emotionally-charged. I went on the attack from every angle. I had not gone off on him, as many feared that I would, when he showed up at the funeral home.

Here is something about the "sperm donor" I should reveal: Oh, how I would love to give his real and full name! He is a police officer somewhere in California. Yep, he protects and serves for *complete strangers* but did not give a damn about, or EVER try to "protect and serve", for Kourtney, his own son! He cannot deny it! I double dare him–any day, any time. Okay, I'll render some credit. He sent money to Kourtney–rather, the army sent money–to Kourtney monthly until he was 9-years-old. The "sperm donor" informed me that he was getting out of the military and going to the police academy. I asked him about support for Kourtney. Never another penny! Oops, my bad.... He paid for a portion of his son's obituary. Gee, thanks! I will never forgive the "sperm donor" for not doing all he could as Kourtney's father, to make sure he stayed on the right path...and just be his dad. When I saw Kourtney was straying a bit and had been skipping classes, I asked his "dad" to allow Kourtney to come live with him in California.

I was noticing some things about Kourtney and I wanted to make sure we could correct some issues before things got worse. To my surprise, he said yes... immediately. However, when I phoned him back to make arrangements, he informed me that he had a new girlfriend and Kourtney would not be welcome! Honestly, Kourtney was still pissed behind the $200 let down. He was happy *not to be* going. I was pissed because once again; he demonstrated just how selfish his ass really is. He put the pursuit of women, and acquiring material things, ahead of raising his son, who was about to become a young man. And then he had the nerve to pass judgment on Kourtney, a human being, a son he cared not to raise and by God was commissioned! He should have been there to do all he could to guarantee his son was successful in life. Kourtney needed him. Yet, like Kourtney said, "He erased me." To all of that madness, I'll conclude by saying, Mr. Sperm Donor, you will by judged by God for your fatherless deeds. The scriptures speak to men like you! And there is this little thing called "karma." So, please believe me when I say that you will get what's coming to you! God will see to that -- and, Amen.

During most of my son's life, I was hurt right along with him, always trying to understand the "Why not?" I spent a lot of money and saying "yes" as he grew up, trying and hoping to cover up the void and hurt he carried with him. And the hurt he tried to hide turned to anger...until the day he died. The only way he knew how to deal with the rejection was to be angry and to claim to hate his "dad". I did all I could do to step up. But I knew that deep down inside, the real truth was that there was nothing I could do to take the place of the one thing he wanted: the love of his father. Not the sperm donor...he was given that name by Kourtney out of hurt and despair because despite everything, Kourt still cared. The truth is that Kourtney had not given up, but, still, deep down, he wanted that father-son bond. For this, too, I say to my 1st Born: I am sorry things turned out as they did. I never intended for his life to be untouched by his own father.

I have just as much contempt in my heart for the "sperm donor" as I do the murderer. There is no forgiveness, no forgetting. And let it be known that neither of these individuals has halted my healing process in any way. What I've said is just to be factual, to tell the story as it is. I know many people believe forgiveness will allow me to really free myself, or at least make me "feel better in the morning." I beg to differ.... I disagree. For me, that is not true. My days are not consumed with thoughts of either of them. Kourtney is now out of the reach of them both. They can't hurt him again – ever. And where my son is, it's my belief that neither of them will make it there. So, with that said, I am free – and so is Kourtney. Let me be clear, too: I'm not saying that the "sperm donor" killed Kourtney. We know who killed Kourtney. But, rather, stating the fact that he played no role, other than that of the absent parent. *He did not care enough*

***to even want his influence over Kourt's life.* And for the years that he did live, the "sperm donor" did not make those years any better or easier for Kourtney. Let's say that even had he been apart of Kourt's life, yeah, Kourtney may still be gone. Simply put, though, there is no excuse; he was not good to Kourtney. And he missed out on so much. It is *his* loss. I feel that I could go on and on with regard to the above, but I won't.... I think I made my point! And, at this point it's between him and God!**

Sunday, September 30, 2007, (did not document the time)

Okay, I just got another visit from Kourtney. I know it's him. He turned my TV off and on about 7 or 8 times. I was on the phone with my Auntie Cat and said to her that there is something wrong with my TV. But I knew exactly what it was about – and who was responsible. It's Kourtney, doing all he can to let me know he is here again. My TV and Internet/computer are connected, and I'm watching my computer screen and there has not been any interruption. But the TV kept blinking off and on along with this loud "pop" sound. I wish he could manifest himself to me. I promise I will not be scared. I'm here by myself. Jaz just left not long ago; she was wearing Kourt's glasses.... I swear, just seeing those glasses is just like looking at *him*. It's the craziest thing. He loved those glasses. Everyone knew it. My dad called last night to say he was having a rough day. And that's how it goes. Some days are okay, but anything can trigger a change...real fast! I'm struggling, but I'm planning on getting out of the house today.

6:58pm

I just got dressed; headed out to dinner. Decided to close the balcony door and found the TV was on. No one ever watches the TV in the living room. I turned it off several hours ago. Okay, Kourtney is showing off. Thank you.... I know you're here. I wonder what I will discover next. More signs? I know this: Kourtney will do whatever he can do. He would not leave me like this, without trying doing something to let me know he is okay. I'm thankful for all the signs received so far.

10:47pm

What the hell is going on? What happened to Kourtney? Are you fucking kidding me? He *is* dead? He was murdered? A friend just left. I got really choked up showing her his pictures and stuff like that. Usually I hold it together well when speaking of him. I guess those feelings have been creeping on me all day long. It is what it is at the end of the day.

Monday, October 1, 2007, 7:04am

Ummm.... Where is Kourtney?

9:06pm

Not a good day, but I've been keeping myself composed all day. This missing Kourtney situation is a lot to deal with - every second of the day and night. It's an incredible time in my life. It's raining today. I hate when the weather turns cloudy. I have to fight even harder. Most times, I lose anyway...so whatever. Christmas is coming. I don't know what we're going to do. I've been thinking about that since he died. I just want to be left alone right now. I don't want to think about all of this and coming holiday season. Living is hard. It's my intention to pray really hard tonight because my mind is drifting yet again. I can hardly control my thoughts. My head hurts all the time. I hope I get the AVON grant and start my group. I need to start writing out the details and how I would like group to be facilitated.

Friday, October 5, 2007, 11:21pm

I have not written in my journal all week because I've been so busy writing others back on Myspace. I found out that Kourtney's old roommate and very good friend had a baby girl born on the same day Kourt was killed (6/11/07). The mother found me on Myspace and she told me that they named their little girl after my son! That touched me because no one had told me. I really like the Myspace thing. People come on and express themselves about Kourtney. It's nice to read....

So far, we have two baby girls named after Kourtney. As I mentioned above, his old roommate's baby was born the day he died. His best friend Ed's baby girl was due in June of 2008, but she was born early. They asked me to be Godmother; Kourtney is the Honorary Godfather. They let me name her. Her name is Kourtney Eryn. I call her by her full name: "Kourtney Eryn", similar to my Kourtney Everett. Some of them call her "lil K-Dot," which is what Ed used to call Kourtney —"K-Dot". Someday, I expect Jaz to give us a Kourtney, too. She always told Kourtney whenever she had a baby, boy or girl, she was naming it after him. I picked out a very special middle name for Jaz's baby. I can't reveal it until he/she is born. But Jaz likes it; it's very appropriate. Now, back to the journal....

Friday, October 5, 2007, 11:21pm continues...

That trial Kourtney was supposed to testify in started October 1, 2007. The idea of it all just eats away at me all the time. I can't wait for our trial to get started. I'm ready.

Saturday, October 6, 2007, 10:53am

I hate the murderer. I hope he is so miserable. I know he is! But maybe prison is a step up for him. I just pray that he is haunted with thoughts and nightmares of Kourtney.

Sunday, October 7, 2007, 6:06am

Before I fell asleep last night, I thought to myself that Kourtney will be forever young. That's a nice thought. I'm up early. Been working on Myspace again. Man, this whole death thing is a trip. I just can't believe it. I've seen so many others on the news. I never imagined my son would make the 6 O'clock news. It's just not a thing to consider for your son or daughter. I'm taken back often to his last full day of life. Death just happens, that's when it's over. You're either dead or alive. I'm alive.... Kourtney is dead.... Wow. What a tragedy for us both. I feel his life was cut short. But I cannot change *anything* about that. I know life and death matters are sometimes left up to God. When his (life) dangled between life and death, God just took him back. Just like that. I have to accept this. I do miss my son, the fat baby boy whom I named Kourtney with a "K," like my name Karen.

10:00pm

Kourtney was only 22-years-old when he was killed. He was not that far from his 23rd birthday. He's not with me. I have to keep telling myself that over and over again. Some days, I'm just ready to drive around and look for him. That's deep denial. The feelings of guilt are back, the feelings that I should have done more to make his life better. Things such as being better educated and move us out the "hood" or being tougher or more demanding with him and longer. He was so grown-up acting though. In some ways, I thought he was ready – and I let go to a degree.

As I walked Kourtney to the front door about two weeks before he was killed, I asked myself "Did I let go of him too soon? Is it too late to snatch him back?" He seemed tougher and colder to me in a way. He was very secure with himself and that was quite evident. He was grown up to me in many ways—showing strong signs of independence and taking care of himself. I know now that the streets start to change your character some if you're out there long enough. The streets were getting the best of my son. I was aware of his lifestyle. You know, how he made money, that he smoked weed. I kept after him about his future. I remember sometimes being mean to him, intentionally, just to make him stop. I thought that if he felt I was mad at him, he would start to make the change. There were times when he knew I was mad or pretending to be...and he would just smile at me or say something silly. I totally forgot about giving him a hard time. Further, I did not want it to be every time he came over, I was riding his back. He and I had good, open communication. And there were times when he wanted to talk about what he needed to talk about. So I would take it easy on him and leave him alone that day. Those were the days when I knew he was deeper than the average kid his age. He knew about things going on in the world. I would get embarrassed sometimes because he was telling me something and I could not comment. He had an opinion on various

topics. He could be so insightful. He really liked the news – more so national news programs like CNN or MSNBC. He was capable of so much more. He kept saying, "I just need to put away a little more money, Mama, and I'm done with this. Then I can get things going the right way." Then he would always add – just to mess with me – "So I can give you some grand kids." He thought that was so funny, because if you know ME, you know the grand kid thing is very serious subject that I don't like to play around with.

Monday, October 8, 2007, 2:57pm

Just got in from work. Thoughts of Kourtney are ever-present. Today, I have no control over what I think. Once again, I asked my self over and over how is it that Kourtney – my first born – is dead? I hate to ask why – but why? I hate this whole process. I hate my life. This whole thing of "who is dead now" and "who is still alive" is backwards in my life. I should have gone before him. Isn't that how it's supposed to be? Just like that and – SNAP – Kourtney was gone away from us at the hands of a real monster. "Jealousy" is what so many people perceive as the so called justification of my son's murder! I hear that all the time even from people who tell me they cool with Kourt and the murderer! Wow... really. I could say more, but I won't. I will say this though: No more hopes or dreams for either one of them. Both their lives are over in different ways. Hey, the murderer... he got what he wanted. So, he should be big enough (which I doubt) to deal with it. Take it and deal with it, little big boy!!

Tuesday, October 9, 2007, 4:48am

I wonder did Kourtney ever think about death? Like, did he realize it was upon him? I'd be willing to bet he did, with such evil thoughts out in the universe. I bet Kourt did pick up one those vibes. That's why I had the dream three nights before he was killed...the evil thinking was prevalent in the universe...and I picked up on it. Today, and once again, I feel so bad for not telling him about the dream. I don't know why I would not tell him about a dream like that! Damn, I'm mad at myself. But, honestly, could I have stopped anything? Probably not. I'm having a hard time sleeping tonight. I just feel asleep at 1am and I'm up already. Tossing and turning is annoying, you know. These bags under my eyes will not go down. I don't want the look of a tired and worn-out grieving mother.

6:30pm

I'm handwriting these notes as I wait for grief support session to start. I just worked on Kourtney's memorial here at the church. But I feel compelled to write. Today is U.G.L.Y. I am very angry and almost in a rage...but only in my mind. I fantasize about the ways I want to torture the murderer – or kill myself! Either one of us would do right about now. I'm just looking for relief. I've been "short" with people the past few days. I feel like I have no real friends. It's cool. I've always taken care of myself. So what the hell? Further, as long as I know Kourtney was loved and had friends, I'm good with that. Funny, though how those "non-friends" will call you when they think you have some money.

Okay, I have to stop there. As I read through my notes into that day, I have two issues going on that contribute to my grief aside of the tragedy to Kourtney. One issue is that I'm on fire with anger and I want to bring serious harm to the murderer. That's all that is on my mind. How I hate him. I hope nothing but bad things happen to him. And I go on and on with the derogatory expressions. The other is quite sensitive and hurtful. I had a friend for almost 20 years. We used to be married to two brothers, which is how we met all those years ago. Even after my divorce, I still referred to her as "my sister-in-law" because we remained very close. That's what everyone knew her as. We had the type of friendship where we could tell one another the most embarrassing and ugly things, the things you dare not tell just anyone. I could tell her if I only had .50 cents until pay day and not feel bad about it. We had grown to trust one another far beyond just a regular friendship. She used to call me her "sister-friend". Our kids treated each other like best cousins, and they maintained their own friendships over the years. She and I were different in personality. I was the very outgoing and fun-loving one; she was the introverted, private and cautious one. Still, we found a common ground and supported each other always...no matter what. We could talk on the phone for hours on end. Jazmyn used to say "Why you guys don't visit with each other? You live right around the corner from one another." And that was true. She and I lived very close to each other, but we did not visit each other regularly. Usually, it was me picking her up to go shopping or to have dinner.

Well, things changed between us soon after Kourtney was killed. The change was not on me; it was on her. I started to notice it had become increasingly harder to contact her literally, day-by-day. I knew this for sure. She had a hard physical job that required early days. So, when she would get home, it was common for her to be in bed and not answer her phone. But I felt it was odd during the time of Kourtney's death because where is my "sister-in-law" at this most-horrific time in my life? I'm her "sister-friend," after all, and I just need to talk. Thing about it is this: Even immediately after the funeral, she and I talked about "regular" stuff and laughed. I was not this incredibly sad person. Well, I was, but I was not hard to be around. I kept my insanity to myself. It was *my burden*...I knew that. And I was carrying my torch, too! As the days passed, it not only became apparent to me, but also to others, that she was not around. Why? Neither had I been talking about her, nor had I seen her or been able to reach her. I could not understand why. Why? We are the best of friends....and my son has been MURDERED. "Where is my friend?" I asked myself all the time.

I wondered if she even really cared. What was this about? Our conversations had become so minimal. And, all I knew is that she did not want to talk to me. But why? I never knew that answer. I started to discuss it more when people asked me about her. And I would be honest. With my hurt feelings and would say something like, "Oh, she don't fuck me with no more." (I'd say it like that on my cocky days.) Or I'd, say "You know, she don't talk to me anymore." As always, they would ask "Why?" I could never provide answer.

The last time I saw her was in August of 2007, when I had a gathering at my house. She was trying not to come, sort of making excuses and never agreeing to show up. It seemed hard for her. Finally, I had enough of her brushing me off. I knew something was not right and I – for the first time in 20 years – got off the phone with her in a rude way. I was sick of it! I just did not get it. It would still be months before she would explain herself to me. To my surprise, later in the evening, she did show up, along with her daughter and granddaughter. I was really happy to see her; I think she was happy to see me as well. I felt relieved and thought, I still have my friend. We took pictures (of course) and the night seemed just like any other. But, then, the distance was right back in place after that day. No phone calls, phone calls not returned. Then I say she is NOT my friend for the first time. How could she be, when she's not trying to support me at this time? I'm suffering and trying to put my life back together. My son is dead. Did she miss the point? I thought she did. But, again, why? But, more than that, I just wanted us to still be cool like we used to be, so we could laugh and talk about hairstyles and bills and men. I thought she would have been my number one supporter during this "dark time" in my life. I know I would have been for her...without question! But she was gone too. I finally accepted I could not call her a friend and that she was not reliable. I thought for many weeks that she would have came and talked to me, not just fade into the sunset. The more time passed and we did not talk, the more obvious it was to me that was exactly what she wanted: to fade into the sunset. She did not want to explain herself to me. Maybe she hoped that I would be so preoccupied that I would not notice her absence. I don't know. Then, after many months of no contact, I got the idea that I should call her and get to the bottom of our "breakup". I was headed to Macy's and called her from my car. I was shocked that she answered. The conversation started off friendly, but I was anxious to get to my purpose. I brought it up by telling her that others have noticed she is not around and that I don't mention anything about her. She stalled a minute. Then I said, with my cocky attitude, I told them, "You know, she don't fuck with me." I could tell that I had caught her off guard. She snapped at me and asked "Why are you telling people that?" I responded "It's the truth, right? You don't talk to me no more." She did not like how frank I had been with people. I could tell that, but my feeling was why sugar-coat it? It is what it is! It was the truth.

That's pretty much what I told her. "So, now, tell me why you're not my friend any more?" She said that she is my friend, but that she has made a life change. She went on to explain how she is back attending her religious services and that it's not something of which I am a part of. Further, that it's her intention to do it the right way. The "right way" meant that if anyone had any knowledge of this organization and were no longer active, you cannot associate yourself with him/her. I told her – or maybe it would be fair to say that I asked her – "We can still talk, right?" She replied "About what?" Whoa! It started to sink in that she had a made a choice and her decision wasn't about our friendship...at least, not in the same way. In my opinion, it was non-existent. I was stunned. I guess that all the years that she made the choice to talk to others that "knew" was okay. She knew full-well those others were not in good standing, yet, still, she talked to them. She was not an exemplified member and inactive in her own right, and that, too, was okay. I guess.... Now *you're* going to judge me? Wow. What kind of friend are you? I'll answer that: You're not a friend. What hurt more was the fact that she had put unnecessary stress on me by not being forthright. She knew how she felt several months before I decided to confront her. To me, she had no real respect or love in her heart for me or my kids. My kids always knew one thing: I had a friend with her. Or so we thought.

The next time I would hear from her again would be over one year later. She called to let me know about a death. We updated each other on our lives. I told her about my big birthday party plans and upcoming cruise and about my boyfriend of eight months. She told me about a surgery she had and about how big her granddaughter is getting. Even during that conversation, I thought of how she never called to see what happened in court – how much time the murderer received –what I said to him. I mean, it was nice to hear from her, and I realized that I had to let all that go. You know, the *why* she didn't call to see about this or that – and be a friend to me – it told me that she only *acted like* she cared about me. She had become a part of my past. But, before our conversation ended, she said in a very serious tone, "Karen, I just want you to know that I love and miss you and Jazmyn so much." I had no response to her claim. My lips were frozen closed. When I was able to say something I said, "Hey, I understand and it's your choice. I never understood why, but it's *your* choice." Then we said goodbye to each other.

My purpose in telling that story was not to make her look bad. But, rather, to drive the point home that no matter what you may go through in your life, EVEN the death of a son or daughter, people will leave you. I had to learn to rely on myself and God. Her departure from my life really made me see that. Had it not been enough that Kourtney was gone? Now her, too? It was, indeed, hurt on top of hurt. But I got through it, around it, and, eventually, over it, as it relates to her. It's a harsh reality to ever believe that in your time of need, you could be

left with yourself. All I can say is just trust in God. He is always there. Also, rely on the unconditional love you have for your fallen son or daughter. That will pull you to safety and keep you grounded for the remainder of your life. Anything else beyond that is a bonus! I really believe that. I had to find a new way of thinking. Not to expect anything, especially compassion or friendship or love. Being a mother who loss a son did not make me more deserving of friendship or guarantee me anything or compel others to be sensitive to my needs (and I was not looking for sympathy). If anything, I had a harder time with people. Or, some people had a harder time with me.

I recall the first time I returned to work. A person who was always cordial with me, and joked around with me, now avoided me. As soon as they saw me, and I was about to speak, they turned around fast and almost ran away from me. Truthfully speaking, there is nothing anyone can say to make me feel better. Maybe people don't know what to say. I suppose. I have a few other friends, and I had to realize and see them for who they really were. I made no demands of anyone, not even my sister-in-law, even when we were still "friends". I just took the phone calls, text messages, comfort, visits, and emails as they came. Life really does keep moving forward. And I knew that no one could baby sit me, even if that's what I wanted. I became more aware of the fact that my friends and family have every day lives to contend with as well. They do...and so do I. I had to continue fighting my battle and get a hold of MY LIFE. My battle was to try to put the pieces of my broken heart back together. I liken my heart to a one-million piece puzzle and the pieces are scattered all over the house, even outside in the yard! As I find the pieces and put them back together, I began taking notice of the "new me" that's coming together. Journal time....

Saturday, October 13, 2007, 12:18pm

The past few days have been tough. I did another TV interview. This interview was about the car rental agency invoice to me. This was the car in which Kourtney was murdered. They sent me an invoice for several thousands dollars, along with about 10 very graphic pictures of the damage and his blood. I was not expecting that. We are trying to get it worked out. I swear, I hate that guy who murdered my son!!! I do. If I don't know anything else, I hate his ass! I got a letter in the mail the other day. The person states they are worried about me. I mean, I appreciate their concern. This person's letter came across as if they expected me to be doing bad. Maybe I'm taking it all wrong. I've put in a lot of work, love, and energy since the tragedy to Kourt. Still, that's not enough. I guess that since I have not had a nervous breakdown, then I must be on the verge. Ummm...maybe I am. All I know is that I'm taking care of me the best I can. Is it okay to expect the worse? I'm experiencing the worse! The worse came into my life, a living nightmare. I bet his "dad" has not given two thoughts about Kourtney. He's living his nice life out in California. It's all about him. He's so sad in character, though. He's going to pay Divine Judgment, just as the murderer! He will see. I hope is punk-ass can't sleep and be full of guilt. He should be. See, I loved Kourtney from day one...and still to this day and forever. I have no guilt. Kourtney is missed by a lot of people, but I don't think no one misses him as much as I do. I talked to him for a while last night. I cried so much as I read the scriptures out loud to him. I can only imagine what part of the Bible he had been reading. Based on his personality, I'm going to say Proverbs and Psalms. I slept better last night and my eyes are not so puffy. Well, got to run. I'm meeting someone for lunch.

Sunday, October 14, 2007, 8:14pm

I've been busy all day today. That's good, huh? Yeah, I miss Kourtney... What else is new? Damn, I can't call him and ask him anything. He's just gone now. I still can't believe it sometimes. I hate the murderer. And I hate this happened to Kourt. It's like he vanished right out of life. It's difficult to ponder that he does not exist anymore. The truth of the matter is that he does not. I know that's why I keep all of his things, to remind myself that he was here...he had a life. I went to a play today at the Fox Theater. Hard to pay attention, despite all the music and folk laughing. My mind was on what Kourt might be doing today and stuff like that. But now he has no life. I can't find him anywhere on this whole planet. The only place I can find physical evidence of him is in his urn in the dining room. That's it. I'm trying to fight the "dark places" in my mind. I know he would want me to be happy. Is there really happiness when your son has been killed? I don't think so. I'm learning how to deal with my so-called life. I hate my life!

Monday, October 15, 2007, 4:43am

I can hardly stand the fact that I have to "remember" Kourt. I have to send comments to my son on his Myspace page. There is nothing I can do, though. Who am I? Nobody...just his mother. I just hope for complete justice for my son! That's the best "get-back" I can hope for. I talk to and pray for my son every night. I have to. Only thing is that it's not a two-way conversation. But I am convinced he has a soul that is free.

I'm taken back in time to the night he was killed. It's true that Kourtney had been pulled over from time to time by the police. Never arrested – well, arrested one time for weed in the car. But I would get calls from either Jaz or other people. People would be like "the police got Kourt stretched out on Fort Street" or something like that. Or Jaz would call me and tell me what she had just heard. Always and immediately I would call Kourtney. He would answer and say something like, "Mama, I knew you would be calling. I'm okay." Sometimes it was not even him who was being pulled over or harassed by the

police. Well, after Kim called and told me that she thought he has been shot and the ambulance took him, I got right off the phone with her. Did I call Kourtney? NO! I called Jazmyn. I could hear her screaming before she even said hello. I guess that was confirmation to her that something has happened to Kourtney, because why else would I be calling her that time of night? After thinking about all that had taken place in the dream that I had just three nights before, it occurred to me a few days later that the dream had come true. And, deep in my subconscious, I knew there was no need to call him because he would not answer that time – or ever again. I believe I knew already that he was dead. I did not even consider calling him. I'm serious. There has never been a time I've gotten any kind of phone call about Kourtney that I would not call him first to verify that he was okay or where he was. Whatever phenomenon that had reached out and touched me that night in the dream was still at work within me. But I did not recognize it for what it was until days later. With regard to the dream, not only did I not tell Kourtney about it, it took months before I told *anyone* about it. I used to think that people would say I was crazy or losing it now. I carried some guilt about it, as if I could have prevented his death. Back to the journal.

Monday, October 15, 2007, 8:38pm

Today I feel strange. My attitude and mood are improved over last week. I still miss my son. I long to see him again. My whole chest hurts when I think about him and I can't breathe very well.

Tuesday, October 16, 2007, (I did not document time, but it's in the morning)

I woke up with a headache today. I'm feeling unmotivated and depressed. I can't deal with folk asking me about the car rental situation. I know I put it out there with the TV interview and all. But for some reason, NOT TODAY! I want to be left alone. I can't believe that some people actually called me and said they were disappointed with the interview because the news camera did not show the inside of the car. Soooo, some people wanted to see my Kourtney's blood on the seat? Ummm, I guess so. Three bullets hit him, but two killed him. I'm so sick to my stomach, and I'm sick of this shit! I swear! It never goes away. It never ends. When does it end, I wonder? I know people mean well, but sometimes the intimate questions are too much. I feel like "Okay, jump right into my nightmare. The water is warm!" I'm not mad at anyone for asking me. People love Kourtney and are curious. It's just hard for me to handle the inquiries, and I get them all the time. I just want to give up on everything. I'm hopeless – and I don't care. Not sure if I'm going to grief support tonight. Not in the mood for anything. I thought this week was going to be better. Yesterday was.

Wednesday, October 16, 2007, 7:08am

I had a hard time getting to sleep last night. I *was* relaxed, but someone called Jaz to tell her about some rumor of some gutter rat chick, saying she is the one who called Kourtney out to be murdered. In other words, this bitch set my son up! Man! That just fucked me up! That is so low-down! This person who called my son out to his death – they are more jacked-up morally than the murderer! They are the lowest of humanity and no one should ever trust a person like that. They are a dangerous type!! I do want to know some things, but I don't need to know every single detail. I know the worse part: He is dead. I'm so sick of this shit, I don't care no more. I wish people would call the police with their tips and information! Real talk. Damn. I know people just want to feel they are helping, but it does not help me, personally. It's just too much to process.

Thursday, October 17, 2007, 6:14pm

Where do I start today? I had a dream about Kourtney, but I cannot recall it now. I hate when that happens. I know I always think about him. Soon as I wake up, and he is the last thing on my mind at night. That's just how it is now. Maybe that will change one day. Talk about life interrupted.... (Chuckle.) I just ride these waves of emotions the best I can. I keep thinking about the court procedure. In a way, I don't even want to go because nothing will change for Kourtney. So, why do I need to go? Hey, they got the shooter and the justice system will take care of him. I don't need or want anymore details about Kourtney's death and how it all came about. I know the trial will be to that extreme. I'm sick of this mess! I'm tired of guessing about what may take place. I'm tired of wondering about it, too. My feelings are so hurt...and I'm hurt for Kourt.

10:28pm

I just returned from dinner. During the last 30 minutes of it, I started to act strange. So, it was a good time to leave; and I did. I'm feeling emotional right now and just need to go to bed.

3:31am

Can't sleep. It's been an emotional night, and I'm up crying right now. Just looked at this picture of me and Kourtney from about six years ago – broke me down even more. Some people suggest putting the pictures away, but I cannot do that. I don't want to. I think I would go insane if I did not see his pictures. I keep having visions of him at the hospital on the bed with the white sheet...dead! That is so terrible. Why? I keep wondering, could this be my fault in some way? I spend hours thinking and retracing my life, trying to figure out exactly where I went wrong. But, even if I find out...what does it matter? He's gone. Here comes the deeper depression. Oh well...I better hold on for this episode!! My nerves are so bad; my stomach stays unsettled. I hate my entire life!!!

Saturday, October 19, 2007, 11:06am

I'm doing better. I did not make it to work yesterday. Friday was a bad day. It felt as if he had just been killed.... Back at day one! I was up most of the night, crying. The thoughts of doing great harm to the murderer enter my mind all the time. Just a roller coaster of emotions plague me. I can't control this.

Monday, October 22, 2007, 5:18pm

I'm in a database training for work that is so hard to sit through. I have a problem sitting still, so it's grueling for me. To add, how about the instructor keeps using examples of dead people and obituaries? Yeah...not cool. But he doesn't know. Yet, I feel strange. I felt like everyone in the room was watching me, to see if I would react. Probably just being paranoid. There are not too many people that can relate. As a matter of fact, I don't know anyone, personally. So, I try hard not to let anyone know what's going on with me. It's *my grief.*

8:39pm

I just woke up from a long nap. The training session is difficult. I'm trying to focus on what I need to learn. That still does not keep my mind off Kourtney or some aspect of the tragedy. I have to watch myself because I will drift. I'm working on keeping positive and pleasant thoughts of Kourtney going, since I can't control my thoughts. And Pray. I love Kourtney. His passing away seems to be this thing where I have to remember all the time prior to June 11, 2007. What's wrong with dying? Everything, especially when it's unexpected! It's all the aftermath that is wrong with dying!

9:46pm

What's going on in my life, I wonder? I sit here in my family room looking outside at the rain (and watching season 2 of "I Love NY"). I was thinking that my life has been long and disappointing in many ways. This year started off so good, and everyone was happy. Now this tragedy that has everyone hurt and shook up. I can't bring him back. I have to accept that he is gone. I can just stop already with the wishful thinking and that dumb-ass dream, wishing I had told him all about it. Maybe...just maybe, he would be here. Is that - or will that - ever be possible? When will I accept there is nothing I could have done? When? Maybe I never will. I'm tortured every damn day! I'm trying so hard to be happy. I know that if I give up, it would be the opposite of what Kourt would want for me. I'm not sitting here today feeling sorry for myself. I'm not even moved to tears or crying. I'm so serious right now. There is no one who has my back, except my kids. And now I'm down by one! Who is really there for me? My supposed-to-be best friend has backed out of my life. I think she could have been there a lot more for me when Kourt first died. We hardly talk anymore. But, hey, I'm not trying to make her or any other female or male stay in my life. BE GONE! During the past couple of weeks, I've been thinking about confronting my so called friend. We talked a couple of times last week and caught up a little bit. But she never calls to see how I'm doing. I think most people know that I'm going to do okay, no matter what happens to me. I always find a way. That is true. Yet this is my hardest challenge. I'm not sure how I'm doing, though. Most days, I think I'm losing. I'm tired all the time. Then, to factor in just every day life...you know, work, the bills, kids, friends, significant other (or lack of). It's hard to handle even a ripple in my life right about now. My tolerance has been zero for bullshit! Any genuine person should have enough human compassion to realize not to bring it to me! But, it never fails...people still try! It's very discouraging. Now I have to try even harder to protect myself, my feelings...and, oh, especially my heart! Still, with all the protection... I still manage to get hurt. My life is so confusing and I'm trying to figure it out. I'm frustrated. I mean, I do smile and laugh; it's genuine. But, there is still that part of my whole being that is broke down and displaced. Shattered! All my life, I have taken care of others and no one to take care of me. The person who tried the most is gone now! (Deep sigh.) It would be nice just to get a life break right about now.

Here comes a "close encounter"....

Tuesday, October 23, 2007, 2:37am

Okay, the TVs, lights, and clocks are off then on again! I said "Hi, Kourtney!" Everything in my house that has a timer or clock is flashing right now. All the kitchen appliances are flashing and so are the lights. I decided to look outside to see if my neighbors' lights are flashing. Nothing...just my house. Then Kourtney decides to get cute with me: Every time I reset my alarm and put my head on the pillow, everything cuts off then back on again! I had to tell Kourtney, "Okay, boy, I have to get up early. I'm going to try and go back to sleep." I think he is done playing around now. "Good night, 1st Born," I say to him.

That "close encounter" was similar to the very first one I had experienced. I hadn't been to sleep so far for roughly 28 hours after he had been killed. I was on the phone crying and telling Kourtney's life story to my friend. I was incredibly upset as I chronicled his life! Mostly, I focused on the things that hurt him – rather the one that hurt him the most. My face was red and burning. The skin around my eyes and nose was so sensitive from constant wiping. I was going on and on about how he did not deserve what happened to him and about what a "deadbeat" his "dad" had been to him. Then I started to get really angry. My rage went on and on.... I was screaming and talking at the top of my lungs. People were at my house; I could hear them waking up; some started

to cry. But I did not stop. I *couldn't* stop. Then I did stop.... The lights and TVs started to flash off and on! My friend on the phone said, "Hey, are you there?" All that rage came to a sudden halt! I stopped in my tracks, my eyes shifted left to right, and my body was frozen in place. I said to my friend "Hey, my lights and TVs.... Something strange is going on at my house...." I could hear a person crying. Its Jazmyn.... She is crying so loud. She has a friend with her in her bedroom. It was, like, 5:30am. As for the close encounter, it was Kourtney's first visit; he wanted to let me know that he hears me and that *maybe* I should calm down. That's how I interpret that occurrence. That was my first "close encounter," but would not be my last. Back to my day-to-day....

Thursday, October 25, 2007, 9:51pm

My cousin Eric just left. Not a sad visit, but he was having a hard time. He cried a little. We were in the garage and the funeral flowers are still there. The flowers are all dried out. I just can't toss them out, not at this time. He and I talked about Kourtney the whole time. He knows, just like everyone else, that Kourt loss his life on some real B.S.!! Knowing what I know about Kourtney and the murderer, it is my belief that Kourt, basically, looked over that trash! Kourtney was about something completely different and violence was not it.... It was money! I hate the murderer. This tragedy has messed up so many people in my family. I hope he has a long, miserable life, and that he suffers. I think the only thing he is familiar with is disorder and hatred! No. I'm sure of it. He is not only evil and destructive to others, but also to himself.

Friday, October 26, 2007, 6:52pm

We went to court today for what they call a "calendar conference". We were told to be there at 9am. However, the judge started his court at 8:30am, seen the murderer, and pushed back the trial date to February of 2008!! I'm not happy about this at all. I'm frustrated—mad as hell to be honest. I was hoping to be done with this before the year ended.

Saturday, October 27, 2007, 12:55am

Just got home from an active evening. Made my final stop at a bar where my sister Angie was with some friends. The bar is in River Rouge...the city where 1st Born's life ended. Whenever I enter the city or the SW Detroit area, I always say to myself "returning to the scene of the crime." But this is "home" for me. I was born and raised here, with the exception of the years I lived in Ann Arbor with my dad while he attended U of M. When I'm in River Rouge, I do avoid the area where Kourtney was killed. I go no where near it! I understand there is a memorial dedicated to him at the utility pole, but I've never seen it...maybe I never will. It does cross my mind to go to the spot where he took his last breath. Ummm...I don't know. Lifeless at the hospital is what I keep thinking about today.... No matter what I did today, thoughts of his lifeless body and eyes stayed on my mind. It's so difficult to think that one day Jaz and John John could have families of their own who will never know their uncle, their uncle who adored little kids. I just pray that they always remember their brother, and that his presence in their minds will not just fade with the passage of time.

Further, I think about the fact that Kourt never had a chance to be a daddy. He would have been a good one, too. Though he talked about it, he knew it was not the time. He would say "I need to get myself together first, before I get a serious girlfriend or kids." Exactly. I'm very proud of the responsible stance he took with regard to fatherhood. He realized easily it could happen. Additionally, more than being a daddy, Kourtney was scared of STDs. I'm sure that in the minds of some people, he will always be "that guy who was shot and killed at the gas station" 10, 15, or 20 years ago.... But, to us, the people who loved him, I don't feel that will ever be the case. And, for me, it will be next to impossible for one day to go by and not think about who is not around. Him. You know, it's amazing to me how others lived through being shot or stabbed multiple times. One or two bullets ended my son's life...just like that. I think I'm questioning God again. So I'll stop here.

Sunday, October 28, 1:13am

It's just that I never thought about death for Kourtney – and I still don't. My biggest fear for him was to find him incarcerated. But don't have to worry about jail now.... He is no longer with the living; he is with the un-living. The dead. We all will die one day; that's for sure. Like Kourt used to say, "We come here alone and we will leave alone." Kourt was comfortable with being by himself. Life is so full of irony. Now that I reflect over his life and the things he used to say, I must say that he was a thinker. He *did* experience life. Maybe not all that I wanted or felt was *enough life*, but I cannot deny the abundance of life experiences that he had. Most important to me is that he was a young man of faith with God in his heart. I know I get my bad days and feel he was cheated...that's just grief and frustration. However, I do know deep down that God knows best. Still, the fact remains, I'm devastated.... Why else would I be up writing in a journal in the middle of the night? Because here I am...here I sit...yet another night, when most of the world is asleep, I'm typing away. I can't help it. The thoughts will not stop. Sometimes I just have to get up off this chair and walk away because my brain is going 100 miles per hour; my fingers cannot keep up with my thoughts. I may break this keyboard. My fingers hurt; they are tired, but my brain says that I better keep going...I have work to do. This is my therapy. I better do something, because I get those scary feelings and wonder if I'm in shock. Has his death really hit me? Many people say that, in their opinion, I'm doing good. And I guess that's true – if outward appearances count. Who sees me on the inside? It's just me and God. I'd like to think Kourtney knows, too. I cry by myself now. It's *my grief* now. It's my personal tragedy now. The emotional waves come and go, and I relish the times when I can smile at the thoughts and pictures of Kourt. Already, it's been 4 ½ months since he left us. Does it get easier?

11:18am

I'm thinking more deeply right now. My thoughts are more intense. So, I already know how this day will be. I'll do what I can to fight against it. I went to bed feeling very low and that's how I woke up. I'm envious of other parents who have nice lives and have provided a safe environment for their kids. All of my kids seen me struggle. And, although I was able to provide, I know that I could have - I should have - done more. Kourtney tried to grow up so fast, be independent of me, and be a man.... And he loss his life trying to get a start in life. I do feel responsible for that sometimes. I'm glad John John lives with his dad (sometimes), just for a better environment and not to be overrun with the crime right in your face. That's how Kourt and Jaz grew up. I just wish I had kept up with my personal dreams. I believe my kids would have benefited and faired in life better.

Tuesday, October 30, 2007, 5:07pm

I find that I understand the meaning of death more and more. Since Kourt's tragedy, it (death) has been a reality for me. It's something different that I've had to consider, unlike other deaths I've known about. So, okay, Kourtney died. He was in the wrong place and was shot and, as a result, he loss his life...stopped breathing. He died. He used to have a life. Now he no longer has it because of an unfortunate event which caused his death. It's sinking in deeper. Death is the opposite of alive or living. Kourtney is the opposite of me now - and I'm the opposite of him. We used to be on the same side; now we are different.

Thursday, November 1, 2007, 3:20pm

Ummm...not sure where to start. I think about Kourtney all day and probably most of the night, even though I may not write every day about my feelings. Thoughts are on my mind today of what I would like to say to that lowdown-ass, broke bastard who murdered my son. I miss my son. I feel like he is a missing person. He is dead.... Oh my, I said it. Dead. I hate that word. Should I be mad at death? I wonder. No, not based on some things I claim to believe about God and His promises to us, especially that "death is not the enemy." I just miss the guy with the best smile!

Friday, November 2, 2007, 10:11pm

Been out shopping all day long with my sisters, Kim and Angie, and Jazmyn. We had dinner, too. It was fun. With all that fun, the sad feelings started to creep in on me. We've had our time together...on earth, anyway. Things about the Bible... and what God says...are confusing to me. I don't always understand. One thing that is clear is that Kourtney is gone. He won't be here to tell me happy birthday tomorrow! That part of my life is over, too.

Sunday, November 4, 2007, 3:52pm

I've been active all day. My birthday celebration was nice. Well, I've been doing stuff all week. I needed to stay busy. Today, I'm flirting with depression. We just came back from Honey's and Kourtney's room is no longer Kourtney's room and, yep, that bothered me. But I cannot expect anyone to keep a shrine or not make adjustments. It's difficult to be pushed in this position, to make all these changes in our lives. Panic attacks are kicking in today, too. It's a weird day. I'm scared for myself. I just miss my son so much. I literally feel the void. I turned 41-years-old yesterday; I cannot imagine another 41 years without him. How does a mother ever get used to that? I guess that I'm just learning how to live again with my new life. Oh well...this so-called life. (Chuckle.) Kourtney used to say a quote to me from one of our favorite movies *Baby Boy*, "Mama got to have a life, too." I would respond "Mama got a life." Now that life has changed. What used to be is no more with regard to me and him.

Monday, November 5, 2007, 7:37pm

Today, I'm fighting the panic attacks! It happens when one side of my brain is trying to tell me that we CAN find Kourtney somewhere on this planet. Then the reality hits me and I know that I cannot. He is no longer with me, no longer apart of this earth. No mother should have to go through this, but it happens all the time. Hundreds have done it before me and, sad to say, there will be many after me... there already has been. I'm sure all of us go through the same emotions. Trying to accept the obvious. Actually, just trying to deal with it on a daily basis. Staying busy helps, especially those days when I'm fighting for my sanity. I just have to remember in my cloudiest moments to trust God and His promise that Kourtney and I will be a family again – not with my hundreds of pictures, but for real. I just pray "Come on, God. Please don't let me down.... Please. Thank you, God, for the promise of another life. In Jesus name, Amen."

Tuesday, November 6, 2007, 7:04pm

Have some drama today with "the sperm donor". I emailed and wrote his ass a letter after reading a letter he wrote to his brother. I don't have the energy to get into it. He emailed me back. To my surprise, he apologized for the letter incident. He asked me to give him a call, as this subject is very difficult to discuss through email. Oh really? He says it's difficult for him to talk about. And what the hell does he think about me? That it's easy for *me*? Here's the deal: I actually love Kourtney.

So where the hell does he think my head and my heart are?!?! So, he can gone on with that bullshit he trying to talk about! Whatever!

Wednesday, November 7, 2007, 5:22pm

Yep, it's the panic attacks again. I keep thinking that I need to be out somewhere looking or driving around for Kourtney. Then, the reality checks for the 200th time today that say I will not be able to locate him anywhere. Anywhere! No where. That's amazing to me and what a let down all at the same time! See, I don't know what happens after death.... All I can speak on his living here on earth. Whoa... these panic attacks. I cannot breathe, my heart races, and I feel my head swims in circles. And the worst part about it is that I cannot control it! Shit! I can be laughing and okay and then – BAM – I'm in the downward spiral. Once again, I have to break down what death means to me. This allows me to come to grips with what happened because Kourtney had no control over the situation. Sometimes I say to myself, "Something really bad happened to Kourtney and he died as a result. I know that he did all he could to help himself. I don't blame him in any way." Well, I need to get dressed I'm going out to dinner. We are going downtown to The Woodward. See, I still try. I just pack up my broken heart and keep it moving. What else can I do?

Thursday, November 8, 2007, 6:55pm

Not sure where my head is today. I think I'm avoiding his pictures. Sometimes that's the best way to deal with it for the day or time being. Too painful. Nothing has changed for me and I miss him all the time. I've been thinking about the trial. I'll be questioned first. I have an idea of the type of questions the prosecutor will ask me. Not sure about the defense attorney. It's going to take everything inside me not to jump all over that fuckin idiot! I have visions of pulling out his eyes with my bare hands! His dumb ass got no clue about what he did. I think if you're able to take a life for nothing, then *nothing* is what value you give to your own life. I know he killed Kourtney, and he knows it, too; but what he did as well was end his own life! So, right back at him! It's called karma, and it did not take too long for him to get his! Kourt may be dead, but the murderer, well, he is the "walking dead".

Friday, November 9, 2007, 8:24am

Off to work for a bowling event. I did rest well for a change. Somehow, I still feel tired. I think its just depression more so than anything – and me fighting the nervous breakdown I really deserve. My body and mind have to find an outlet. I am determined (at least today) to get through this. Tomorrow is another day... another fight. I'm wearing my Kourtney necklace today.

Sunday, November 11, 2007, 1:36am

Hurt....Yes, I am. Jaz and I went to Kourt's old girlfriend, Mercedes', birthday party/dinner at a popular sports bar. Mercedes had a T shirt made with pictures that she and Kourtney had taken on her birthday in 2006. She also wrote a letter to me, about Kourtney. Jaz started reading it; I had to walk away. I just opened my cell phone to his picture and gazed at it. So sad. So many people loved Kourtney. I hope he knew that. As I gazed at his picture, his smiling face back at me, I said to him: "Kourt, I'm so sorry. I hope I did not make life bad for you." Kourtney had no destruction or malice in his heart. I'm not saying he was without fault or was perfect. But I said it – and I'll say it again and again – Kourtney had the love of God in his heart. He was finding his way. Life can be hard, even when doing things the best or right way.... Still, there are challenges. I know that from my own life. My son is with God now; he is peaceful. He has joined our other family. He now waits for me and the rest of our family. The devil used the murderer. Now the devil has the murderer's soul for eternity. I believe that. The dragnet the murderer set up for Kourtney is the one he fell into! Man, my head hurts so bad now. Losing a child is the worst thing to happen to any parent. Even if I hated someone, I would not wish this heartbreaking burden on him/her. Does the pain ever completely go away? I don't think so. Got to learn how to deal with my new life – whether I like it or not.

Tuesday, November 13, 2007, 8.42am

Yesterday, I found out that another young man was murdered in the same neighborhood as Kourtney, in the River Rouge or S. W. Detroit area. I know his parents. We all grew up together. My cousin Lauren is the victim's Godmother. This young man and Kourtney were cool with each other. I believe he is about 2 or 3 years older than Kourtney. The victim was also cool with my sister Kim. His grandparents live right up the street from Kim, which is where he was killed. Yes, right in his grandparent's front yard. Shot in the head. His grandfather found him. I thought about going out there, but I started breaking out in hives just knowing how the family is feeling right now. This is all too much, and I'm trying to reach Kim. The last time I spoke to her, she was upset. I'm going to get out there by tomorrow to check on everyone. I know just what to do.... But, oh, how I wish I didn't. I prayed so hard last night for Kourtney, myself, the recent victim, and his family. I also prayed that I'm approved for my grant through AVON to start my own support group. I have not heard anything back. I have not given up. I know there is something I can do to help. When someone carries out a murder, it's out of the control of everyone. I find that I continue to pick up the pieces whenever I can. I manage to find one and a place where it fits, or I toss it out. Welcome.... Welcome to my new world.

I know there is no way Kourtney would have ever wanted or intended to leave this way...or leave us this way. But, again, we can only control ourselves. The murderer made his decision. He carried it out with nothing but pure evil... disguised in human form. In November of 2007, when this other young man was killed, I felt even more determined to do something for the community. I was on my second attempt with AVON for the $5000 to fund my group. Still, I had not heard anything, but I waited and remained hopeful. There would be another chance to apply in December, with the final opportunity in April of 2008. As a devastated and heartbroken mother, I could directly relate to other parents of murdered children. I felt that I had a solid plan to provide some comfort and relief. If only I could get the AVON judges to believe in me. That would be left to be seen. All I could do was wait it out and continue to work on myself. All along, small talk about writing a book would come up. Typically, I would brush off quickly. Not that I didn't think it was a good idea. I just could not see how what was contained within the pages of my journal would be of interest or help anyone. I only felt that it was my help alone. And, often times I did not view it as therapeutic in my own life.

Tuesday, November 13, 2007, 8:42am continues

I continue to fight all kinds of emotions and impulses. I will be so glad when it's over, "it" being the trial and sentencing. Much of my time is spent having visions about it, worrying about the outcome. I got that back-and-forth thing going on inside my head again. One side is resistant to what's really happening, the other side is all reality-based. As a whole person, I have to rely on reality to keep me from going off the deep end, never to return. I'm going to tell my therapist about this. But, for now, I just talk out loud to Kourtney. That makes me feel "normal". Since he and I would talk on the phone more than we saw each other face-to-face, I felt it okay for me to hold my phone to my ear and pretend we are engaging in conversation. Whatever works, huh? Yeah, I think so. I still pray at night with Kourtney and read scriptures out loud. As his mother, I want to make sure I'm doing my part to appeal to God for my son in the event there are any reservations. Here is the good news, and I need to remember this more often. Kourtney told me...he told me shortly before he was killed that he had been reading the Bible more and praying. He asked did I believe him. I was like, "YES, boy! You had a spiritual upbringing, so your foundation is there." Further, I went on to say to him that if he took one step towards God, then God would take two steps towards him. I encouraged him to find his independence and to make good life changes for himself. We talked about future plans often. I appreciate Kourtney for always listening to me. Never being disrespectful, even if he got mad at me about something I said or in which we disagreed. He would listen, take the information he needed, and move on to make his own final decision.

Wednesday, November 14, 2007, 9:16pm

It's been a busy day. Much of what I did today revolved around Kourtney. I had to take his social security card back over to the funeral home to get his death certificate corrected. I originally gave them the wrong number and they misspelled my name. Now that I think about it, when the corrected copies come, I will mail one to his "dad". See how he likes that!! Since he says, "It's (Koutney's death) a very difficult subject!" Whatever! I'm not even sure if I wrote about the drama from last week with him. But I had to check his ass! He asked me to call him, but I just could not. It's too late...Kourtney is gone! I asked him in the email why he even showed up at the funeral. But whatever...no need in me getting all worked up over that. I've got bigger and more important fish to fry. God will deal with the "sperm donor".

I was contacted by the TV news. They want to do another story on the car rental agency and the bill in excess of $8,000 that they sent me. I really did not want to do it because it gives me additional stress. But I did agree. A few of us wrote letters and emails to the car rental agency, but we received no response yet. The news reporter said that a lot of people were outraged by my story and had contacted the news room. So, we are scheduled to do a follow-up report. However, there is nothing new to report. I'm checking into setting up a donation system through the bank. If anyone wanted to donate, they could. I feel funny, though, about asking for financial assistance. My step-mom, "DD", gave me the idea of setting up a website so folks could donate online. It's been a long day, though. I had an appointment in Southfield, MI. Afterwards, I got back in time for Jaz and I to go downtown for dinner and pastries at a shop in Greektown! All of the deserts are so gorgeous. It's a shame to eat them! I just like looking at them. (Smile.) On the way home, we stopped at Honey's for a while. There were some miscellaneous things of Kourtney's that I packed up and brought home with me. I don't think there is anything else to clean up. That's it, huh? Man...I just don't believe it. The whole time I was at Honey's, I kept waiting and looking around for Kourtney. I just knew he would walk through the door any moment. That did not happen. It will never happen again. The more I think about that fact, the harder and faster my heart beats. Then there's the shortness of breath. I try to play it off in the face of others, excuse myself to another room or something, and pull myself together. I don't want anyone to see me in distress or struggling. I'm always putting on the front that I'm okay. I know it's on me and God. I don't want to bother anyone, either. This is my problem.

Since I've been home, I talked to John John for a while on the phone; took a shower and washed my hair; went on Myspace; laundry; and now, as usual... watching Martin.

Thursday, November 15, 2007, 3:06pm

I had to find a new therapist/counselor today. We got new insurance at work. I can't get my next *"much-needed"* appointment until Tuesday, November 20th. On the way home today, I stopped at a market. I had a craving for vanilla and chocolate wafer cookies. The market was busy with people preparing for Thanksgiving next week. My thoughts were with Kourtney and how this will be our first holiday without him. Wow.... How about he has not had any dinner of any kind in five months now? Amazing. I had to get a hold of myself in the market. Those thoughts induced another panic attack, along with dizzy spells. As hard as I tried, I was in the midst of something. Next thing you know, while I'm trying to clear my mind and make it out of the market, I have thoughts of the car with all the bullet holes and Kourt's blood. I got sick to my stomach. I'm dizzy and alone. I know I'm not going to make it out of here, is how I felt! I'm scared, and I felt that people are looking at me. I make it through self check-out quickly and almost ran with my bags to my car. In my car, I just stop trying to hold back the inevitable...yep, the tears. Then I began to feel stable enough to drive home...so I did.

What I found to be true through this whole process is that anything can trigger a thought that will lead to an emotion or reaction. It's not about needing attention or wanting someone to feel sorry for me. It is just what it is: the grief process. The more time gets behind you, the better you get at dealing with the loss. How can you ever get over the loss of your child? That's impossible. To me, that's the good news...the love remains. But the strange thing is that there are actually people out there who think "Shouldn't you be done with that by now!" Are you serious!?! In the words of a pastor who I heard preach at the funeral of the young man that was killed after Kourtney, "You'll never understand unless you've sat in the front row!" The point the pastor was making is that unless you're son or daughter has died before you – because that's how you make it to the front row of the church – then you will not be able to relate. Not to minimize the death of anyone, but when a death is tragic, unexpected, with the elements of VIOLENCE AND A CHILD involved, there is a difference! I have experienced the hurt by other deaths in my family, but, I have to say that nothing compares to the death of Kourtney. Nothing. I'm sorry. That's just how it is. Again, I'm not comparing or minimizing the death of a parent or friend or an uncle. My point is that it's so out of order. It's backwards for a parent to prepare a funeral for a child. My dad told me a story of a man who loss his parents, his wife, and his son (not at the same time). He told my dad of all those ones he loved so much, the death of his son has been the hardest to deal with. And I know why. It's because, as parents, we protect and provide for our children, and can never break up with them. We sometimes get divorced, but our children will always be. We expect our parents to live full lives, then we lay them to rest. But our children will always be. *That's what we believe*. That's what I believed. The

death of Kourtney has taught me that anything – I say anything – can happen to anyone at anytime. How vulnerable we all really are. Since we don't expect it, we don't say I love you enough – or do all we can – because we think there is always tomorrow. What I'm getting at is that I'm learning not to beat myself up over not saying each and every day that I loved Kourtney. He knew that I did. I showed him. "*Saying* and *doing* are two different things," in the words of my grandmother, the late Henrietta Duffie. And, of course, the "I wish" syndrome will kick in…. I've come to find out that's normal, too. The next day, or next hour, I'm back to an inner smile for Kourtney. Or at least I'm peaceful about him, if only for a little while. Now, back to the journal.

Saturday, November 17, 2007, 7:04am

Oh, Jesus…. Here I go again – looking for Kourtney. I know damn well he is nowhere around.

November 17, 2007, is a day close to mental breakdown. It's hard to put into written words my emotions. As I read, I would have to say that I'm out of my mind. I'm confused and preparing to do things that don't make sense, such as going to Macy's to buy his favorite cologne. To do what with it, I never said. I just headed to the mall to make the purchase. Pulling out his clothes and setting them up, along with his shoes, as if his body were in them. I really needed some help. However, my next counseling appointment is not until Tuesday of the upcoming week. I think I needed a real psychiatric intervention at the E.R. I don't know what the rest of my weekend was like because I didn't journal again until Monday, November 19th. So, let's see where my head is now…

Monday, November 19, 2007, 9:10am

Starting my day off with thoughts of my very own fallen angel. The dark angel… Kourtney. I will be attending the funeral of the young man killed the other day. I went to the funeral home last night for the viewing. He looked very nice and handsome. I hugged his dad and I could feel his pain. I know that "look" of being in a trance, like you're not really there or here. Yeah….I know that all too well. I've been praying for them. There is a party going on somewhere tonight. It's for all the young men who have loss their lives…all to violence…and Kourtney's name is on the list, too. I kept one of the fliers to put in Kourt's scrapbook.

7:32pm

Well, I went to the funeral; it was sad. When I heard his mother yell out for her son, it was so hard to listen to her despair. Harder for me, knowing that she better hold on to God because there is no one to help you, really, not when you're alone. Take it from me, those times do come. What you going to do then? At the family dinner, when the mother seen me, the first thing she yelled out to me was: "Tell me what to do!!" I was stunned as I made my way through the crowd to her. We just hugged and cried and held hands so tightly. I'm not sure what I told her to do, but I know that I said that she DOES NOT HAVE TO FORGET ABOUT HER SON... EVER! That I know for a fact! I showed her my heart shaped urn I wear around my neck. I told her Kourtney is everywhere with me. This is his body inside this urn I explained to her. We exchanged numbers and promised to stay in support of each other.

She and I do stay in touch. We both belong to a national organization, "Parents of Murdered Children". They have monthly meetings. She and I check on each other by phone or text message. Let's see, today is Saturday, February 8, 2009. As I was headed in for the Saturday night worship service, I just saw her last night going into her parents' house – the house where her son was killed – which is right across the street from my church. I told her all about my book endeavor and we plan to see each other at the meeting next Thursday night. It's evident that she and I have come a long way from the tragic events of 2007, the events that rocked our world and turned it upside down and inside out! We are still a work-in-progress. I think that would be true of all parents in this same situation. It's not something to get over. You just learn how to deal with it.

Tuesday, November 20, 2007, 6:36pm

I've been out shopping for Thanksgiving dinner. *Not a good look,* as I realized every second who will not be at dinner. So now, here we go! Here comes these special days when I know we would have seen each other. Now it's just not possible. How? Why? The tears filled my eyes in the market and how glad I was that I only needed a few things and able to get out of there. The way it is for me is like this: Kourtney is gone away from me forever. He does not require a meal today or any other day. He does not require anything this earth has to offer. Well, maybe that's not completely true. The love of a mother or father will always be. I told my therapist today about the panic attacks. She showed me some breathing techniques. She also gave me a great idea for Kourt's funeral plants and flowers. It's been 6 months and all the flowers are still in the garage. But she suggested that I create a compost pile and return all the flowers back to the earth for new things to have life! Wow.... I light up like a Christmas tree. I told her that is a wonderful idea! Her suggestion got my biggest and truest smile in a long time. I hope to get started on that project this week. Just thinking about it feels good to me. I'm so glad I left the flowers alone and did not throw them out. Although, Jazmyn teases me by saying "Kourtney's funeral is still going on in the garage," I knew deep down something would have to be done with the flowers. I could not hold on to them forever. My therapist said that more than likely I did not throw the flowers away is because, to me, it probably felt like I would be throwing Kourtney away. She was right! Gee, she's smart, I thought to myself. (Smile.) Making a compost pile with the flowers was more like a ritual, definitely most appropriate for my feelings. Still, I miss Kourtney...I do. I can only hope now that he thought I was a good mother. Sometimes, I feel I could have done better. Maybe that's natural after this type of loss. I gave him all I could, and I encouraged him to be independent and to lean on himself. He was independent in so many ways. But now I see that being 22-years-old is still *a baby*. I just thank God right now for Kourtney. Thank you, in the name of Jesus—Thank you!

Wednesday, November 21, 2007, 4:47pm

Today seems strange. It's ugly, cold, and raining outside this Thanksgiving Eve. I'm wondering about being thankful and find myself questioning everything – life, living, death. What does it all mean? Yeah, I'm happy about being alive, I guess. However, lots of people say "Death is the beginning." So, I guess it's okay to be dead, too, huh?

Thanksgiving Day, Thursday, November 22, 2007, 10:34pm

Well, I made it through the day. As the evening went on, I started to feel sad about the tragedy. Much later, after dinner, Honey, John John, and I went to the movies. That was good, kept my mind off Kourtney, whom I only thought about every few minutes instead of every other second. I keep picturing Kourtney driving up to that gas station and the drive I took to the hospital. I find that I can hardly stand looking at EMS trucks. I've seen two tonight. I see more and more that this is a tragedy to my life, too. So what am I to do? My circle of friends is limited. I'm glad I have only depended on God and myself. I do know that others have their lives. I do understand. I don't expect anyone to see after me. It's my burden, and I've got my life, too. I'm really trying...I am, but, at the same time, I feel so *un-noticed* in this world. Am I being punished? I know three people for sure that I matter to...and now one of them is gone. So, that leaves two people for sure, and I'm nervous. My life has been full of disappointments. No matter how nice or right I attempt to make things, I get the short end of the stick. And how much shorter can the "short end" get than losing a child? My therapists brought up the Bible story of Job and, yes, I agree. I understand all of that. But will there ever be a blessing for me? Where is my beautiful blessing? Nothing can ever replace the loss of Kourtney...NOTHING! So, I must be in store for something quite grand. I think I deserve it. I hope God does, too.

As I look back over my life, all that I've done has been in the name of love. I'm not having a pity party, I swear. But tonight, I just feel alone and sad. The day has been of good food and family - you know, the things that make you feel happy to be with family and friends. But for me.... (Deep breath.) I just had to suck it up.

Yep, I took the pictures and smiled for the camera, ate, and we all told stories about Kourtney, and laughed. But me? Oh, me.... On the inside, I'm screaming to be alone. I can't take all of this "fun times" and family gatherings. This one person is missing...it's my son...its Kourtney.... And will he ever make it back in time for dinner or any other meal or holiday or event? NO! No, he will not. What must I do to keep myself going? I'm trying to fit into my new world. Do I really have a life? What's my future? How do I ever really have fun again–I mean, for real?

Thoughts of Kourtney seem to take over. On my drive home from Honey's tonight, I feel all the more prepared and hopeful to get my support group started. I feel like I need to be doing something to get this thing started in some way. No word from AVON yet, though. I've got to teach broken-hearted mothers to stand on their own again. I know I can do that. It's what I've been doing for 6 months...and no break-down yet. I play around with the fire but am not consumed–yet! Further, I made a promise to Kourtney that his death would not be in vain. It's what my co-worker said to me at the funeral home. She said, with tears streaming down her face and reaching out to hug me, "Don't let his death be in vain." I said I would not. Even though, at that time, I had not a clue how not to let it be. That stuck with me. That's been so important to me; it made sense. The passion of ideas are within me, but I can't get them out. I'm fighting through all this grief. Seems like the only thing I can do is journal.

***The only thing I can do is journal.* Journaling has saved my life! The very thing I didn't give much credit to, only as my 24/7 outlet and sounding board, has set me free in so many ways. It took me a long time to see how therapeutic writing or journaling is – to me, it feels like magic! My expectation on this unseasonably-mild winter night, February 10, 2009, is that Kourtney's death will not be in vain. When this book is complete (in what I hope to be the near future) and reaches the hands and hearts of others, I can say to my co-worker and the world, proudly to Kourtney, to myself, and be ever grateful to God that "Kourtney's death has not been in vain—and this book is just the beginning." Amen. I find the more I write the pages of this book, the better I feel. It's overwhelming for me sometimes. I sit here and bang out these pages with a lump in my throat. I'm amazed, and I sometimes cry, smile, laugh, and get mad. Sometimes, if working at night, I sip some wine or drink a beer (low calorie, of course) and let my iPod play all my best songs. I keep a picture of Kourtney right in my eyesight as motivation. I glance over at it, give him a wink, and keep on going, like I did just now. OK, journal time....**

Thanksgiving 2007 continued

No need in saying I want Kourtney back...because I know better. He is gone. Always in my heart...always and forever. I have to love him the same but show it in a different way now. This is all new to me. He is forever with me, and I protect him all I can now. I protect his memory, his character, and his reputation. My heart is heavy tonight, and I can feel the weight of it for real. Not because it's a major holiday. I cannot imagine that I'd miss him anymore today than I did yesterday or last week or when he first died. So, today being Thanksgiving, or next month being Christmas, means nothing to me. I do, however, realize that during the big holidays, I know we would have spent time with each other for sure. We could count on that. We would have talked and laughed. With that in mind, yes, I'm sad and hurt about that. But, all and all, I miss him no matter what day or time it is. So, what to do now? Where do I go from here? I've been thinking about going to church. The pastor who spoke at the funeral earlier this week gave a message that was not only for the family, but for me, too. I had heard about this pastor through Jazmyn. She said he was a powerful speaker and she asked me to attend his church a few weeks back. I think I may. Could it be true that I need better guidance and not rely on myself so much? This whole life and death thing confuses me. "Forgivness"? I can't even go there. But I know I need to address it at some point in the future. I mean, I pray all the time...always have. I pray for things to get better for me and anyone else who is hurting over Kourtney. There's this black cloud hanging over me and I can't escape it. How do I escape and be free for real, free like Kourtney but still on this side of the world? Is that possible? Is there any relief for me, I wonder? When? Well, time will tell, right? It always does.

Yeah, I did attend that church. I did join, but it was not until January 31, 2009! All that time went by. I would think about it and make plans to go, maybe not to join, but just to hear a good, spiritual talk to strengthen me. I never made it. The first time I went was a couple weeks before the day I joined. I felt it was where I should be. On January 31, 2009, it was a huge crowd at the Saturday night service. Forty people were to be baptized and everyone took communion. When the pastor asked if anyone wanted to join, something in me just pulled me to the altar. I could not believe that I was standing up walking to the front of the church. People were clapping and singing. My cousin was crying and saying, "Kourtney, she did it! She did it!" The night God put on my heart to write this book is when I knew I had to go. I had to complete my circle. I knew that in those moments of despair and grief that Friday night, not so long ago, was the time. I got my answer. I don't know that a prayer had ever been answered, but it was loud and clear to me this time. I'm doing everything I can to protect my blessing, too. I continued to be encouraged and grow spiritually as I prepared to fall in place in my new life.

Sunday, November 25, 2007, 11:55am

I'm taken over by emotions so suddenly today. I decided to take the advice of my therapist, Susan. I'm going to start the compost pile with Kourt's funeral flowers. I don't know.... Maybe I did feel like I would be throwing him out to the trash had I just thrown the flowers out...as if they did not mean anything. His funeral plants and flowers meant so much to me. I can't explain it. Well, I started with the plants on the balcony. The leaves are dried up from the much cooler weather. I clipped most of the brown and greenery and put them inside large plastic bag. When I got down to the garage, where the flowers are, a different feeling comes over me. I could do nothing but break down in tears. I mean, after all, some of his clothes in boxes are noticeable, not to mention a picture of a birthday cake that says "Happy 17th Birthday, Kourtney." I managed to work through this, taking apart two of the flowers that were attached to easels or potted. I had enough, though. I said out loud to Kourtney "I'm doing good. These beautiful flowers are going back to the earth and something new will have life." I guess I made a step in the right direction, huh? I stopped because I realize I can move on this in my own time. It's the holiday season, and I'm glad I'm not a big holiday celebrating person. I've made friends with a guy whose 20-year-old son was shot and killed. There was a conviction in that case – a life conviction. I just pray we get a life conviction, too.

10:47pm

Good night to my most favorite angel!

11:23pm

Well, I'm still up. Not really sleepy. I feel tired, but I don't want to get in bed. It's snowing outside. It's sticking to the grass and cars; it's like a rain and snow mix. I hope it does not freeze up. I'm too scared to drive when the weather is bad. I remember when the weather would get bad and I would tell Kourtney all the time how he needs to be careful, slow down, and watch for black ice. I really used to worry about him (I think he used to drive too fast.) Well, don't have to worry anymore. I still wish for my old life back. I know...move on. That's all I can do now, because time does not stop or slow up for anyone. My so-called life. Where is the happiness? Where is the peace? Where is the understanding?

Monday, November 26, 2007, 2:25pm

It's cold and raining today. How I long to be somewhere nice and warm, with my toes in the sand and just think about Kourtney. I miss him a lot today. The physical pains are back again. Today, when the thoughts overload my mind, the pain literally starts. I keep thinking about going to church. I need some explanations. I have questions on some very serious matters. The pastor said at the funeral last week that it's his responsibility to bring the word and to teach. I need some teaching. My thoughts are overwhelming at times, and I get scared because I don't know if I can save myself. I fear I may go too far and not make it back to my "right" mind, or worse. My mental stability is in question. No one knows that. I don't talk about it to anyone. It's my secret.

4:38pm

Okay, I have a word now: "Incomplete". I woke up from a catnap and "incomplete" is how I feel. I mean, of course, I miss Kourntey. I feel the void, but still I needed a more descriptive word for my emotions. Incomplete! Jazmyn just brought up an idea I have been tossing around. My dad asked me about it as well, few months back. The idea that was tossed around was that I try to publish my journal; turn my entries into a book – to help others. I took a moment the other day, read a couple entries, and I think what I have will only help *me*. I like what I read, but not sure my notes will be for someone else's struggle or their interest.

Tuesday, November 27, 2007, 4:31pm

I went to my therapy session today. I like my new therapist. She is good. She confirms to me that it's okay to miss my Kourtney forever! She does not make me feel like I need to try to let him go and get over him. Of course, for me, that would never happen, anyway. So, the sessions really feel like *my sessions*. Today, for the first time, I exhibited anger and revenge. I'm going to continue to work on ways to honor Kourtney and his memory because his life is not about the tragic events of June 11, 2007. His life was about everything else. He had a nice life and a good heart, and I'm proud of him. I'm still thinking of a game plan for my support group. I know there is a need for it in my immediate area. There have been more murders in the SW Detroit area. Also, that NFL player, Sean Taylor, was murdered. I want to help someone and I feel that I can. Therefore, I have to get this together. How do start without funding?

10:11pm

So, where do I start? I seem to have all the ideas, motivation, and love to do this project, but what should I do first? I'm waiting on AVON and hopefully I will be awarded the $5K for a community service/outreach project. I believe helping others will help me. I have to do more to honor Kourt's memory and help the other parents in the club. I'm lost...maybe just daydreaming because I want to feel better so badly. It seems that I can make myself useful. I know Kourtney would prefer that. He was always helping. So, in that spirit, if nothing else at this time, I hope I can find a way.

Wednesday, November 28, 2007, 10:45pm

Just got home. Was out having drinks with a friend. Just trying to relax a little bit...ease my mind and talk with someone that I have something in common with in my new world. My friend's son was murdered, too. We just chilled at a lounge inside MGM and kicked it on another level. It was cool. Umm, I should go down to the garage and work on Kourtney's compost pile. Those flowers are a constant reminder. Well, whenever I go down to the garage, I'm reminded that something *did* happen to Kourtney. Still, I just can't let them go. Maybe I'm still hanging on to anything from his funeral. Oh my...I got to go now.

Thursday, November 29, 2007, 9:57pm

Ummm...not sure where to start. So many thoughts of Kourtney...isn't that always the case? Sometimes it's hard even write about him. Today is one of those days. I just got finished updating some stuff on his Myspace page, with pictures and different music. My life... his life ...everything...is so different now. Hold on... he does not have a life anymore. He used to, but now he doesn't. My son.... My son, only 22-years-old...gone way too soon. I often feel like I want to do what that lowdown idiot did to my son. But I know that will not bring Kourtney back or solve anything. I think or fantasize...but it's all just fantasy. I know that. However, when I told my therapist about my feelings of anger, and what I think about, she told me that this is how I get through the grief process. "Bad," or even violent, feelings are a part of it. I just don't know sometimes. But this I do know: I have not talked to Kourtney since June 10, 2007! Amazing. I don't like this one bit. I don't. Can I change anything? No, I can't. I can change me? Well, that's happening, anyway... with or without my permission or wanting to.

Friday, November 30, 2007, 11:01am

I had to run home from my office to get something. I had a thought or a word that describes my feelings today. That word is "haunted" or "haunting". It's because I continue to feel that I don't know where Kourtney is. I know, I've said it before, but he's like a *missing person*. I can't find him. I have not heard from him. He can't talk anymore. He has been silenced and muted! This is what I thought of, seeing him at the hospital and funeral home: He was muted. He could no longer talk. That's a tough way to look at it, but it's true. He cannot talk anymore. In my dreams he can talk. Like the dream I had a few nights ago. He was on the phone talking about $1,000 dollars, he smiled at me. Nice.

9:09pm

Tonight...boring, to a degree. Was suppose to go out, but that plan fell through. Tentative plans for a "girl's night" here at my house, but we are expecting a snow storm, so I don't think that will happen, either. I think I should get out of here before tomorrow's storm. I feel as if I'm suffocating. I need some air. I just lit a couple candles and I looked at Kourtney's face, with the candle-light glowing on his face. Peaceful, yet confused. Well, I'm supposed to attend church this weekend. I need some help. I have some real questions and I need some real answers. I'm so mad that my son does not have a life anymore. Literally, his life was taken. It was intentional. His life was stolen from him – and from me! My hope and dreams...and his...gone – just like that. All because this fuckin' punk could care less about his own life and drags my son, (and me) into his world of hate and confusion! For real.... I cannot escape this. I'm left here to pick up the pieces. I'm also here to make sure there is justice for my son, store all that I can about his life in a safe place, and to get help with my own shattered life. I know the murderer should be feeling pretty stupid right about now. If he doesn't, he will. Oh, he may never admit it, but it's coming. So, all the better, he is locked up. His life is not his own anymore. He is trapped inside himself, where there is no love, total hate, and dysfunction. The bottom line is that he does not love *himself*. He cares nothing about his own status or his life. How can it be expected of him to care about the next man or woman, for that matter? He is in the right place. The only place for him is jail for now, but it will in the end be prison - until he dies! No better for him. That's what he gets!

When I think back on those days when I would write things about the murderer, that was a time when I was lost and burdened so heavily with anger and sadness. And, based on the time frame, I know I was where I was mentally because of the healing process. Not enough time had passed when I could let that line of thinking go. Sure, even today, I think about the murderer...more about his actions against my son. I no longer get so fired up like I used to. I've come a long way. I think about all the comments others have told me over the months and it's always the same thing: Kourtney was killed on some real bullshit. That's the worst, you know, and sometimes provokes a level of anger that's indescribable. As I said earlier, the comments were even coming from associates of the murderer. I don't pretend to know every single detail about my son. But I do know this: I knew his core character. I raised him. As much as he desired not to get any attention – he got it anyway. In the words of my cousin Lennie "Enjoy your life, because you never know when you will get a hater in your midst." Exactly. There's a whole other world in the streets after a certain time of night. There are no rules. I believe that had become quite clear to Kourtney. He had enough — for real. I can say that, based on our discussions over the past year before he was killed. I almost said "died," but Kourtney was KILLED! To me, there is a difference. Death is final. It's the last thing we do in life.

Sunday, December 2, 2007, 7:40pm

It's been kind of a sad day. I've been lazy this whole weekend, doing nothing but eating junk food and sleeping. Finally, Jaz and I got out, went to an early dinner and did some shopping. We ran into a guy in public. I know others are concerned. It's hard for me to hear the details all the time, not to mention the lies and fucked up rumors! I try to come to the defense of every lie or rumor. I had to realize I can't. It's a struggle all the time. Why does it seem as though it's getting harder instead of easier? I was told it would get easier as time went on. It's been 6 months and where is my real and steady relief? My hair is coming out, I'm eating all the time, and getting fatter. Wow, next Monday will be December 10th, the supposed start date of the trial. I wish we were going. I'm ready. Now we have to wait until February 19, 2008. But that date will arrive, too! Here is one of those stupid rumors: The murderer will be released in February of 2008. Yeah right.... Even if he is not found guilty on Kourt's case, he still has to stand trial in March of 2008 for the other murder case. I pray and pray and pray for Justice for Kourtney! That means everything to me right now. Out of being nervous, I will accept a plea right now, but only for a good number of years. Nothing less than like 50 to 60 years! This will ensure he serves a good amount of his life in prison, we avoid what could be a lengthy trial, the details, etc. I'm not looking forward to that. I understand that his attorney is begging for a plea, but I've not been contacted yet; so we will see what happens.

John John is growing up so much now since Kourtney left us. He's trying to look out for me in so many ways. He is always concerned. On the way home from McDonalds, he asked me about the car rental bill. We talked about it for a while and he gave me his opinion. We both wished this: that the murderer receives a significant amount of time in prison. We always do.... But I ended it by gently saying to him, "Well, Kourt is gone now and there is nothing we can do." It was a sad moment. Later, John John says that he doesn't want anything from me for Christmas. That was really sweet.... I told him it's not for him to worry about these things. Yet, though he did not know it, I had gotten all the things he asked for last month. So, he is all set. He is doing much better overall and in school. He and Jaz are getting closer, too. That's a good thing. John John, being the younger brother, was always looked at like a baby, the little annoying brother who drove Jaz and Kourt crazy. But John John is really growing up and maturing. I think he's trying harder since the tragedy that happened to his big bro. I always tell them both that their big brother left plenty of things they can learn from and we can "use" in our lives by applying those things he showed us and told us. There are so many ways to honor Kourtney. I believe that for the past 6 months I've done just that.

Monday, December 3, 2007, 7:10am

Wow, dreamed of Kourtney all night. Another dream of him as a little boy. Very cute. In the dream, I hugged him; he was the same Kourtney: He was busy and mischievous. He is missed terribly. Hard to know that he won't be around anymore. So, thank God for those dreams. In my opinion, we are too young of a family to have experienced this type of tragedy. Certainly too young, at 22-years of age, for Kourtney. I really need to pray and workout to rid myself of stress, and clear my head.

7:48pm

I think that I'm back in the "denial phase" of this grief process. There is no way I'm accepting that Kourtney was killed – murdered! How? Why? Is it really true that we will not share anything else again? Ever? How can that be? I just think that something is wrong, and that I've gotten some incorrect information. One part of my brain is fighting with the denial and tells me that, yes, it's true... he is gone. Gone forever. That cut so deep. I just called his cell phone and there is a recording which says that his cell phone is "no longer in service." Oh my God! It *is* true. My hurt is very deep today, and I'm trying to stay busy. It's that mind-twisting hurt today. I've been out Christmas shopping and, for the first time, I'm not buying anything for Kourtney. It's so wrong what happened to him. All the wrong or right will not bring him back to me, though. I have to find another way to make things okay again. Just thinking about him standing at my front door, my hope level soars! I'm so desperate to see that boy again. At times, I feel relieved knowing he is not sad or hurt or disappointed or worried in this cruel world. But the part of me that loves him so much says that I want him back. I don't mean to interrupt his peace by calling on him, but my emotions of denial are very strong. I have remained calm and manage to smile in the presence of others. Deep down, though, I'm very troubled over what has happened. Rightfully so.... I should be. A co-worker gave me a grief chart. It's a cool reference, too. It's true. As the chart states, the symptoms and emotions can come and go at any time. This means that I could go back to shock at any time. Based on this chart, I would be in the "low or depressed phase". Eating and weight gain are playing a big role in my life right now. I know I should be working out. Burning some calories will also help to burn off some stress and clear my head. I really have to fight. I mean, fight for every little piece of sanity and peace that I can manage to grab — I'm grabbing! I fight every day to stay in control. I know I'm by myself. It's my burden. It's just Kourtney, God and me. But, where did Kourtney go? It seems God is here. I am not. "Dear God, please carry me and Kourtney". I'm at war, except I'm the only foot solider. I hope that I win. I hope that I can find some peace and enjoy what's left of my life. This has to be the ultimate low of any human being that became a parent. I'm seeking spiritual guidance. However, once again, I did not make it to church yesterday. I wanted to talk to that pastor. My question is when can I see Kourtney? Also, is it really true that we will see each other again? There is so much on my mind. When I realize there is nothing I can do, here comes the anxiety and panic attacks! It's been 6 months since I've seen Kourtney. I'm speechless now. Got to go.

The waves of emotions are tremendous on me mentally - and physically exhausting. These waves of emotions go up and down all the time. The gears can switch at any time. Control has become a big part of my world. Still, to this day, it's hard for me to shop in the men's department at Macys. This is where Kourtney shopped all the time. I have to go to that department for John John. It's uncomfortable. I try to move as fast as possible, but have to remain fair to Johh John, too. Just a few days ago, Jaz and I were in Macys. We were done, for the most part, and I decided to go over to the smoothie bar for my favorite "Strawberry Blast!" She said she was going "right over here." I said, "Okay." She walked away and, as the clerk finished making my smoothie, I looked up and saw that Jaz is right back. I'm like, that was fast. She admitted that she started to feel funny and didn't like being in that department. I told her, "Yes, I know. Everything looks like Kourtney." It's an intense reminder of him. And that's the thing: I never push myself. If I cannot handle a situation, I get away or avoid it. Sometimes the wave of sadness may pass within minutes. Sometimes the wave of sadness may last all day and night. It varies. But, I know for me, it's not good to remain in an environment that evokes sadness or crying. I return, if need be, when I can face it.

Tuesday, December 4, 2007, 8:09pm

As I got ready for bed last night, I broke down to tears. Jesus, my son is gone! And, I miss Kourtney so much. The crying spells are hard to get through at times. My whole face hurts...and my throat. Most times I end up with a bad headache. I could tell that a crying spell was coming. There was too much going on, and I was feeling the way I felt early on in the grief process. I went to counseling today and sounded off! I've been very angry lately. Nothing matters anymore. I could win a million dollars...won't or can't get me Kourtney back. I want nothing more than for Kourtney to come over. That's all I want. But I know better. I know now it's all about my dreams. Yep, that's where he and I rendezvous. I told my therapist about all my dreams, too, how I dream of him as a little boy and at 22-years-old. I express thoughts, too, of "the sperm donor". I think how I should have made him more accountable. But he will *pay* – if he's not already paying. He will pay - just as the murderer will pay. Oh, he is already starting to pay, too! So I say fuck both of them! Real talk. Those are two people I know for sure that didn't give a damn about Kourtney.

Wednesday, December 5, 2007, 8:04pm

I'm trying to get my support group started *without* the AVON grant. I'm writing out the mission statement and stuff like that.

Thursday, December 6, 2007, 7:11pm

I made some progress in preparation for the support group today. I am trying. I hope I can make this a reality, starting at the beginning of the year. I created a flyer of interest so that I can determine the need in my area. I set up an email address and put some info on Myspace. I have a third Sprint cell phone that is not in use. I've assigned that number as the support number. I don't know what to expect. Last night was rough on me. I cried so much, thinking of the reasons I'm trying to start this support group. The only reason is because Kourtney was killed. How I wish I was not considering any of this. But I am. It's a horrible reality. It is.

Saturday, December 8, 2007, 6:31pm

Today is interesting. I'm in deep grief, trying to be happy. I'm hosting a birthday party for Kim, along with a fight party. Yep, I'm a boxing fan. It's a Mayweather fight on HBO PPV. Now, this *should* make me happy, but it doesn't. The last time I watched a fight Kourtney was alive. It was on May 5, 2007, and I hosted another fight party. My, how time changes so quickly. As I type in my journal, I'm listening to a song currently playing on his Myspace page called "The Struggle is Over". My mom called me this morning to let me know she was contacted by a young lady who had been looking for Kourtney. I gave the young lady a call. She told me how they were friends as middle school youth, but she had moved away. They had been in contact with each other for maybe a year or so. Then, suddenly, she just did not hear from Kourtney anymore, she told me. She looked through the phonebook for any "Duffie" in River Rouge, and that's how she got my mom. My mom told her the news. I went ahead and called her back; she and I talked for a while. She told me that she will be at the trial in February. Her name was Kieta.

I finally met Kieta in the halls of The Frank Murphy Hall of Justice in February of 2008. She held true to her word and was there for the trial. Kieta stayed in contact with me, too, and remained a good source of support. I knew she had been a good friend to Kourtney, and I liked knowing that. Even after the trial, she and I would stay in touch by phone, text, and Myspace. Then, in June of 2008, I received what I thought to be a call from Kieta. I could hear my phone ringing, but I was in the shower. When I noticed it was a missed call from Keita, I thought to myself, Oh this is a good time to catch up. We had not spoken to one another in a while. I knew she had been sick a few times with asthma attacks and she would call from the hospital to let me know about her condition. Well, when I got dressed, I figured it would be a good time go outside and call her back as I soaked up a little sun. I also noticed, too, that a voice message was left. I just assumed she'd left a general message. I did not listen to it but instead called her. Now I get her voicemail. So, I think we're going to play "phone tag". Then my phone rings again; it's her number on my caller ID. I answer "Hello." The voice responds, "Ms. Duffie." I know right away

it's not Kieta. Curious, I said "Hi." The young lady says I'm Kieta's cousin; the smile that was on my face dropped and my heart started thumping as I listened to her explain who she was; she had come to the courthouse with Kieta. All the time I'm, like, "Yeah...ahhh humm." Finally, she says it: "Kieta died last night!" Instantly, I started to cry and went back inside the house. I gathered all the facts at my desk. She said that she would contact me with the arrangements. I immediately called Jazmyn, then my mom. Then I prayed for the comfort of her family. I talked out loud to Kourtney and Kieta. I asked Kourtney to please show her the way...now they are friends on the other side. I smiled with the thought of that, but all the time I was crying more and more. Like I said before, you never know the last time you see someone that it will be the last time.

The last live image I have of Kieta was on March 12, 2008 – the day of sentencing. I would be delivering my victim's impact statement...and, yes, once again, she showed up to court. After leaving court, we decided to go up to the utility pole and have a balloon release where Kourt took his last breath. Some of us were crying, including Kieta. My Auntie Cat led us in prayer as we let those black, red, and white balloons fly into the air! All of us looking upward, tracking them. We all felt good about what we had just done. Confirmation of that came from horns blowing as the trucks and cars drove by! I say to Kourtney, "You are so free now!" As the crowd split up and we went our separate ways, I start to realize that there is nothing else to do. A friend of mine, Mel, and I walked to our cars and talked. We decide to go to lunch back downtown. Everyone started to pull off and make plans to continue to celebrate. I looked over at Kieta. She was in the back seat of a car and the car was pulling off. She and I waved a slow goodbye. I smiled and she wiped away tears. That was the last time I saw her alive. The next time I saw her was at her funeral home visitation. I touched her hand and I whispered to her "Thank you." I told Kieta "Thank you for being Kourtney's friend – and my friend, too." Wow.... It's the little things when it comes down to it, huh? I'm so overwhelmed with grief just writing this. I just give the praise to God right now for love, real friends, and mercy.

Sunday, December 9, 2007, 8:48pm

Not sure where I am mentally. I know this: I hate the murderer! And, more importantly, I miss Kourtney. Last night, before the party started, Kourtney came to visit. Kim and Jaz actually saw the image walking over me. I was on the phone with Comcast because the PPV was not coming through on all my TVs. They could hear me walk through the house because I had on a charm bracelet. When they looked up, they could not see me, but instead they saw a huge image hovering over me. They both started to cry. Kim described something gold around his neck. It was intense for both of them. All I know is that when I turned around, Kim was peeking and looking strange from around the wall. When I turned around, I had no idea what had just happened.... I was still on the phone. At first, I believe Kim thought I had let a guest in. She asked me, "Who was that?" I was like, "What are you talking about?" Then it all became clear to them what they had witnessed. We've also had some Kourtney sightings lately with the young children in our family. They tell stories of Kourtney playing and holding conversations with them. What is remarkable about this is that these kids are like 1- and 3-years- old and they had no relationship with Kourtney. They are pointing at his pictures when asked who are they're talking to, and they are calling out his name as the person that plays with them! This is amazing and heartwarming to me. The irony of last night is that just moments before they "saw" Kourtney, I was in the laundry room and I asked Kourtney (out loud) to come and see me. Little did I know, he was already here. I'm thinking maybe he wanted Jaz and Kim to see him so that I would believe. But I have to let Kourtney know that I believe him, anyway. I don't know for sure what happens after life.

I do know that when the time is right, Kourtney and I will sit down and talk again. I believe that. That time will be forever and no end. So, until then, I will do my best to hang on, be positive, and do all that I can to cover my pain and sorrow until I can't handle it any longer. Sometimes, that means NOT writing in my journal, not looking at his pictures, not having the fantasy that he is still here. Hey, I have to do whatever I have to do in order to keep my head above water. To keep breathing in and out!

Monday, December 10, 2007, 12:29am

...and I cannot sleep! Sleepless in Detroit, huh? Not cute at all! Already, I'm feeling like not going to work. I know I'm dealing with a major depression. I refuse to take pills, though. I have to fight on my own. Like Kourtney...he fought to the end. He did all he could do. So, it's the same with me. I fight.... I will fight until there is no more. I'm having PMS right about now, but I'm not at all emotional. My emotions stay hidden behind smiles, and I become the "hostess with the mostess." It's a lot of pain and feelings of being lonely or alone. Nothing can replace Kourtney; the void is there. His life was stolen away from him and repayment will NEVER suit *that* crime. It will never be enough. I would not care if the murderer died 100 times worse than Kourtney....What he stole can never be given back to me. I mean, I will take what I can get in terms of sentencing, but that really does nothing for my heart.

I'm 41-years-old now. How much longer will I have to suffer this way? All day and night wishing and hoping and thinking about this boy, my son. I know it will never completely end. I cancelled my therapy appointment for this week. I just don't want to go. I find I have to force myself to do just about everything. I better make myself journal or get out of the house or else I'm going into a deeper depression, making things worse. I may carry out one of these thoughts of suicide! It's a scary time for me once again. I think to myself, what if I cannot help it? What if a breakdown hits me - then what? What of my life and the delicate balance I already play between life and death? For that matter, I play with fire — not burned — not yet any way. I have not been able to take any real time off work — not the time I feel I need after this happened. I would not get enough money to cover financial obligations. It's pressure and stress. A careful balance of more pressure and more stress.

John John suggested I start a home business. That "sounds good," I told him, but I have trouble just managing day-to-day in any setting. Maybe my support group will help me. You know, it will keep me busy and, while helping others, I will help myself. Sounds like a win-win to me. Maybe I'll try to publish these notes I've been writing since July, 2007.... Who knows? Maybe another parent in grief can identify, find some comfort in my words, and know they are not alone. Umm, I don't know about that...someone reading my diary. I really wonder if anyone would find it that helpful...or even interesting. I don't know. I'll keep thinking on it. I think that's my problem: I'm always trying to plan too much in advance. I can't do that anymore. Its one day at a time now. Things are so different. Just one day at a time...until further notice. I mean, thinking about the future does have its place I think. I get too carried away. I just need to stay focused on no more than 2 to 3 days out. That is quite enough for me. Earlier today, I could not even remember the numbers in order - you know, just how to count. Just as I was about to tell Jaz there is something wrong with me, I was able to regain my focus. I could literally feel my brain trying to give me the next number, but it would not come to me. I'm a ball of confusion and insanely distracted. I know I'm tired. What can I do? I do the best I can. Once again, my brain is on super speed and I cannot sleep. There is so much madness going on in my life. Sleep depravation is a side effect of grief. Soon I'll have to be up for work. I would leave out early, but it's icy outside and I'm scared to drive. Maybe I can fall to sleep and go in later when the salt trucks are out. It seems that everything is a struggle, except for being restless and eating junk food! Well, I'm headed back to bed to see what happens. R.I.P., Kourtney.

Talk about being distracted. One day, I drove right pass my house in broad daylight. Did not even realize it until almost one mile up the street! That really scared me. I started to think that maybe I would run a red light one day just because either I'm not thinking or so deep in thought and not concentrating on driving. There were times that I would be driving and the tears would start up. I knew it was best to get home. Those were the days when I could not control my emotions. "Control" has become my protector.

Monday, December 10, 2007, continues 3:46pm

It seems that I understand death more and more. It means in part that I will never see Kourtney again. He is gone from earth...forever. I'm here and he is *there*. Wherever "there" is, right? Everything I do now is in his memory, honoring him, and keeping his spirit alive.

10:09pm

Okay, Kourtney is dead? Oh my...we're either dead or alive, right? It can be no other way. And for each of us, it's one way or the other. I swear, I want to tell that lowdown bastard that took my son's life something right about now! Actually, I want to do more than tell his ass something. I hope Kourtney haunts his dreams so bad, he is afraid to fall asleep. Whatever punishment he receives will not be enough, even if it's natural life in prison. That is not enough! There is nothing he can do, nothing he can suffer, that will make me happy, because nothing will bring Kourt back. His life was over in a matter of minutes. That's all it took. All it takes is a deadly weapon in the hands of some idiot with nothing to lose anyway and it's done! I hate so much that my son crossed paths with this fool! I'm so full of anger, and I wish there was something I could do. But there is nothing I can do. The only real satisfaction would be to get my son back, but the sad, so sad reality is that cannot happen – it *will not* happen. His life has been cut off by a person who had no right to his life, to determine when he dies. I wish that bullet would have boomeranged and hit his black ass or the person who called Kourtney out to his death. That person should know they are just as responsible for my son's death as the punk who pulled the trigger!

It makes me feel so sorry for Kourtney when I count down the last hours of his life. No one knew what was being planned and plotted against him – except the murderer and the person who called Kourtney to that gas station. I hate even more that at least one other person knew – and maybe even a few other lowdown niggas – and helped the murderer orchestrate and carry out that madness on June 11, 2007! How could they just sit back and do this? Do they sleep at night, I wonder? Are they really okay with their role in this, their decision in this? I hope they are haunted, restless forever, and eventually called to justice. I want everyone involved called to justice! They must pay.... I'm paying in every way. I'm living proof of the tragedy committed against my son. I have his pain now. I'm not sure how to release it, or even what to do most days. I just walk around and do the things *I think* I should be doing, all the while not feeling stable. Trying to enjoy my life and constantly seeking outlets is the task at hand. I need to bring some peace back to my life, or at least have some of the pain subside. But, somehow I just don't see that happening. Why did this happen, I always wonder? It's a mystery and puzzle to me. I don't like questioning God. I'm lost, though. What do I do now? I keep saying I'm going to church. I can't say what's holding me up. Maybe I'll be okay one day. Maybe....

Tuesday, December 11, 2007, 11:48am

I'm not at work today and I don't feel well...not well mentally. I'm so sick of work right now. But, as I stated before, I cannot afford to be off work. I'm so scared because I feel as if I'm on the brink of a breakdown. Right about now, I'm hating my life once again. I'm so angry today. I'm mad at the world!!! I'm mad at everyone!!! I'm doing everything I can to hang on and find some normalcy in my life. It's next to impossible for me. I can't win. I have no way out. And I'm a loser...a loser because I lost my 1st Born.

1:34pm

I just had lunch, and I'm feeling somewhat better. Perhaps part of my problem is that I feel guilty when/if I don't devote enough time to Kourtney in thought and prayer. I thought about that last night, telling Kourtney out loud that I can't spend every-waking-second thinking about him, and that I have other things to get done. God knows, I mean no disrespect to Kourtney...no way. I know for real that Kourtney understands. I'm struggling with the idea, because it's true: I do feel guilty if I'm not thinking about him or praying or journaling. I love Kourtney; there is no question about it...and that will never change. Never. Now, one would think, since I'm aware of that, I'm giving myself permission not to be guilty. My Grandma Duffie, "Big Mama," also loss a son, my uncle Chris. He was 17-years-old when he died. He had been sick. I recall her saying that since his death, there was not a day that went by that she did not think about him and still cry about Chris. I wish I could ask her something, such as how to cope day-to-day. I remember my uncle Chris very well. We were buddies. I was 5-years-old when he died. I remember seeing him at the funeral home, coming home and hiding under Big Mama's living room end table. I also remember years later, when Chris would come to visit me in Big Mama's kitchen. It scared me; I went running out of the house. I will always remember that. Now, if and when Kourtney comes to see me, there will be no running. I've been waiting. I'm on constant watch for him. I never know when or where I may see him because I don't know anything about the afterlife. One thing about it is that we are all going that way. All of us will one day. Kourtney went early in life, however. At some point, he would have traveled that path.

Saturday, December 15, 2007, 6:34pm

So much has been on my mind, to the point that I cannot even write about my feelings. I feel like, in many ways, my life was already disappointing enough – then my son is murdered!! So, now what do I do? It's been six months now and I do not feel any better.... I cannot say it's gotten any easier. I'm more depressed and it has nothing to do with Christmas. I'm not a big holiday person to begin with. Today started off okay, but it took a turn and went downhill. I'm surprised that I can even write today. But I felt like I should or wanted to.... Who knows? I don't. The weather is not good today. We are in the midst of a winter storm advisory. John John and I went out earlier and got some shopping done. The snow is accumulating fast, though. I got scared and was ready to go home. Life has been so discouraging. This murder has complicated things on another level for me. I can't deal with all of this right now. Do I have a choice? No. Well, sort of. But I don't want to get into that right now. Is there anything that can make it better for me? Doesn't seem like it. I'm so burdened with grief *and* my life. There's so much to sort out to try to find my way again. I feel different all the time. I envy Kourtney sometimes because he is peaceful and away from the B.S. of the world!

Sunday, December 16, 2007, 8:43am

Wow, it's so pretty outside...all dressed in white! The snow has covered everything; it's perfect. As I look outside at the blowing snow and the drifts, I think about Kourtney (What's new?), and I once again force myself to accept his death. What is the real meaning of "death"? Death in my opinion is nothing. Yeah... nothing. No matter what I think of, death is nothing; it does not exist. It's fearful to me that Kourtney will one day become *someone they used to know.* Maybe he already is in the minds of some. He's no longer around, and he's not coming back. Death is final. I have to keep reminding myself that Kourtney did not know what was going to happen to him. If he had, he would have never been caught off guard. Simple as that. It's just so hard to accept he is gone. And there will be no new memories to create. Dealing with life under these circumstances has been so very hard. If I'm not journaling, I'm praying. I pray for many things, but JUSTICE is my focus right about now. I pray the bastard gets life! The life *without* parole! There is no plea deal being offered and our prosecutor feels confident that she will win the case. So, I'm satisfied. I just pray for justice and leave the revenge to God, whom it rightfully belongs to! So there! Kourtney believed in God and was a person of faith. I'm confident about where is soul rests. God knows our hearts, and Kourt's heart condition was right. That makes him favorable to God. That's why little kids are having play sessions with Kourtney. He is peaceful, not a care in the world. I wish I could say the same for me. I'm worried, scared, freaked out, and in a constant state of panic all the time over his death. I pray for peace of mind for myself, too.

10:12am

As I look outside at all the snow falling, I hear the sounds of snow blowers when I realize for the one thousandth time today that he is gone. He's so far away from me, but yet he is still close. I can't explain it. All of my senses are in tune with his death. I can feel my brain flutter, my heart race, pain in my chest, and I'm sometimes speechless. I stumble at times, just trying to figure out how to talk, or even think of anything to say. It's fair to say that my mind is blank. I hate what the truth represents in my life now. I'm tempted to go and see another physic reader, because I have so many questions. I think about church all the time. I don't know where to turn...

4:13pm

I guess this means that Kourtney has lived his life, right? He almost got 23 years. Almost twenty-three years is what *I got*, too. That's it. I'm trying to find a way to put this into perspective and what makes sense to *me*. I need to continue to collect in words and information; that means something to me. It may only mean something *to me*. All I can handle is what makes sense to me. I can't stand thinking that he died...that he *is* dead... how about he was killed.... I hate that one most of all. Isn't it true that we carry our children's burden? I think so. Kourtney's burden is mine. I don't want to remember him. Why do I have to "remember" him now? Not fair. What else can I do now? Nothing...just remember all day long. Oftentimes, I find myself sorting fantasy from fact. Unfortunately, for me, my brain rejects the facts and that confuses me. I go back and forth too much.

Monday, December 17, 2007, 4:30pm

I've not had time for a real "cry session". Since that is the case, one just hit me right in the middle of a business call! BAMMM!!! Tears flowing.... I had to end the call. But I do feel a little better now. I think about my support group all the time. I still have not heard from AVON. I guess they don't like my community outreach idea. Oh well. I like it, so I'll have to figure out a way to make it happen.

6:23pm

I went on the AVON website and noticed I could reapply.... So I did. This time, I was able to provide more information, more details on my plans. I hope my initiative is noticed this time.

Wednesday, December 19, 2007, 5:57pm

I went to my cousin Lennie's birthday party last night. It was at the bowling alley, the same one I have been thinking of having Kourtney's next birthday party. I want to have a party – or some form of celebration for him – every year. Thinking about death more and more drives me crazy. But I have no control over this. Not right now, anyway. I have to keep on explaining to myself that his body has stopped working and that means that he is dead. My cute, chocolate lil baby boy. He was so, so cute... right from the start.

Thursday, December 20, 2007, 11:00pm

Don't know where the time went today. I spent about three hours on the phone with my Auntie Cat. We had a really good conversation. I still feel lost, though. Nothing ever really helps. I mean, sometimes, yeah, I'm okay; but it's never 100%. I suspect that I'm the only one with these intense feelings. If he had a father who truly loved him, there would be another person with whom I could relate. I was up in the middle of the night crying. I can never tell when the tears will start. There are times I can hold them back. I went out to the mall tonight in search of a gift for Honey. She asked for something by Gucci, *Rush* or something. I could not find it. I'll try again tomorrow. I'll be so happy when the Christmas season has passed. I hate being in Macy's men's department. Kourtney used to shop there all the time. My mind drifts, and I feel even more depressed. I'm so tired worrying about everything, such as to re-fi my mortgage payment. If I can get my payment lowered, maybe I can be off work for a few months. Some *real time* off, which I've never taken since the tragedy. I just feel like giving up. What matters now? Keep having flashbacks of the blood on the seat of the car. That's my blood, too, you know. His heart is part of my heart, too. When he went to cremation, a part of me went to cremation as well. I'm all tied up in this thing with Kourtney. Maybe it will get better. Right now...not better. The past few weeks have been tough. I do good on the outside, but I'm fucked up inside! I can't sit still or sleep. I can only hope and pray that after the trial, which is rapidly approaching, I'll be better.

Friday, December 12, 2007, 11:21pm

Just came in from dinner with my buddy Greg. He has been a good friend. We actually talked for 4 hours. We laughed, as well as had a serious talk. After I left dinner with him, I stopped at the mall for some late night shopping. I went to Macy's and JC Penny's. My brother Ken came home from prison today. I understand he is having a hard time adjusting to Kourtney not being at Honey's. I'm like this: "Welcome to the club." He hasn't had a chance to deal with Kourt's death. He was locked up when he was killed, so he did not make it to the funeral, either. I feel bad right now. His grief is kind of new in the sense that he just came home. Oh well. I don't know. I know this: I'm getting so damn fat, and I'm sick of me! I need a gym membership, and I need get my ass up early and workout! All this depression and overeating is showing up on my body. Not cute. I don't like it. The aftermath of his death is something else, I tell you. These horrible feelings soar through my body...top to bottom! Sometimes all I can do is shake my head in disbelief. Hard to believe that someone wanted to kill him. It happened, though. I'm so sorry Kourtney will never be able to accomplish his dreams and realize his full potential. Wow...Merry Christmas, Kourtney.

9:48pm

So sad.... I'm depressed – and I know it. I've been trying to dismiss it for weeks, but I know what's going on. It's not the holiday season making it worse.... It's just the tragedy. Why did he have to die? Most days, I don't know if I'm coming or going. It's a lonely kind of night. Oh well.

Sunday, December 23, 2007, 11:48am

It hurts to look at his pictures today. It's real pain that I can feel in my chest and my throat. Life is so crazy. I would have never imagined that I would have a child to precede me in death. On my obituary it will read something like "Karen leaves to mourn her first born son, Kourtney, who proceeded her in death on June, 11, 2007." (Deep sigh.) I now carry all of Kourtney's disappointments, heartaches, his stresses and worries. It feels as if his life has crash-landed on me.

Sunday, December 23, 2007, 11:48am, and I really get deep into the anger and the "I wish" thoughts. You know, I wish he were still alive, I wish I had done better for my kids...I wish the murderer is miserable (although that's probably true). Based on what I read on this day, it was a pretty bad day. I seem to repeat the same things over and over. I can just about imagine how I was typing, too – with such force that it seems that I can do damage to the keyboard! It's just one of those moments. The worse "I wish" is that he comes over right now and tell me it's all been a long and terrible dream and that it's okay now. That is such a tease, a tease that lasts for all but 3 seconds, literally, because I know better.

Monday, December 24, 2007, 3:10pm

Well, today is Christmas Eve. It's my dad's birthday, too. I'll call him in a little bit. I had breakfast this morning with my friend Mel. We went to Cracker Barrel. Then I went to pick up John John. We had our Christmas gift exchange early afternoon. We decided not to open gifts the way we would when Kourt was with us. When Kourtney was still alive, our traditional way would be to do so at midnight. After we opened our gifts, we headed back to the mall, then to the grocery store. I'm pretty tired today. I made sure everyone told Kourtney "Merry Christmas." I kissed his urn. I told him "Kourtney, you're the best, the perfect son."

8:23pm

It was also my decision to keep things quiet around here. I did not want to make a big deal out of this holiday. So, we have been downplaying everything, just to try and keep our emotions in check. There is no big dinner around here or nothing. Furthermore, we went to Southern Fires yesterday and had soul food. Southern Fires is one of Kourt's favorite restaurants. Often times I sprinkle his ashes in the grass or let blow in the wind when I get there. Tomorrow, Christmas Day, will be just another day to me. Maybe next year, 2008, will be different. I don't know. Who knows if I'll even be alive next year? Life is so fragile. How vulnerable we all are.

Tuesday, December 25, 2007, 6:24pm

Okay, it's here...the biggest holiday of the year. And guess who does not care? Me. It's just a regular day for me. I'm staying very quiet. For me, it's just another Tuesday and I'm not at the office. We plan to go to the movies. Jaz and I want to see Denzel's new movie *The Great Debaters*; John John wants to see something else. I did talk to Kourt's best friend, Ed, for a long time today. I feel so bad for him. He says it feels like Kourt died just yesterday. It's very sad for all of us. Well, I better get dressed. We are keeping the candles lit for Kourtney all day today.

9:48pm

We just returned home from the movies. The movie was really good!!! Denzel did an awesome job. John John saw the Chimpmunks movie; he said it was funny. I wish.... *Don't even get started*.... I know the real deal in my heart.

Wednesday, December 26, 2007, 11:29am

John John and I just got back home from the Macy's after-Christmas sale. He is ready to go back to his dad's house now. So I'll go ahead and take him back. I have an early dinner date, too.

I'm a little tired today, and I hope to be in bed early tonight. I talked to my friend Mel in the middle of the night and again early this morning. We were talking about how Kourtney did not give up and probably felt he still had a chance (to live) to the very end. He was still fighting with the few seconds of life he had left.... He was trying.... That's part of the message I gave Ed yesterday, that *we* cannot give up. And that Kourtney fought, fought to the end – until he could not fight anymore. He did all he could do -- until his brain was no longer connected, until his heart could not beat, until his eyes could no longer see...until the very end. I'm proud of Kourtney.

8:37pm

I just got home from dinner with a friend. Everyone comments on my "strength". I know what they see. It's my outer appearance. I have the ability to talk about him and show his pictures without breaking down. Hey, all I know is that's MY son! I love him. Believe me, I welcome all opportunities to talk about him. I'm so afraid he will be forgotten. I think more and more about where Kourt stood with God. God sees our heart. My only conclusion is that Kourt was in a good place with The Lord. This is based on the condition of his heart. I am convinced. He was a young man of faith. He believed. He was raised with God as his foundation. He never lost sight of the bigger picture. Every day...closer and closer to the trial and I'm ready, too! I'm ready for a conviction – a life conviction – so that I can move on with my life. Another thing I told Ed yesterday: "We don't leave Kourtney behind; we do take him right along with us. We recognize him in the things we do. We celebrate and cherish the memories we have. We thank God for the time we had! Now, that message is for the ones who truly love Kourtney.

At this very moment, as I journal, I'm grooving to the new Keyshia Cole song "I Remember". Sources of strength and motivation come from unlikely places sometimes. I'm home alone right now and the music volume is turned up loud. At the same time, my fingers flurry across the keyboard as the million thoughts of Kourtney invade my mind. Wow! I actually had time for another thought other than of Kourtney. I must drink two more glasses of water before I go to bed. I'm working on slimming down my waistline. All of this "emotional eating" has come back to haunt me! I read on Yahoo News today that a good way to slim down is to make sure to take in at least 8 glasses of water each day. I do so to ensure that my body does not store up the little water I do manage to drink.

Seems like everything I do is connected to the tragedy in some way. I'm starting to think about relocating again. Part of me is done with Michigan. I need some time off work, but I cannot afford it. My mortgage.... Man, to hell with this mortgage is how I feel right about now! I'm so tired. I'm up most nights – every night. I work and worry over this trial; I'm in grief; I'm depressed. I have no way out. Maybe I need to go see the doctor – tomorrow! I keep rejecting depression pills. But could medication be of some help to me? I've neither allowed myself the time nor the chance to deal with this. So, what should I do? That other shit I tried, leaving work early when my doctor put my on a reduced schedule (at my request) didn't work. I think I need the whole 12 weeks or longer off work! I'm run down... and I feel it. My body is different. *Everything* is different. I do know why!?! I don't need a professional to tell me that. I don't feel fazed by anything. It's like "Yeah Whatever."

And that's how it was for a very long time. It did not matter what I did for myself, or what someone tried to do for me. I felt I had no outlet. In every direction I turned was a dead end. I could get no relief. I could not adjust. All those changes were forced on me. That's how I felt. And I resisted. Just like Kourtney, I fought...fought 'til the very end. I fought to the death of the old me. I had to give in. I had to make the change. But it took time before "the surrender" came upon me. The grief process *will* take place. The grief process, as ugly as it can be, has to work its course.

For me, I was doing well in many ways, but I knew I still had serious emotional issues to work out. I had been contemplating suicide way too much. This was even in late 2008. However, you would figure that in late 2008, what was going on in my life should have made me stable and happy to a degree. But I wasn't. I had some good things going on, but I could not get away from the war that

was being waged within me. The thoughts of suicide only increased; these thoughts became more intense with the passage of time. The more I felt no relief was in sight, the more at-risk I became. I started to plan it (the suicide) out. I wanted to carry it out so that Jaz could still collect my insurance money. On the other hand, sometimes I did not care. I wanted the world to know just how hurt I was and that, yes, I loved my son so much, I wanted to be with him. That made sense to me. But it always came back to this: What of Jaz and John John? I have to be with them, too. They still need me, right? The answer was always yes. So, I would let the "dark thoughts" go. But they would return a day or so later. I guess the devil was working on me. I was allowing it, too. I was so confused. Even when I was with family and/or a friend, I was alone. No one understands me. That's how I felt. I felt shut out from the world, alienated by those whom I thought loved me most. I never wanted to feel that I was putting a weight or burden on anyone. So I kept my feelings to myself.

But I was the one in my own way. I had to learn how to move out the way. The new me wanted to come out, but the old me was stuck. I was stuck like a stick in heavy mud. It was hard to move me. Nothing moved me. Part of me wanted to accept, adjust, and advance. The other part of me wanted nothing to do with anything except to relish in thoughts of Kourtney...all day and most of the night. Those very thoughts had gotten me into a place where I was not sure if I could recover. And this is while *life appeared normal*. But, the truth, I was fearful of myself. I was scared and had convinced myself I was alone. I was afraid to let go of my past. After all, you know who – Mr. Kourtney – is a part of my past. How could I leave that life? All those months and it was never clear to me that time was marching onward and that I had allowed myself to miss the bus! Being grief-stricken can do that to you – and more if allowed.

On the days I was not contemplating suicide (which were not many), I would pray really hard. I started to pray in a different way. Finally, I reached out for help! When I realized what and why I had been praying so much, I knew I was in trouble. There was a bigger me on stand-by, but I did not want to know that person. At the same time, I knew I had to release and submit to God. My other options were either a mental institution or defy the gift of life and kill myself...to end my pain. I knew what my choice should be. It was the same thing I told Kourtney, "If you take one step towards God, He will take two towards you." The sweet surrender. When I took my one step towards God, it was the same night this book was born. He blessed me with the ability and the strength to try and make a difference not only in my life, but, in another person's life. I never thought I could help anyone, not even myself. This was especially true in my suicidal state of mind. My spirit had abandoned me and I was empty. That night, when God granted me peace – when I opened my heart to peace – I went to bed so calm, my mind and body rested. I say the book was born that night because, in my tearful prayer, I asked

God to clear my path and remove negativity from me. I told Him that I wanted to live; I wanted to know what my purpose was on this earth. I had become so bored with life. I depended on the entertainment of others to get me through. Before going to bed, I followed through on a promise I made to my dad: I told him I would contact an author, Elizabeth Atkins, who lives in the Metro Detroit area. At that point, I had printed 140 pages of my journal. But I could not read it.... I did not *want* to read it.... My journal was about 250 pages (but it grows every day). I went to my desk after praying and emailed Elizabeth Atkins. To be honest, I thought I would not hear back from her. Thinking she was a busy professional, if I did hear from her, it would be a long time from now. Further, I felt that I didn't have a story to tell that will help others. Still, though, I had made an effort. I went to bed at ease. I got up the next morning and checked my email. Well, what do you know? I had received a returned email from Elizabeth! And here we are today. Praise God! All Glory to God! My faith reaffirmed! I had to make it completely right. So, I went to that church I kept talking about – Triumph Missionary Baptist Church. I joined and promised to get my life in line with God's purpose. I knew I was in the right place at the right time. The night I joined the church, I had no plans to join. But, when prompted by the pastor to step forward if interested, it seemed like I floated right up there. I was not even sure what I was doing until I got to the lower level for paperwork and officially joined. Surely, it was one of the best nights of my life...and will always be.

Let it be my guess that Kourtney's soul is at ease, too. I ask myself: Did God provide all those dreams of Kourtney to help me along my journey through grief because He knew I needed them? I believe that to be true. I ask myself another question: Did those "mysterious encounters" occur because I had continued to call for Kourtney? Not letting him move on, so he stayed around trying to help me? I also believe that to be true. I can only imagine the night I joined Triumph Church, Saturday, January 31, 2009, Kourtney and his other angelic friends were praising God, playing their harps and trumpets in celebration! I believe that his angelic friends were so very happy for him, knowing that his mother made it through the storm and defeated the devil. And one day Kourtney will have that beautiful duty to greet his mother at the gates when she crosses over! Yeah, that feels right to me. Now, back to the journal.

December 26, 2007, 8:37pm continues

I just don't know how much longer I can hold on. I'm tryin' – I think. Kourtney was a solider. I should be like him, huh? I think so. He still felt he had a chance by trying to escape the gunshots! He did all he could do for himself. I know that for sure. Just this moment, my thoughts have switched to the thoughts of the Pacifica he was driving on June 11, 2007. I think about him ducking and dodging those bullets and trying to drive away – all at the same time. I know he was scared. I realize that I must deal with every aspect of the tragedy. And it's all negative and BAD to me. Some things are more difficult and intense. But those things, too, deserve my attention in order for me to help myself or anyone else. Speaking of helping others, I have not heard anything back from AVON. I even wrote an email to Oprah, and I'm certain I'll never hear anything back from her either. She probably receives millions of emails per day. I feel so desperate; I don't know where to begin in an effort to start this support group.

I think about the last time Kourtney and I rode in that Chrysler Pacifica together, which turned out to be the last time we rode in any car together period. We were talking about him buying a car. I was telling him how I thought he wasted a lot of money; he agreed. I remember this song on the radio, "Gotta Go" by Trey Songz. Kourtney was moving his head and snapping his finger to the beat. I was driving and looked over at him. I told him I liked that song, too. Then he said to me, "Mama, what you know about that?" We both laughed. After he was killed, I listened to that song all of the time. One day, I listened to it for several hours on repeat from my computer. It's kind of interesting because the story line of the song is that the guy does not want to leave, but he has to go right now; yet, he will be back before you know it! Further, in the song..."these streets be calling me." Thoughts of that day in the Pacifica, that being the last car he would ever drive, not to mention being killed in, seemed to haunt me. It used be that every time I would see a Chrysler Pacifica in traffic, I would stare at it, recreate the shooting, Kourtney speeding away from gas station – only to make it across the street at the utility pole. It was worse seeing the pictures. Here's what I mean:

Thursday, December 27, 2007, 11:59pm

Today has been one of those days when I totally realize exactly what death means. Jaz is having a rough day today. She has been crying all day long. There is not much I can do. So, I just hug her; we talk about Kourtney and try to make jokes after the serious stuff is over. I try to hold up and, to my surprise, I do. I don't want her to see me breakdown. We both realize that we have no one. The man of our house is gone. He was our protector. Now we're waiting on John John to grow up. But, at only 13-years-old, it seems like it will be an eternity waiting on his maturity. Kourtney was that father figure for Jaz. Long before his untimely death, she told him that she wanted him to give her away at her wedding. She also told him that her first born would be named Kourtney, whether a girl or a boy. Since he is gone now, I told Jaz that I had figured out a creative way that he can still walk down the aisle with her. So, it *will* happen!

Today, I could easily be full of rage. But I manage to stay under control. My head has been hurting all day. I'm tired, but I'm not sleepy and I'm hungry. Oh boy, now I need some control on the bad eating habits. I think about joining the gym all the

Original photographs taken by insurance adjuster in June of 2007, however, the Feb 09 date shown on the pictures is the date I downloaded these pictures on my computer.

time. Just trying to figure out how do I live my life now? I guess the way I've been living it since the tragedy, a day at a time, an hour at a time...whatever it takes to get me to the next point. I'm worried about me. My support system is not/has not been steady. Could it be that it has something to do with me not reaching out but instead keeping to myself? Yeah, probably.... But I do wish at times that others would reach out to me more. I mean, who is there to talk to me in the middle of the night? People say "anytime," but do they really mean that, I wonder? You know, I wonder if I called someone at 3:30am on a Tuesday morning, would they answer the phone? I just have to continue to rely on praying to God, my journal, and ME! I worry, too, about sounding like a broken record. This is all so confusing to me. I did not make a counseling appointment for this week. I don't know...just not feeling it. I wish this would all go away. I want to be left alone. I am alone. I'm not sure what to think of my life. I feel transparent, like others can see right through me. That scares me so much. A mental break is what I need. But how do I turn off my brain? It goes on and on. It never stops. Is there anything in this life, other than my kids, that's just for me? (Deep breath.)

Friday, December 28, 2007, 3:56pm

I cannot believe this. He *is* gone. For always.... That's it. Yeah, whatever!

8:20pm

Damn, this world is so crazy and imperfect. I don't think I was supposed to know when Kourtney died. Why did I have to be a witness to him being dead? When he died, I should have been long gone. This is out of order. It's not normal. I just want to try once again to understand how the hell do you go from laughing and talking – ALIVE – to just a few hours later to doing nothing – DEAD? I cannot help but feel that was not for me to see what I saw in the hospital. Believe me when I say that I'm doing all I can to keep my sanity and not go off the deep end. I feel like that song that says "If I Had a River" by George Michael (I think). Yes, I would skate the hell away from here – and stay gone! I mean that. I'm supposed to be meeting some of my family and friends at MGM Club Ignite later tonight. Yeah, I'm going. Why not? I had to call Christina at the funeral home today. I noticed the paint/engraving is coming off the urn when I clean it. A replacement has been ordered. She told me that the manufacturer has had some complaints about the white paint. I don't want his ashes disturbed, but oh well.

Sunday, December 30, 2007, 11:04am

Don't know where to start. Not looking at Kourt's pictures today. I guess it's one of those days. Not that I'm avoiding him...well, I am. But I got to keep *me* in check. Today's concentration is to try to limit my thoughts of Kourtney as much as I can. Can you say "control?" Control. I'm headed over to my aunt's house for a "girl's party" at 5:00pm. So, until then, I'll try and relax and stay on the phone. I should pray more, too. My prayer routine is typically in the morning and at bedtime. Did I forget that I can pray *anytime*? Here is a gentle reminder to self: "Feel free to pray anytime." (Smile.)

Monday, December 31, 2007, 1:56pm

So, from the looks of things, I'll be headed into the New Year of 2008. Kourtney only made it to 2007...only for 6 months into it. He and Ed had so much fun New Years Eve 2006! I remember me and him on the phone, hearing the excitement in his voice. I said to him "Boy, you sound like you're 10-years-old." He did have some fun in his life. I hate the murderer!!! I think I'm giving up. I sit here and think back over 2007. So much gained and too much diminished. I could never have imagined this. So much to deal with at one time. Seems like as soon as Kourtney was killed, me and my so-called "friend's" friendship started to NOT EXIST. I also broke up with a guy, like, a month after Kourt was killed. And all of that was coupled with my biggest loss and having to deal with my grief over Kourtney. That's why I say people don't care. They don't. I'm like Kourtney on this one: People be out for themselves. I better learn to trust only me. People let you down – and lie – all of the time. Unpredictable. I mean, I never tripped over that breakup. It was not the best time, no doubt. More than anything, I was shocked at the timing. But, since it did happen, it made me realize that anything can happen and that it's not best to feel someone will always be your friend...even in the worst of times. People will leave you. I know – it happened to me. My son taken away from me and two other people (so-called friends) disappeared from me in my darkest hour. Wow, a crucial time when I needed my friends love and support....

I do have expectations and would like accountability from people when we claim to care about each other. That is not unreasonable on my part, is it? I think God has his own way of showing us who is really down for us. I've never wanted sympathy. I didn't want anyone to feel sorry for me. I just wanted, and expected, people to be there for me. Be my friend. And, to be fair, there were a few who were consistent with me. But, you know, I had to realize, too, that others had their own "Kourtney grief" to deal with. I bet, sometimes, thinking about being around me, or dealing with me, was so hard for others. All the more reason I tried so hard to be "normal" around family, friends, and co-workers, for that matter. I did not want to scare anyone off...or be judged. And there were some folk out there who I would say had judged me and still do. If I got upset over something legitimate, they would say things like, "Well, you know she's been going crazy since Kourtney was killed." Are you serious?!!!! That is so outrageous to me! Or they would say things like, "You know, give her a break. She's dealing with a lot. She's just lashing out since Kourt was killed." Yeah, I am dealing with a lot. But I don't have to be handled with "kid gloves". And

there are things that happened/happen to me that provoke an emotion that has nothing to do with my son's death. I need to make that known! I may think I'm having a nervous breakdown, or sometimes even WANT one, but it has not happened. And now that I've let God back into my life, it will not happen! That's that. Now, back to my final entries for 2007....

8:19pm

I may stay home tonight. Pop a bottle of champagne and let some of Kourt's ashes blow off the balcony. I have the option of going to three parties or to church. I invited a friend over. But I want to be alone – I think. I'm sad. There is nothing for me to celebrate. This year, 2007, did not end on a good note. I never could have guessed this year would have been so horrible. I'm afraid of thinking about the future. One thing I am thinking about is a 7-night cruise. I would like to go right after the trial.

9:25pm

Okay, I'm home alone. I just did some work on my computer. I'm watching the Pistons whoop Milwaukee right now! DEEETROIT Basketball!!! The score is 94 to 59! This will be 9 straight wins. I'm also doing some housecleaning. Getting my 8 glasses of water in, too! Thinking and talking out loud to Kourtney. I asked him if he is seeing this game. John John just called. He is at his best friend Chris' house for their house party. He really wants me to come there, and I do want to go. Part of me is not in the "5,4,3,2,1...Happy New Year!" feeling. Tanya is Chris' mother. Her brother was murdered in August of 2007, and their family is hurting, too. They are all together, though. It's just me – with me – tonight. Jaz is gone to that church,Triumph, the one that I keep saying I'm going to attend. That's cool for her. I'm glad she is finding her way and doing what she needs to do for her life.

10:40pm

I'm feeling okay, just watching TV. The house is clean. Not much longer and it will be a new year. 2007 will always be the year that I will never forget. I'm taking Kourt right into 2008 with me. He will always go with me. I remind myself that what happened to him is not his fault. I keep that in mind and try and move on and be better, to keep the dark thoughts away from me. I promise I'm trying. I will continue to fight, too. That's a lesson 1st Born left for me, the family, and our friends: We fight.... We fight until there is no more. So, I can't kill myself...Jaz and John John still need me. I'm still here.

Tuesday, January 1, 2008, 12:45am

Damn, I had to say goodbye to my son in 2007. That year is gone now. 2008 came in uneventful for me...just like I wanted it. I'm glad I stayed home tonight.

The storm started about 45 minutes ago. I've just been chilln' in bed, runnin' back and forth to my computer. What's new, huh? Feeling sleepy. So I'll give falling to sleep a try in a minute. I'm so happy the holiday season is over!! YES!!!! I made it through. Sure, a little sad, but not as bad had I not prayed and prepared myself mentally. I know what's best for me, which is why my phone is powered to off right now. I really don't want to get the phone calls "Happy New Year!" Whatever. I know they mean well, but it does not help me. So, I'm chilln. *I love you, Kourtney.*

Wednesday, January 2, 2008, 4:48am

What do you do when your hopes and dreams have been snatched away from you? Create new ones? How can I make new hopes and dreams for Kourtney? I don't think I can. I know in my heart that Kourt would have never wanted to cause any kind of burden or heartache for me. What happened was out of his control. Still, I have to find a new way of living. Continuing to be stuck on what used to be is not working. I know that, yet I still can't help myself. Most days, I want to give up; in some ways, I have. I'm trying to stay strong for the trial next month and I pray that it's not rescheduled again. I need that trial to be over...so that I can start over. Things are not the same. That means that I cannot go back to my previous way of living or thinking. My previous life included Kourtney. Now he's gone. I was so irritated and cranky yesterday. I think I was mean to a friend. Others need to realize I'm not capable of tolerating any B.S. at this time – or ever again. I just can't. I got shit to do and problems to be sorted out. Peace and happiness is what I'm after. Seems like these things will be impossible for me to have in my life. I wish I had someone to turn to.... Seems like I don't. That's why I rely on me. But now I'm wearing me down. Still no word from AVON on the grant. I just feel like giving up on that, too. Don't think I'll ever get used to this.

3:42pm

What the hell have I done with Kourtney's funeral pictures! I'm in a frenzy. More stress! Sometimes I never know what kind of thought or action will set me off! Guess, that's why I'm writing. I hope I find these pictures. I have them on a CD, too, but not sure if I saved them to my hard drive. This is driving me crazy. Well, let me get back to my search for the pictures.

8:56pm

I miss Kourtney so much. All I can do is shake my head. Just got home from dinner with my friend Mel. He has been so helpful. I'm nervous about the trial. I may call the prosecutor's office tomorrow to see if they are considering a plea deal.

Sunday, January 6, 2008, 9:35pm

I think I'm missing some information over the past couple days. I had an issue trying to save this document. That worries me. What if I loose all of this data! I must start saving a backup copy, like at work or something. These pages are too valuable and priceless. I hope to read my journal one day...maybe. Hey, maybe someone else would like to read it, too.

Monday, January 7, 2008, 7:44pm

Finally, I was able to speak face-to-face again with a childhood friend who loss her son to gun violence in November of 2007. That young man and Kourt were friends. I was telling her about the group I want to start, but I'm having some difficulties in doing so. I told her I'm kind of giving up on the idea. She told me not to. We need the group, she said. I know there are many more of us out there. I heard on the news this morning that a 22-year-old young man was murdered overnight! It never stops.

Tuesday, January 8, 2008, 3:18pm

On the way out to dinner with Jaz and Angie. We've been talking about Kourtney all day. What's new, for me, anyway? If I'm not thinking about him, I'm talking or praying about him. Had to get my brakes fixed yesterday. My friend Mel did the work for me at his auto shop. There is something about him that reminds me of Kourtney. We are good friends. We always talk about Kourtney, and he did not even know him. He just took an interest and has helped me see the inside world of street life. Thanks to Mel, I understand some things better - and Kourtney's prospective.

7:54pm

Mary is Ed's sister. Ed is Kourtney's best friend. I just left this comment on Mary's Myspace page:

"Hi Mary. I can do nothing but cry when I read your comments on Kourt's page. Tell Ed that Kourtney and I are honored about the naming of his baby. Kourtney will be there, kissing her cheeks and playing with her. Not sure if you heard about the little kids in our family that did not know Kourtney but are telling stories of them playing with him all the time. It's amazing. We all know that he loved little kids and babies. Is there a due date for this bundle of love? Tell Ed I said congrats. Kourtney is smiling down and will do whatever he can for us and the new baby. Thank you for everything, Most sincerely. We love you and Ed.... Karen, for Kourtney with love."

Ed is Kourtney's best friend and he took Kourtney's dog, Ruby, after he was killed. I feel so bad for Ed because he still suffers—he loss his friend and brother. He and I had a chance to talk on Christmas day, and he feels guilty because he was not there to help Kourtney. I told him, as his mother, I feel the same way: Not being there – and he was alone.

On that day, it became overwhelming talking about the fact that Ed and I both had feelings of guilt because we were unable to help Kourtney. I started crying so hard, so much so that I could not continue in my journal that day. And that's the worse. I think all parents of murdered children go through that: The guilt of not being there. As parents, we are always there – no matter what. Then – this one time in their lives – they could not call on us. They were alone. I always keep in mind the "grown-up" words of Kourtney. He used to say: We come in the world alone and we will die alone. There are just some things that we will do alone. This brings me to something my pastor said recently: He explained why God needs our Mind, Body, and Soul. I can't remember what he said word-for-word but, in essence, he said: In death, our minds will stop working and our body will shut down and that leaves our Soul, and our Soul is what goes back to God (*Thank you Jesus!*). That's why we have to be right with God - for the purpose of our Soul. I'm comforted by the fact that Kourtney had been praying and reading the Bible prior to his untimely death. The very Bible he had been reading from, the one that I found in his bedroom, is the Bible I take to church with me and sleep with, along with his picture. Journal time...

Wednesday, January 9, 2008, 6:53pm

Trying to stop crying is close to impossible today. I cannot believe my son is dead - my first born, Kourtney. I want to plan a trip for after the trial, so that I can spread his ashes in Miami and in the Caribbean Ocean. He wanted to go to Miami so bad. He had me looking up prices for about 3 months. Poor Kourtney. He felt so alone the last week of his life. He had recently stated that Ed had to take care of things. T & Joe were locked up. His roommate, Larnell, was around, but I guess they did not see each other too much. Jaz also told me he said he felt like he had no friends around anymore. There is so much of life that he is missing. Or could it be that I'm missing it for him? That's a big part of it for sure...you know, that I'm missing it *for him*. I just wish he were still here. This grief process is cruel. It's forced reality.

Friday, January 11, 2008, 12:55am

I'm tired but don't want to go to sleep. Been up looking at his pictures for hours and listening to all my favorite songs. At this moment, I'm listening to the new Prince song "Future Baby Mama". I like it. I just posted a bulletin on Myspace and sent an email regarding the upcoming trial information. Found out earlier today that Ed's baby is due in June! The baby will be named "Kourtney," whether it's a boy or a girl. Ed misses Kourt so much, and he has to let go of the guilt. There was nothing any of us could do to help Kourtney. Kourtney did all that he could do. He tried to get away. And probably his last thought was that he had gotten away.

10:52pm

It's been a busy day. I sent out three separate emails with regard to the second "Baby Kourtney Tribute" and court trial information. I'm experiencing some strong "hate" emotions toward three individuals. I feel that I hate them so much, I don't want to mention their names.

Sunday, January 13, 2008, 8:00am

The weekend has been nice. John John was here. We went to the movies last night, out to dinner, and then over to Angie's "tattoo party". After shopping at the grocery store for a few items, we made it home about 11:30pm. Talked to my friend Mel, then I went to sleep. Soon as I woke up today, Kourtney is instantly on my mind – as usual. I'm worried about his friend Ed. I've been praying for him, as well as the brothers T & Joseph. Their trial is currently underway. I hear so many rumors. It drives me crazy. A police officer told me that it's not uncommon to "blame the dead guy." Why not put it on the guy who can't talk? Can't do anything to him, right? I don't like that, though. I don't want my son's name disrespected, particularly when he has not committed a crime and is not here to defend himself! I have mixed feelings, and this kind of thing bothers me.

OMG!!!! Kourtney is in the room right now!!!!! I'm so excited I can hardly type this. Okay, here is what just happened: I came into the family room to journal, which is where my desk and computer are located. John John was asleep, so I turned off the TV. About 10 minutes later, John John, still in same position, grabbed his cell phone to check a message; I was still typing. Suddenly, the TV came on, then off, then on, then off. I knew the TV was being turned off and on because it makes a "bleep bleep" sound when turning on or off. This did not alarm me because I thought John was having trouble with the TV picture or something. Then John John started staring at me. He asked me, with a puzzled look on his face, "Please tell me you did that, Mama." I responded "What?" He replied, "The TV." I realized at that time, when I came in the room and turned the TV off, I had left the remote control out of John's reach! So, *who* is playing with the TV? It's Kourtney again! He is here visiting us. I love it! I told John John to stretch his arms out in the air and move around since we can't see Kourt then maybe we will touch his spirit. John John asked me if I noticed the very bright light on the TV before it came on. I said no. He said that a very bright light appeared on the TV screen before it came on the second time. I think John John was a little freaked out. It was heartwarming for me, because I know my son lives on.... He lives on! He has a soul that is free. So, I say out loud, "We love you, Kourt!"

8:00pm

It just occurred to me that not only was Kourtney too young to lose his life, I'm too young of a parent to be dealing with this. I was 40-years-old when he was killed. It seems like I will never get through this. This is what death is, huh? We all have been introduced to death in a way that none of us have ever experienced. This has been, and continues to be, such a shock. Just thinking about him and his personality. The things that made him laugh...the things that motivated him... his serious manner...his becoming a man. All of that makes it that much sadder for me. He did not deserve what came to him. That violence and hatred. No way. I will never believe that. At Angie's party last night, her boyfriend, said to me that all they do is talk about Kourtney around the house. He said the kids and Angie go on and on about him. It makes me smile because I know he was loved and still is. Kourt did not like a lot of attention. He was a quiet movement, determined to make something of his life. He was much deeper than most people knew. I know he had been reading the Bible and praying. I always like to think he was reading Proverbs. I say that because he liked to dwell into more serious matters, those that required conceptualization and thought processes. I know for a fact, that as for the street life, he was tired of it. He also expressed that to Jazmyn.

I often wonder about what his life would have turned out to be had this not happened. I think about him as a husband and a father. It's 2009; in July, he will be 25-years-old. That's hard to believe. Would he look a lot differently.... Probably not. I wonder what changes he would have made at this point. I'm sure these types of feelings are normal for any grieving parent. It's always the "What if?" Unfortunately. Yeah. But could it be true that the *misfortune* of the situation is really an *opportunity* to become better? That's how I feel. It's still being connected to my son. Is it not true when they say, "Children...the gift that keeps on giving?" Yes, that is true for me. The love that will always remain in me for him motivates me to want to do better and to do more for others and myself. It's all out of the tragedy that befell my son. For me, that is unconditional love. That's never ending. How beautiful is that! I went through some very dark times. Sometimes I was scared for my life. But I always knew deep down that I did not want to hurt myself. It would be during my weak times, overwhelmed with feelings that there was no outlet, when I felt I was truly at risk for giving up. And it could have happened, had I not made some serious calls on God for my life. Like I stated before, I knew I needed a clearer view and path, which only God could grant me. He was waiting on me, and I had to open my mind to receive The Gift.

Sunday, January 13, 2008, 8:00pm continues

My biggest challenge is to stay busy. All I know is that I better stay busy. I get afraid for me when there is nothing much to do. That's when I get flooded with all kinds of thoughts. Idle hands.... An Idle mind could be "the devil's playground." I'm not even going to play around and underestimate myself. I'm trying to find progressive and constructive projects to keep my mind busy. I still miss Kourtney – all the time. But that's just how it is now. All I can do is continue to do my best. Be a fighter...like Kourtney. Never give up. I think to myself sometimes that I would gladly change places with him...so he could live more of life.

Monday, January 14, 2008, 6:00pm

Missing Kourtney is like the counting time – it never stops. It hurts. I'm really learning what it is to truly miss someone. Never thought that it would be *my son* on the 6 O'clock news. Doesn't this kind of tragedy happen to other people? Well, obviously, I'm "other people" now. It's an emotional evening. I have been busy, though. May see my friend Mel tonight for dinner. He has been a great source of comfort during a very confusing time in my life and give me good "inside information". We talk for hours on end about the tragedy and similar situations.

6:20pm

You ever love someone so much that you do the wrong thing? That's how I feel when it comes to Kourtney. Not everything I agreed to was wrong. But I know I could have demanded more of him. Some things I simply gave in to...just to make him happy. Now, looking back, at least I know he had some happy times. Mel said that I helped him "get his 'shine' on." Funny!

Thursday, January 17, 2008, 3:15pm

All of this is so confusing. Is it true that I'm trying to keep Kourtney alive by living his life through mine? Could that be what's going on? I don't know the right way to let Kourtney go. It does not make sense to me. I know what other people mean when they say Kourtney would want me to live my life, and that I should be happy to know we will meet up later. But, right now, I'm here – and he is there. How do I live and breathe right now? I can hardly do it. Maybe I won't be "right" until we meet up again on the other side. I've been sick a lot this week. In the midst of this separation, I will call it "love sick." Will I ever recover from this one, I wonder? I love my son so deeply, and, when he was taken from me, the love grew even more. My belief is that it grows because of the *fear* of leaving him behind or forgetting about him...which I know, at least in my case, is impossible. But tell that to my heart. I'm in a panic frame of mind all the time. You know, always thinking I'll forget the sound of his voice and stuff like that. I know for sure that I will never forget Kourtney. Now, how could that be possible? It's impossible. But, still, I have that fear. Or is it guilt? Guilt that if I'm not thinking about him, writing about him, or talking about him, I'm doing something wrong, that I've left him behind and forgotten about him. No matter what I'm doing, in some way, he wiggles into my thoughts. It's not a bad thing. It's just that sometimes it's too much. I think about his smile, and I get nervous because I know what's coming next. Yep, the tears. And if that goes on too long, who knows?

I don't always break down or give way to tears when I think about him. There are good days when I think of him. I smile and know that I've been so blessed to be his mother. Wow, it's been a little over seven months and Kourt has not called. There is this gigantic void that exists in my heart. What's a mother to do about that? Lately, I feel like I'm losing my mind. It's my intention to get away from Michigan for a few weeks. Maybe go out to Vegas with my dad before this trial gets started. I know the trial is going to take a lot out of me. I'm searching the Internet for a good travel deal – I'll even settle for a quick get-a-way.

Friday, January 18, 2008, 5:15am

I slept good last night, and I'm up early. And that's okay with me. I did some of my office work from home already. I'm about to get some breakfast, shower, and drive to the office. I prayed so very hard for Kourtney, my family, and myself. I'm concerned about the trial all of the time now. I'm worried and scared. I want justice for Kourt. I also did some Bible reading out loud with Kourt. I've missed a few nights of reading with him. I'm happy to report that I have no head or stomach aches this morning. At this very moment, I am not nervous. Ummm...I kinda of feel like me, tired but not wired up! I miss Kourtney, and I suppose that's how it will always be. I don't see how it could be any other way. And, you know what? That's fine with me. In time, I'll learn how to adjust with the ups and downs. It's really a day-to-day effort to deal with the horrible pain and hurt that is constantly with me. If I get one of those hurricane cycles of emotions, my body is filled with *physical* pain. It's a trip. I know Kourtney would be so sad (and maybe he is now) if he knew all I'm going through. I want to be my best. I really do. I don't want to give up...but sometimes I do. And maybe giving up for a few hours is okay. I don't know. This is new to me. I wish I knew what was going on with AVON. If I don't get the grant this time, I can apply one more time in April. My private counseling session is cool. Sometimes I like it. I just want to set up my own group so that I can help others.

7:28pm

It's been a long day. My therapist called me because I missed my appointment. I appreciate her concern. I had to take a nap today after work. Now I'm sleepy again. But there's no time for a nap. Going out tonight with my sister Kim and a few others may join us. Emotionally, I feel a little better. I got a letter from one of the brothers. Joseph gave me a bit of information that I guess made my day...to a degree. He told me about an encounter, or fight, he had with the murderer while they were in the county jail. He said he tried to choke the life out of him. He said he put a serious beating on that fool. Seems like everyone I told was so happy to hear the news. I don't want him dead. Though, if he is killed, I would not care. I want him to live a long, miserable-ass life! And I hope all the horrible and vicious things I hear about prison happens to him! That's what the fuck he gets...and good for him. Fuck him! And maybe that's what he'll get, too!

8:16pm

Okay, just got a call from Jaz. Someone told her that a guy they know is locked up in the county jail, too. He reported that there is so much love for Kourtney, and niggas been beating (the murderer) ass so much that he won't even come out of his cage! Yeah, that's good. They got that nigga scared; now I'm happy for real. His punk ass took my son away from me...and me from my son. I want him to suffer. He don't need to die! He needs to suffer. He needs to be alive every day...to realize he has nothing to look forward to.

Sunday, January 20, 2008, 11:20pm

Today has been a lot better for me. Not sensitive or emotional. Talked to my dad for a while. Not sure if I'll go to Vegas prior to the trial. He pointed out a truth to me, which is that we are all trying to find our own way dealing with the loss of Kourtney.

Monday, January 21, 2008, 4:24pm

Today is going okay. I took Jaz and John John to the Henry Ford Museum for Martin Luther King Day, then to Buffalo Wild Wings for lunch. Since I've been back home, I've been sitting at my desk, browsing the Internet for something interesting to read and short vacation for myself. I need a life-break for real. I just want to think, just sit, think, and relax...without the worry of work or being at home. My dad says I'm welcome to Vegas any time. However, he feels that since I'm stressed now, I'll unwind, but that I'll re-stress myself out. I swear he don't get it. I'm looking for a break right now. I'm going crazy on the inside. I'll just look for somewhere else to go. I've got my eye on this Bahamas cruise. I hope and pray that after this trial, I'll be better. My heart is heavy now. I'm not so emotional, just burdened with sadness. I'm hurt and confused over what has happened to Kourtney. I cannot change anything. He had his life as short as it was. And, no matter how shortchanged I feel his life, I cannot bring him back or extend his life. What's done is done. (Deep breath.) Right now, I want to relax.

Jazmyn & John John, January 21, 2008, Henry Ford Museum, ML King Day. They were sitting in an early model airplane! This is one of our favorite places.

Thursday, January 24, 2008, 3:49pm

I received an unexpected blessing today. I needed to alert a group of business-level associates, to let them know I would not be available during the court trial dates. I actually work for this group part-time from home. So, I sent the email. I got a response from a board member. He told me that his nephew was shot and killed. His name is Scott and was only 17-years-old. He asked if I wanted to talk to his sister, who is Scott's mother. I was like, "YES!" Instantly, our sisterhood was acknowledged. It felt so good to talk to someone and know I'm not getting on their nerves or sounding like a broken record. It's good to relate. We talked on the phone for a while, too. I see now more than ever that I need to get my group started. No word from AVON, though. I have not written in my journal in a few days, due to heavy grief and crying spells. I've just been trying to keep my head up. We are going to the Bahamas next week. I'm so happy that I can take Kourtney's ashes to the Caribbean.

Speaking of unexpected blessings: You never know where you may come into contact with a brother or sister who is in "the club". I remember one time when I was up in the middle of the night. As usual, when I wake up, I head to my computer. But it's not always to journal. This time I got on Ebay. I wanted

to bid on an item, but I had a question. So, I wrote the seller, expecting to get a response much later in the day. To my complete surprise, I got an almost-instant response. Delighted, I wrote right back, expressing my surprise and thanks for the information. Further, I noted to her that I did not think I would hear back so quickly. She responded something like this: "I'm always up in the middle of the night because I miss my son so much." I responded with, "Where is your son?" Her next response totally shocked me. She told me that she is up because her son had been murdered, and that she could not sleep for, like, 3 years since it had happened. My heart started beating fast, as I hurried to tell her that is also my reason for being up at 4am! We exchanged emails for a while. She, being further ahead of me in the grief process, was able to offer some good advice and tips on coping.

6:32pm

I wish my son were here. I still cannot believe he is gone...no longer among the living. I guess that means he died.... That dreaded "D" word.... Yeah, DEAD. Kourtney does not seem like the type to be dead. Not even sure what that means. I truly hope he enjoyed his life for the most part. Jaz just mentioned that Kourt used to love vanilla milkshakes. I was like, "He sure did!" Wow, just thinking about him with a vanilla milkshake in his hands does something nice to me inside. He was so special - and still is. We miss him all the time. Sometimes I miss him so much that I try not to think about him...so that I don't have to hurt so much. It's hurtful, such deep hurt to think about him and who he really is. Or "was"....

I find that I've tried to keep Kourt alive by speaking of him in the present. Or it could be a way to ease the sting that stopping his life at 22-years-old reminds me? So, I keep count most times by saying is age now in the present day. Since he has been gone, two of his birthday's have gone by (and in July it will be 3 of them). In my mind, this year (2009), he *will be* 25-year-old. Sometimes, out of fear of being judged, I say, "You know he *would have been* 25 this July," or something like that. That actually makes me feel uncomfortable, because I'm not being true to myself and my feelings. And life rolls right on, steadily marching onward and forward. Gee, just 22 when his life stopped, just learning how to be a man and trying to find his way. So much has happened since his untimely death. And so much more will happen.... What that means is that I'm learning and coping, always moving forward.

Saturday, January 26, 2008, 10:23am

Here is what's bothering me the most over the past few days: It's hard to accept what happened to Kourtney BECAUSE he and I cannot sit down and talk about it. I'm just left with hurt feelings and a broken heart, trying to carry on and do all I can to be happy or feel okay. Most days, that does not work. But what can I do?

I suppose that I can do nothing. All I know is that I want the pain to stop. It never does, though. I *should be* excited right now. Our Bahamas trip is in 5 days. And, yeah, I am happy about getting a break from the day-to-day routine.... But where is my Kourtney? He's still dead. I have packed up several small bags of his ashes to put out in the Caribbean. My efforts to cheer up and stay busy are just that – efforts. I stay busy...nothing changes...my efforts to cheer up are just worthless efforts. I think I want to put my condo up for sale when I get back. Time off from work for a while is what I really need and want. If the condo is sold, then I can free myself from some expensive financial obligations. I worry about everything all the time. I know the world will not stop. But whatever I can do to slow things down in my own life, I will do just that. If that means giving up my lifestyle to deal with my mental issues, then so be it! I live *my life* – no one lives it for me – just like I don't live the next person's life. So, whatever decisions that I make, it's *my* choice. I have to go with what feels *right to me.*

Sunday, January 27, 2008, 8:02am

I think I slept pretty well. Earlier yesterday, I slept a long time. It feels like Kourtney is with me. I don't know.... I just *feel* something around me or in my presence. Already I can tell it's one of those days when I want to "avoid". Avoiding the pictures is how I will best make it through this Sunday. I say this because I looked at a picture this morning. It felt as if I were kicked in the stomach a million times and then got hit in my chest a million times with a sledge hammer!!! There are those times when I get sick to my stomach, and it seems like I'm going to throw up at the slightest thought of what happened to Kourt! I don't know what to do when these physical pains attack my body. I'm lost. I'm scared. Scared of whom? I'm scared of *me*. Staying busy could be the answer today. Am I going crazy? Earlier today, I pulled out Kourt's clothes and set them up at his favorite spot in the family room. I keep walking in and out the room, trying – and hoping – to catch a glimpse of him with the clothes on. Jaz thinks I'm going crazy or slipping away. Maybe I am.

5:57pm

I miss Kourtney. I hate everything that happened to him. And now I hate my life!

Monday, January 28, 2008, 6:21pm

I'm having a hard time today. I had to call "my sister in the struggle," Eva, today. I cannot believe or accept the fact that I'm never going to see Kourtney again. Why? Oh my God.... Why? I'm devastated and hurt. I feel wounded to my core! Nothing makes it better...nothing. There is a giant hole in my heart, and my brain has been sucked out by a high powered vacuum. The void has entered my world and sucked out someone so dear and special... my son...my first born child. I want to talk to him. But I can't! I want him to ask me to do something for him...like get some information about Miami...anything! Please – *anything.* That just won't happen, will it? It won't. At work earlier today, I was so upset, I had to write this:

Okay, I'm tripping out this morning. I've been up since very early this morning and in my office right now. I cannot believe Kourtney is gone. I feel like I'm going out of my mind. I must keep taking deep, deep and rapid breaths because I'm increasingly unclear and unfocused. I'm busy at my office today, and I hope that helps me out. I keep looking around for Kourtney. I know he has to be somewhere. The part of my brain that actually functions in reality tells me that he is NOT! I want to tell that part of my brain to "Shut the fuck up and let me have my crazy ass fantasy!" So, I go and look out in the parking lot and look out my office window. Maybe he's waiting for me at my car or standing in the hallway because he's forgotten where my office is located. This is crazy. I need to get a grip. No one knows the tricks my mind plays on me. I'm scared to tell my family. I'll probably get committed. It's now January 28th, 8:38am. Will I ever make it? I try to hang on...if not for me, I do it for Jaz and John John. They would be so devastated if they loss Kourtney and me. I keep praying and praying and trying to settle myself down, to meditate and look forward to different things in life. But how about this: My life sucks! My son was murdered! I hate my life. I can't find peace. The world is against me. Maybe after the Bahamas trip, I will feel better. The trial is fast approaching, and I think many of my feelings will go away.

9:36pm

Am I trying too hard to understand death? Trying too hard to come to grips with what has happened to my beloved first born son. Something tells me that I will never really understand most of this tragedy. Besides, I will never *accept* what has happened to him. I am smart enough to know that if I ever make it to "acceptance," that does not mean that I have forgotten him. I guess, in some way, I must make peace with what has occurred. Strangely enough, I have had some moments when I am peaceful. However, it never lasts for long. It's been an emotional day. I've been praying more and more. I just don't know about life...bad times...and how to effectively deal with this. *I* would rather be dead than Kourtney be dead. I feel so bad for my son. He did not deserve what happened to him. No one deserves to be murdered. But, since that punk ass nigga did it, I hope that nigga is raped and beat up, then finally killed – in the most vicious way possible while he is in prison! FUCK HIM!!!! I hope Kourt haunts his dreams. I hope he haunts the corners of his weak-ass mind day and night, that he never feels safe again! Not even in his new cozy little cell!

Tuesday, January 29, 2008, 5:34am

I'm all dressed for work. I slept pretty good...much better than recent nights. Well, I'm out of here tomorrow. A major snow storm is predicted for this part of

Michigan, and we will be long gone to the Bahamas. And, still, even with that excitement, I'm flooded by thoughts of Kourtney. Some people say that I "think too much." Maybe that's true. I'm going to work on being better to myself and praying. I don't know what else to do? Nothing makes me happy. I feel like giving up on everything. But I'm still here....

Wednesday, January 30, 2008, 5:30am

Don't know where to start. Kourtney is gone?. I'm really trying...I really am. I don't know what else to do? Today, I've been back and forth with the "He's in a better place...." Is he? Is he happier? I guess that if he is next to God, then it is better there than here. I had a thought when I used my credit card yesterday: When I was at the register, I realized that Kourt had never even applied for credit. Wow. There is so much that he will not experience. No kids. This is all a shock to my system, because of all the things I thought he would have in life....murdered was the one thing I never considered. His having no kids means he will not have to go through the worry and hurt that sometimes come with being a parent. I mean, like the way I worried over him from time to time, always wanting better for him and not wanting ANYTHING bad to come to him. Still, one event, I would have never wanted for him came to him, nonetheless. I often wonder what Kourt was praying about? He told me that he had been praying and reading his Bible. Maybe he got his answer. Not to say he requested to be murdered, but maybe he asked for peace in his life. Maybe - just maybe - he wanted a way out of this cruel and cold world.... No more for him. If he truly were an angel, he would have a hard time performing his God-given duties here on earth. It's my fantasy (or belief) that when these special "dark angels" have trouble on earth, God finds a time to bring them back to Him. After all, Kourtney was only *on loan* to me, right? He really *belongs* to God.

11:26am

I've been writing some good and powerful notes to say to that fuckn' loser...that monster...the murderer! I hate him. I swear I do! My Kourtney is gone because of him. I'm leaving for the Bahamas today, and I had to pack up my son in the form of dust in order to take him with me. I hate this whole grief process. But what choice do I really have? None.... Kill myself? Yep. I think about that sometimes, too. A few things stop me, though. First, my two kids are still on earth with me and, second, if I do kill myself, I will not be able to reunite with Kourtney on the other side. It's a horrible and incredibly sad thing to see your son or daughter in a casket. Well, I'm going to soak up some island sun, relax, clear my mind and get mentally ready for the upcoming trial. Damn...it's so hard to grasp that he is really gone. Simple as that: He is not with us any more. All of us miss him so much. He is so special and unique. He had become a man.

And it was off to The Bahamas. It was a much needed vacation. Prior to the trip, I was under considerable stress and worrying all the time about the trial. The fear of not getting a conviction and finding no justice for Kourtney was overwhelming. This took over my thoughts day and night! I felt that I was going to jump clear out of my skin! Or kill myself. The suicidal thoughts were not that intense at that time, but I would think about it as if I had no other alternative. Several months later, it would seem it was my *only* option. It was not so easy to dismiss the urge to "do it." But, upon return from the Bahamas, I was so relaxed and my confidence level was high. I said to myself and Kourtney, "We are going to win." I knew it...I could feel it. When the trip was over and when I arrived home, I knew I had made the best decision to take that trip. I'm so grateful that my family traveled with me with me! They helped me so much! Now, that's LOVE!

Monday, February 4, 2008, 2:54pm

Well, The Bahamas was nice and warm! What a beautiful trip. I put Kourt's ashes out all over the islands! I really relaxed, partied, enjoyed the food and everything, including the cruise and ports of call. I took it all in. I realize that we are about two weeks away from the start of trial. I'm ready...so let's get to it! I've been praying for strength and confidence and courage, all the things I will need to be firm when I confront that bastard. Always – always – praying for Justice for Kourtney! I miss him. What makes this process more difficult is that he cannot tell me what happened. For once, a problem occurred and he and I cannot talk about it. It's just over for him. His life ended in a terrible way. So undeserving.... When his heart stopped beating, part of mine did, too! I miss every day life for Kourtney, you know, the things I feel he is missing out on. Him not being here for us anymore.

Actually, he was the head male of my household, and he took that leadership role without question. I think his personality type was that he felt a sense of satisfaction knowing that he was needed. Some people are like that. They like to be needed. He was reliable. He was a "real" kind of guy and a faithful friend. That's a major loss, because true friends are hard to come by. Someone that is there for you 100%. They "got you" no matter what. That's exactly the kind of young man Kourtney was/is. And he NEVER expected anything back. He never looked for anything in return. He gave and gave and gave. Selfishness? No, that was not in him. I'm very proud of him. He still had that affection for me and our family. But I know the streets made him tougher – or a little "colder," let's say. He had to be like that I suppose. The haters are everywhere. He knew that. That's why he wanted out of that life. He knew it had played it's time out in his life. He despised what he had subjected himself to, and, in his mind, he was done.... But the fast money kept a grip on him. I just wish we could talk about this matter. Will I ever get that chance? Will I ever find some peace...or is it me against the world?

As I finished typing the above entry, a day when Kourt was alive comes to mind. It was a day, maybe sometime in 2006. I had rented a Chrysler 300C for him. He LOVED that model car. But, any how, I was sitting at my desk and talking on the phone. I noticed he kept pacing back and forth. He would walk pass and glance at me, and, when I would look back at him, he would turn his head really fast. So, I continued to talk on the phone, but kept my eyes on him. He walked to the front door and looked back at me. I tell my friend to hold on and I say to him, "Kourt you need me for something?" I know there is something on his mind...I know him too well. But, he said "Umm.... No, Mama."

Still he paces, then goes to another part of the house, then back pass me again and hangs at the front door, while taking quick glances at me. I ask him again, "Kourt...is everything okay? You're acting strange." He smiled a little bit and said "No, Mama." Then he has this funny look on his face. I decide it's time to end my phone call. I end the call. I pretend to ignore him and start typing on my computer. Finally, he comes over, stands in front of my desk and says "Mama." I look up. "Yes, Kourtney" I respond. I'm, like, and to myself I say, "I knew it." He starts to chuckle and I say, "What's wrong?" "This is like pulling teeth," I say to myself. But that's how Kourtney could be – especially with me. He knew there was accountability with me, and that he had to answer to me if no one else. I still had the ability to make him nervous, like he was 8- years-old. So, I give him a break and I start to guess what's the problem. I start off, "Is someone pregnant?" He flashed that cute smile and said, "Naw, Mama. You ain't going to be a grandma." I smile really big and I tell him, "Well, anything else I can handle." We laugh and I guess things, such as, maybe he got a traffic ticket or he has problem with a young lady. Finally, he tells me that he got into an accident with a semi-truck and the front end of the 300 is ripped off! I immediately come to my feet and, before I could yell at him, he stated "I got the money, Mama, to get it fixed. I'm just waiting on the part to come in." I slip on any shoes I could find to run out to see the damage. The faster I walked, the faster he talked, telling me all the details.

What could I say? He was not hurt, no one else was hurt. Also, he had already taken the car in to be repaired and ordered the part. Now, I have to admit he could have hid the damage from me and never told me. But his conscience would not allow him to lie to me or keep it from me. He knew he could not be in my face and not let me know what had happened, even at the risk being yelled at or disappointing me. He knew the truth is what I respected and expected. And for that – being honest with me – there would be no punishment. Now, as we stood outside and I looked over the damage, I did give him a good talking to about being a safe driver, staying alert, and about when driving next to big trucks, we could easily get into their "blind spot". I believe that's what happened in this case. As Kourt attempted to turn, the truck came over on him and forced him into a street sign. Thoughts like that come to the front of my brain all the time. For some reason, it was on my heart to tell that story. Now back to the journal....

Tuesday, February 5, 2008, 5:33pm

Thirteen days until the start of the trial. I sent out a text to everyone in my cell phone book. We need to increase our prayers. It's time, and I'm so ready! I visited with a person that my family has been close with it in what seems like forever. The father of that family died while I was gone to The Bahamas. The mother of this family used to baby sit Kourt and Jaz when they were little. I forgot that years ago their oldest son had taken his life. As I sat there, I realized that the mother knows my pain. We both loss sons in a tragic way. I've been texting all day with a friend. Her son was murdered 5 months after Kourtney was murdered. We've known each other since elementary school. Also, my cousin Lauren is Godmother to her son. Since my Bahamas vacation, I'm not nervous or anxious. I'm ready for battle! Believe that. I'm there all day and night for my son. I'm ready. I promise myself that I will not be scared, but, instead, I will be full of courage and show all who look at me where Kourtney comes from. I'm very serious. I know I've shown some of my character. However, they have not heard me speak! I continue to pray and ask God to grant me the peace and ability that I'll need to be articulate my feelings like no other time in my life! I need to deliver a message from Kourtney, and I've also been praying for God to give me that insight. Please.

Wednesday, February 6, 2008, 5:11pm

I'm doing okay. I'm better today that's for sure. I know the vacation helped. Today, I was so busy at work. Maybe being preoccupied is helpful right about now. Twelve days until trial, and guess who is so ready? ME – that's who! I feel confident and unafraid. I'm so proud of myself. Believe me when I say that I'm staying on top of my praying and meditation to remain focused and confident. I just posted some Valentine's Day graphics on Kourt's Myspace page. He is forever loved. Today, I called a radio station to qualify for a trip to The Bahamas. I was the lucky caller. As she collected my information, I informed her that I just returned from a trip to The Bahamas. But, if I win this one, I will use it for my post-trial celebration! She asked me what would I be celebrating, and I told her that I would be celebrating justice in the wake of my son's murder. She then told me that her brother was murdered in 1991 and that it has taken her mother a very long time to get better. Her brother was being a good citizen by assisting a young lady who was about to be raped! The young lady got away and he was killed at the age of 29-years-old! For whatever reason, the two young men who committed this crime had been charged but were allowed to be bonded out of jail. Their families put up their homes and posted the bond. After that, the two have never been seen again! No justice!!

Wow, that phone call reaffirmed my fears and rocked me a little. Her story reminded me that anything could happen – that anything not in our favor could happen. The legal system is this huge and strange monster, and sometimes mistakes and injustice happens. It's true that the justice system can grossly lose it's sense of balance. And, although the fear was present within me, it did NOT take long for my confidence to return! I prayed day and night and repeated to myself, "We got this! We will get the victory and JUSTICE for you, Kourtney!" I would be in a meeting at work and in my mind I would say over and over "We got this! We will get the victory and JUSTICE for you, Kourtney!". In my car I

would almost shout out loud, "We got this! We will get the victory and JUSTICE for you, Kourtney!" I'd be on the phone with whomever and say it over and over in my mind.... No disrespect to anyone, but I was in my zone! I'd be in the shopping mall and, in my mind, I would say – come on and say it with me – "We got this! We will get the victory and JUSTICE for you, Kourtney!" And we did just that! Praise be to God! We got it!

Wednesday, February 6, 2008, (continues), 8:46pm

Had a real breakdown, an emotional-ass breakdown! I finally found the funeral pictures. I like to see them from time to time. I have a few in my cell phone and on my computer, but I had some other really nice ones. (If that makes sense: "Nice" funeral pictures??) I have some good up close ones, as well as some showing the flowers. I just need/want to see them. Maybe it's to convince myself that "it" really happened. (Deep breath.) I don't know where the breakdown started from. I was really okay...but that's how it goes. The tears...then the downward spiral just happens. Just like that! I'll be so glad when this trial and sentencing are over, I'M CLAIMING VICTORY AND JUSTICE FOR MY SON AND OUR FAMILY AND FRIENDS! I prayed out loud and talked to Kourtney. I told him I'm not giving up – EVER! I have not given up, although sometimes I feel down. I'm confident. And I'm not afraid to claim victory and justice right now! I feel so right about this proclamation. I know this feeling.... We are good. It's just a matter of going through the process. Note to the murderer: Nigga, you FUCKED UP! You fucked with the wrong guy. You may have killed him, but YOUR STUPID ASS LOST THE MOST! You are the walking dead! You will see that.... Believe me. You will see that. You will understand that. Note to my son: You rest in peace and paradise until we meet up again! I love you.... But you already know that!

Thursday, February 7, 2008, 8:11am

Another wintery morning. I don't like driving in the snow. I slept good. Cried a little bit while praying. But that's the way love goes, right? That Janet Jackson song just popped in my head. My body feels tired and overwhelmed, but my brain is where it should be. So, by the time I hit the shower, my body will catch up. Nothing but positive thoughts for me today. I have claimed victory and justice in the courtroom with regard to the murder of my son. I know that justice will be served in the face of the monster that deserves nothing but misery. I'm sure he will get it, too. So there!

8:24pm

So, this is how it is, huh? Kourtney...just gone. He's really gone. I feel so bad for him...and me too! I wonder if it ever crossed his mind that he would be killed or die young? I wonder what his thoughts were on the way driving to the gas station.

I can see him now...leaned back in the driver's seat...windows up, with the air conditioning on (he hated being hot)...music on, no doubt, but not too loud (since it was late). But I can also see him as being relaxed and calm and cool, like he could be so well. THEN – all hell breaks loose on him and, just like that, his life was over! Wow.... Are you serious? Yes...very serious. It was over for him. Done. He died. He was killed. All I know is that part of me went with him. It's very painful to deal with...every day...each and every second of the day...and the night, too!

I'm looking at his favorite spot: the loveseat in the family room. I always find myself looking over there, hoping to catch a glimpse of him sitting there. I'm so desperate for anything related to Kourt to happen. Is that sad or desperate? Maybe he will be smiling. Or maybe he will be taking a nap. It's been 9 months and I've not seen him in the family room yet! But I forget how he plays with the TVs around here.... That's a trip when that happens. He has not been to see me recently, but I always ask him to come and see me...please. I know Kourtney, and he will do what he can. So, I don't trip when I don't get a sign from him. I tell people that. "Don't trip, because we know Kourtney will always do what he can...just like when he was here with us." It's so weird, being forced to deal with these feelings and knowing he is not around. I can't see him or call him. Can he see me? I have no choice but to try and accept this, but I just don't think that will happen...ever. I just learn my new life now – a life without Kourtney.

All I can do is celebrate his memory. You know, the life he had with us. I'm so thankful for all the pictures. I remember when I almost took a picture of him at Jaz party (the night he was killed). He had them Cartier round frame glasses on. The glasses became a part of his personality. I have no pictures of him with the glasses on. I wonder, was he wearing them when he was being fired upon? He had them on him because they were returned to me by the police, along with $330 cash, a couple of lighters, and his wallet. He went through a horrible experience. It did not last long.... I'm so happy to know that. Life is full of the unexpected, huh? I never ever thought I would receive a phone call telling me to come to the hospital. I did not think he had died. The worst I thought was that he would be on life-support. But, dead? "He didn't make it," as the ER doctor told me. I almost fainted. Someone just told me my son was dead.... Not Kourtney.... How can that be? Why? He's dead...he didn't make it! Kourtney looked like he was asleep, as if he could get up any second and walk away. But he was so far gone from me... so far that I could not even begin to imagine. This world – or people, should I say – can be so cruel...so cold. Living is hard. The street game is hard because there are no rules.

Sunday, February 10, 2008, 9:51am

It's been a weekend of "I don't believe it" syndrome. Where I have to think two, three times that Kourtney is dead. He is gone. The part that makes it harder is when I factor in his personality. It seems to be one thing just to say his name.... Many people are named Kourntey, male and female. But then it comes up that MY KOURTNEY was killed! *My Kourtney*...really. Those are scary moments. The grief is so intense...on any given day and at any given time. I ponder on all the things that should have taken place in his life. I could scream until my lungs collapse! So many opportunities and dreams, not just delayed but disappeared right along with him. No more new memories.... I have what I have and what others tell me about him.

Today I have to go shopping with Jaz to help her pick out an outfit for a flight attendant interview she has coming up. I'm still a little angry with John John. He got kicked out of school again. Eight days until trial. Detective "H" stopped by Friday to drop off some papers. It's on now! There will be no change in the date of the trial. Jaz and I both will be called to testify. I know she will do well. She loves her big bro, and he loved her. We will keep it 100% (as Kourt would say). I will be confident and looking good! I've been shopping for a pantsuit.

3:29pm

Jaz and I just got home from the mall. I hope she gets this job. A new start for her may be what she needs. We went to dinner early and got on home. It's freezing cold outside.... I think 5 degrees! That's a long way from 80+ degrees in The Bahamas last week. It doesn't matter – at home, The Bahamas, hot or cold outside – Kourtney is forever on my mind. When I pray at night, I have started to ask God to send all my love to Kourtney. I know He can do that for me. God will get my message to him!

Monday, February 11, 2008, 10:22pm

Today was okay. I got somewhat emotional at the mall. While I was there, I ran into a high school friend of mine. Since I have to testify at the trial, I was at the mall shopping for a suit to wear on the first trial day. We both cried as we discussed the tragedy and the upcoming trial. Tina prayed for me on the spot – right in the middle of a busy store! She was like, "I remember when you were pregnant with Kourtney." She also has a son named Courtney. As for the trial, I hope they allow me to bring in multiple pictures of Kourtney for the jury to see. After all, they will see that loser sitting there. I want them to see that Kourtney had a life and that freak-of-nature stole it from him.

Tuesday, February 12, 2008, 4:37am

Jaz just woke me up because it's time to drive her to the airport for that job interview out of state. I prayed for her all last night, and I hope she gets this job. I truly hope it's what she wants. I told Kourt last night to hang out with his sister while she flies for the first time by herself. Well, got to run it's time for her to go.

7:55pm

Well, Jaz is stuck at the airport in Indiana, due to a bad winter storm. Not sure what time she will get in. She forgot her cell phone charger and her battery is low. So, she's been calling from a pay phone. On this call, however, she borrowed someone's phone. She said the interview went well. If she takes this job, she will have to leave Michigan. I know she will do just fine if she decides to take this route. I've been crying a little bit today and texting folks. My girlfriend Gina is going to host a dinner for us after the first day of court. That is so sweet! That will make it easier for all of us. I appreciate so much what everyone has done and is doing. There is no way I could ever measure my gratitude. I'm forever grateful.

Wednesday, February 13, 2008, 9:31pm

Okay. Here we go! Five days until trial! I am so ready for legal REVENGE! I'm ready for justice for my 1st Born, my sweetheart. Happy Valentines Day, Kourtney! I miss him so much. Gee.... Why did this happen? Why does life have to be so hard and sad and disappointing and hurtful and just plain unfair? Why? I will never understand. But, I guess, like many other parents just like me, there are hearts a aching all over the world tonight!

I'm grooving to sounds from my computer play list. I'm grooving to a song by Phyllis Hyman called "No One is Wanted More". I love this song. I have to stop and snap my fingers to the beat between typing words. (Ha, ha, ha.) I have to laugh at myself. I love Howard Hewitt, too. I used to play him a lot when the kids were growing up, and I still do to this day. I remember one time when Kourt told me that he went to school with a Howard Hewitt song playing over and over in his head. We laughed. That song just went off. Now a song made over by Mint Condition is playing. They did a remake of The Isley Brothers' "Make Me Say it Again". It's very mellow and relaxing—like most of the Isley's Bros. music. I feel okay in this moment. Music seems to help me. That's why I play it most times when I sit at my desk.

Back to business, though. I'm feeling very confident about the outcome of this trial. I KNOW we are getting justice for Kourtney. And, although most times I've felt that I want "an eye for any eye," I truly see that with that type of justice, you know an-eye-for-an eye, the whole world would be blind. But that nigga is gonna pay for what he has done. So, if it's HIS life in prison until he dies, then there it is! I think the slow death he will suffer is more torture than someone shooting him. Let him suffer his day-to-day locked up in his cage! I hope he enjoys his new life: Playing with the fellas! That's what the fuck he gets! This is what he wanted. He hated Kourtney just that much: to trade his life for Kourtney's. Wow, Kourtney must have impressed his ass for sure. But I'm so ready. Let's get it on! On one hand, I'm on top of the world with confidence. Then, on the other hand, I'm at the bottom...hurting so much over my son. I just got off the phone with Kourt's Godfather, Ray. I told him everything I do requires much effort. The only thing that is effortless is crying. Dig that! That's just how it is, you know. That's my life. There is nothing – absolutely nothing – that I can do to change it. I try to reject it. With everything I have in me, I try to reject it when the pain comes in, that deep down, intense pain. And what I do is I roll with it. Or the alternative – give up. I do realize that that if I "do something" to myself, I will never see Kourtney again! And thinking about Jaz and John John I realize that, no, I can't stop the beat of my own heart! I may come close in thoughts, but I know I'm stronger than that. I have to see my Kourtney again...I have to. This can't be it. It's not enough. Everything just ended and changed just like that. Just over. I say this over and over: I feel so bad for Kourtney. I really do. I can't help but wonder what he was thinking about on June 11th. I bet it never crossed his mind that he would not be alive the very next day...not even for another few hours. Damn! Damn, Kourtney! I guess it was your time. Was your work on earth complete? I suppose so. I know that God could have spared you, but it was His ultimate decision to take you back. Sometimes I wish I never brought Kourtney to this horrible and cruel world. And, then, his life ended in such a violent and cold way! I feel guilty about my other two children. I brought them to this world, too. Anything can happen. Now they have to deal with life, as well. Being so young, they have a much longer time to deal with their brother's untimely death. We are a young family. I was 40, Jaz turned 20 the day before he was killed, and John John was only 12! Incredible! Sometimes, when I think of Kourtney, I just think he is in a very deep sleep. But, most times, my feeling is that he has a spirit that is happy, active, and free. This all becomes confusing to me from time to time. I question things. After all, what do I know about death? Kourtney knows about life *and* death.

Talked to the prosecutor about the case. She hopes to have it wrapped up within 3 days! She says we have what is referred to as an "ID case". She says she is not long-winded and will get to the point. I'm like, "Hey, let's get it on." There are also eye witnesses from the barbershop incident. So, it's a mutherfuckin' wrap! I do keep in mind that this case will go to the jury and they don't know Kourtney any more than they know that animal. Still, I feel good! The jury will be mature and fair citizens – and I stay on my knees in prayer! I continue to send texts and emails to my family and friends. We have to stay on top of this. I was just notified that I can only bring in one picture of Kourtney, and that it has to be a picture of him alone. Oh, no problem.... I have hundreds of pictures of him! I have not decided which one, but I have a good idea of the one I will use.

Thursday, February 14, 2008, 5:34pm "Happy Valentines Day" and What-the-fuck-ever!

I feel like someone blew a big-ass hole right through my heart!!

7:13pm

I'm a little nervous thinking about the case. I talked to the prosecutor again; one of the witnesses from the barbershop is freaking out, saying they don't want to be involved. I'm a little confused because I was told their testimonies were sworn and could be used, regardless. So, I don't know. I'm trying to stay focused. I'm being told all kind of things, and I've become more and more confused. I'm so worked up now to the point that I'm in panic mode! The confidence I had is not gone, but I am worried. Shit! They told me if this particular witness does not cooperate, they can jail them. I was like, "Don't do that." I do understand their fears. They live and work in that area. I believe there has been some threats on their lives and things like that. I don't want anyone else hurt. Their testimony helps support the "premeditation" element of the case. The detectives will continue talking with that person and get back with me tomorrow. I hope it all goes well. It's all too much to think about not winning the case.

Saturday, February 16, 2008, 9:18am

Update! I'm calm again. However, the detectives are still working with the witness from the barbershop. The four witnesses from the actual crime scene are on board!!! I got on my knees and prayed for all the witnesses. I prayed and requested God to watch over them and to protect them and to please bless their lives – PLEASE! It's what they are doing that means so much to me. They did not plan to be there, anymore than Kourtney knew he was going to be killed there. It just happened, and here we are. So, I appreciate their courage and stepping up to do the right thing for Kourtney! It is justice for Kourtney! I hope to have an opportunity to speak to them in person.

But, Mama is ready! I have purchased new suits and got some things lined up from my already existing wardrobe. It's hard to know what day I will take the stand. The jury has to be selected first, so I'm not going to wear my "testimony suit" on the first day. I'll wear another pantsuit.

Last night was cool. My cousin Lauren had a birthday party at her house and my sister Angie had another tattoo party at her house. So, I was busy last night. Lauren had a delicious birthday cake. I went to Angie's and she made me the best sour apple martini! I got home about 12:45am this morning. I wonder where is Kourt's spirit? Is he here with me as I type in my journal? Perhaps he is sitting in his favorite spot. Part of my new prayer is that I ask God to send all my love to Kourtney and a kiss him...because I know He can do it!

7:20pm

Just woke up from a nap. Immediately I think of Kourtney. Hard to believe it's him who was killed. Ummm, shopping...shopping for the right kind of clothes to wear to this trial. First, it was me shopping for a suit for him to wear for HIS funeral, then it's me shopping again for a dress to wear to HIS funeral...then it's me shopping yet again for things to wear to the trial. It's all so crazy!

Sunday, February 17, 2008, 11:08pm

Having a hard time falling to sleep. There is so much on my mind. I'm distracted. Fighting depression. I can hardly finish a thought before another one jumps into my head. All this back and forth and up and down. I'm drained even before the start of the trial. I've been praying all day. I was up in the middle of the night praying and, before I could close out my prayer, another thought or worry popped in my head. Do I ever get a break? Seems like I do not! I'm out of sorts. Out of my element. This is all new. I asked God for forgiveness and a sense of calm. I know He knows what I'm going through. I'm trying harder and harder and more and more to only rely on myself. I have not demanded anyone of their time. I know that other people have their lives. This weekend, I had the worst feelings of being lonely. I'm going to try and get back in bed. It's too late to take a Tylenol PM. What does it matter, anyway? It won't work.

Monday, February 18, 2008, 3:57pm!!!

Yes, ONE DAY left and it's on! Trial starts tomorrow! I find that I am so anxious. It's hard to sit still. I just got home from getting a manicure and thoughts of Kourtney are never-ending and intense. I have his Myspace page open now and playing this song "The Struggle is Over"! I'm on "full" right now. I'm more ready than scared or nervous. I am mentally focused. I'm getting justice for my dear, sweet 1st Born. Damn, I can't believe I had to identify his body and had to sign papers to say that this is my son: the deceased. Those images have been with me a lot the past couple of days. But that's what happened, and I cannot change it. I'm dealing with it.

6:31pm

Well, I framed the pictures of Kourtney. I'm taking a three with me, as I can't make up my mind. Of the three, I think it will be either the picture of him in the red Jeep or his "dark angel" picture. Everyone loves the "dark angel" picture. It's one of my favorites, too. I just got off the phone with my cousin Eric. I got emotional. Still, I'm ready. This is it. Just a matter of hours now. I've been waiting all these months, and now it's almost that time. A friend told me to get a bottle of wine and just chill tonight. I'm doing that. I plan to be in bed no later than 8:30pm. I've received lots of phone calls today. Everyone is prayerful and ready! I'm listening to a song right now by Teena Marie entitled "Dear Lover". I'm surely staying calm and getting into my zone.

TUESDAY, FEBRUARY 19, 2008, 5:35am!!!!

Finally, the day is here! I've been waiting 8 months for this day: the first day of court! It's on.... I'm ready! I know everyone is praying for the right outcome. I know that today will feel long; a lot of waiting; I'm prepared. This is for Kourtney. Well, it's about time for me to start cooking breakfast for me and Jazmyn. I need to get focused and clear on today's tasks! This whole week should be interesting and emotionally draining. I will keep in mind that it's only temporary, that it will not last forever. It's a process. Just like anything else. Here are my words to Kourtney this morning: "Boy I'm going to fight and not give up. I'm there every step of the way. I love you, and I'm so sorry this happened. But you are lucky in a way because you have no worries. I can't wait to see you on the other side." R.I.P. Kourt!

My thoughts go back to that morning. It was so quiet in my house; it seemed like peace all around. I was particularly calm. I prepared a full hot breakfast for Jaz and I, complete with grits, meat, eggs and cheese toast. (The cheese toast is a Duffie family thing. It's a certain way to prepare it along with the right kind of cheese.) John John was unable to attend the trial. The judge said no one under 18 in his courtroom. Jaz and I ate breakfast, showered, dressed and left the house feeling good! I drove. We headed to downtown Detroit on I-75 northbound. Other family and friends followed me in their cars. We had a small convoy. And, as I passed the street where Kourt's life ended, I looked up at the "Schaefer Street" exit sign and shook my head. I thought to myself how funny life can be. How things had changed in my life...in Kourt's life, literally, from one second to the next. And now I'm on my way to The Frank Murphy Hall of Justice in pursuit of *justice* for my son. I remember looking around at other drivers on the road and wondered where they might be going. Most are probably going to work or going home after working the midnight shift. How many were going to court because their son or daughter was murdered, I wondered?

The first day at court went something like this: We arrived and went through security. We all headed up by elevator to the 4th Floor. When the elevator door opened, a female was standing there and she said out loud something like, "Here she is." or "They're here." She then ran to get someone. I guess to show them Kourtney's family. It was obvious that it was someone from the murderer's side. The first half of the day was full of arrivals of supporters from both sides. Most had to stand in the hallway because another case was concluding. I was allowed in the "witness room". So was Jaz, along with four young men (the witnesses) and their mothers. We walked in and out, talked to our family and friends, and, of course, took bathroom breaks. Already, some drama was jumping off! A few people were arrested. Just stupid stuff was happening, such as fights and just plain shows of ignorance. I was informed that the judge found out about the drama and was also aware of the drama that happened with our River Rouge court days. As a result, he only allowed five people from either side inside the courtroom. I had to decide who the five people would be. Wow!

Right about lunch time, the potential jurors were escorted up. Everyone left for lunch; some went home. We knew there would be no testimony. A large group of us braved the cold and walked a few streets over to Greektown and had lunch. I pondered over who my five would be. The five included ME, since I would be staying in the court room. So, I had to give courtroom privileges to four others! That put so much pressure on me. At lunch, I told everyone that if they were selected, I would call them later in the evening. I was very upset about that decision. So many people have supported me and my family – and loved Kourtney – I knew they wanted to be in the courtroom for him. But, still, I could only pick four. My mom decided to leave and would not be back. She did not want to hear the details of what happened to Kourtney. Jaz would be stuck in the witness room until she was called, if at all. So, I did not have to factor her in...yet! My choices ended up being my two male cousins, Lennie (from my mother's side of the family), Eric (from my dad's side of the family), my sisters Kim and Angie. This really cut down all the drama for sure. But, still, many of Kourtney's supporters remained in the hallway and waited.

Ironically, at the same time as our trial got started, Joseph and Terrence's trial had been going on for weeks. So, plenty of neighborhood folks were all over the courthouse. Their trial was on the 5th floor. Most people believe and say that the reason Kourtney was killed was because of the crime in which the brothers have been charged. The brothers were charged with the murder of a young man from the neighborhood and the attempted murder of a guy who was with him. All I know is that all these young men's lives are ruined. They are either dead, or the "walking dead". ***In prison for life*****! After we returned from lunch and waited around, they finally told us that they have a jury selected. Opening arguments and testimony would start first thing in the morning. I was glad to hear it. We left and everyone headed over to my friend Gina's house for a dinner she had prepared for us.**

Wednesday, February 20, 2008, 8:14pm

Well, the murderer and his family got the reality check they needed! The murderer had the disposition of a "defeated" person. He is so guilty, not even his attorney would come to his rescue and just left his ass out to hang! The case is now in the hands of the jury. It was great testimony. The medical examiner's report was one of the most difficult to listen to. The first police officer on the scene testimony broke me down and I burst into uncontrollable tears. I had to leave the courtroom. I was crying so hard. My sister Kim, my victim's advocate, and a sheriff followed closely behind me. Jaz was already in the hallway talking (she could not come into the court room yet – she was still waiting to testify). I stayed out in the hallway talking for about an hour...until I could recover. My victim's advocate, and I just talked. We even laughed about stuff off the subject. I'm so tired tonight...

and exhausted. I think we will get a verdict tomorrow. I know it will be GUILTY OF MURDER IN THE FIRST! He murdered my sweet dear 1st Born, the guy with the best smile in the world...Kourtney! I'm too tired to write anymore, even though I really want to. I'm also having strong thoughts that I need to add to my victim's impact statement. Then I need to get in bed.

Okay, so now I'm face-to-face and eye-to-eye with the individual that committed this horrible transgression against my son. I take the witness stand...in the suit that I know for sure Kourtney picked out for me! I'm sworn in and a little nervous. All eyes on me. I say to myself, "We are here Kourtney." I repeat it a few times: "We are here Kourtney. We will have the victory and JUSTICE, Kourtney." Then I look directly at the murderer. I roll my eyes so hard at him. Jesus! If looks could kill!!! I feel the tears fill up in my eyes. But I don't care. The questioning starts and a picture of Kourtney in the red Jeep is blown up so large – right before our eyes. Like magic, he is in the courtroom. The prosecutor, Ms. "Z", asks me simple questions. However, these simple questions, ones in which I certainly know the answers, evoke emotions. I keep my eyes on the prosecutor as she paces the floor; my eyes are on the picture of Kourtney, too. She asked me did there ever come a time when I had to go to Henry Ford Wyandotte Hospital to identify my son? Instantly, I start to cry. In a fragile voice I answer "Yes." I'm handed tissue by a sheriff. She then asked me what's my son's name as I identified him on June 11, 2007 at Henry Ford Wyandotte Hospital. I slowly respond "Kourtney Everett Duffie." She continues to ask me things like his age at the time of his death, his date of birth.... I said simple things, but it hurt incredibly to respond – and more so with his picture blown up so big and in that unknown environment. All my senses gave way to the moment. Every part of me could not deny that this is so very serious. This is real. There is an individual sitting only a few feet from me who killed my son! He could not even look at Kourt's picture. I seen him glance at it and quickly turn his head away! He should have been made to look! But I knew it was the guilt in him that would not allow him to look at Kourtney. He kept mouthing the words to me "I didn't do it." Man, whatever! Every time I looked at him, I would turn my head and roll my eyes at him with such contempt! The defense attorney declined to ask me any questions. I was then excused and approved to stay in the courtroom.

To everyone's surprise all testimony was finished in the early afternoon! One day and pretty much it's over. The judge gave the jury their instructions, then he lit into the murderer! Whoa! The judge ripped into him so deep! He told him that it is no question in his mind that he "assassinated, ambushed, and executed Kourtney Everett Duffie!" It was so powerful. No one had EVER described what happened to my son with such passion and anger! Not even me! All he (the murderer) could do was hold his head down. I don't even think his attorney held his head up! No longer was he taking loose his braided hair and twisting on and

off rubber bands. He was stunned! Finally, he listens, I thought to myself. As the judge continued to lecture and scold him, you could hear a pin drop or, as the old folks say, "You could hear a mouse pee on cotton!" All the murderer could do was stand there and take it! He knew it was over. His family knew, too! And, to be honest, for about ½ second, I was not Kourtney's heartbroken mother.... I was just another human being watching the physical and mental demise of another human being. I almost felt sorrow for him. It was sad, indeed. The judge yelled at him and brought out just how unintelligent he truly is! He could not even answer questions. It was obvious that he could not even comprehend. And his attorney did little to help him! It was pitiful to watch. The judge was relentless and did not ease up at all! It was not the time for jokes or to be happy or celebrate. Lives have been ruined and families are traumatized! Who won? There are no winners. How could there be? To add, this was not a "family feud", as others tried to make it out to be. It was amazing to me how the other side tried to intimidate us or start problems. As if we should not be there for Kourtney! Nothing – I mean nothing – could have kept me away from anything related to MY SON. I guess people like that make up the rules – or try to – as they go along. Then, when it's them walking in my shoes, or shoes like mine, they will get the fuckin' point! The same legal system they disrespect and defy, they will want justice and cooperation! It would be just fine by me had I never laid eyes on any of them! Especially, the murderer, because had I not, then my son would have his life. The murderer had no right – NONE – to do what he did. Kourtney's life was not his to govern over. Not in any way shape, form, or fashion. The murderer stepped off into God's territory, and he will pay Devine Justice as well.

Thursday, February 21, 2008, 5:31pm

VERDICT IS IN! GUILTY – MURDER IN THE FIRST DEGREE!!! Oh, my...I don't think I've ever cried so hard! It was so overwhelming, how they just dropped the axe on that nigga! I'm so happy...so happy. One of the Michigan State Police troopers approached me and said the jury has reached a verdict. Then Ms. "Z" came and told us. That same trooper told me that during the investigation, they had literally talked to hundreds of people and everyone had something good to say about Kourtney. That makes it just that more difficult to accept what has happened to him. But today, the legal system came through. The jury knew. They were smart! I knew they looked like a good group when I first saw them, when it was 52 of them reduced to 13. Everything worked out perfectly. Finally, some evidence that somebody in his family is a human being...some tears for the murderer. Finally, they pay him some attention and stop worrying about what we're doing. One of his family members keeps making threats and Jaz responded back. But it don't matter. It is a wrap for his black ass! He is done! His life is over! He is the walking DEAD! Sweet Justice...so sweet for my Kourtney...for *our* Kourtney! Praise God!

Everyone came over to my house. They've been here since this morning. We got the verdict at 9:05am. I'm told that Wayne County has a new record set for our case being over so fast. Fastest trial, fastest jury verdict.... That's so awesome! The jury deliberated 1 hour and 50 minutes. The case was really cut and dry. Well, I'm tired and my eyes are so irritated. We have been drinking and eating and talking and crying and praying, and more and more people keep coming over and calling. Kourt's Godfather, Ray, asked me out to dinner to celebrate, but I'm just way too tired. I feel some life coming back into me now. Maybe this means some measure of peace for me. I hope so. It just hurts so bad that he's gone. (Oh, here comes the tears.) He is missed in the worst way – terribly missed. But I have faith that he and I will meet up again...and never part. God came through for his special son. Who is a very unique young man that I named Kourtney. His name meaning in part "from the Court." His name rang with Truth & Justice this day! I thank God for Kourtney. I'm much happier for the 22.9 years he allowed me to establish myself has his mother forever. I realize I could have never known him. So, YES, thank you, God. Thank you for lending him to me and my family and friends. I can't blame God for wanting him back. I had to break away from company to type this.

This is verdict day, February 21, 2008. Look how absolutely exhausted and tired I looked. I don't even look like myself. That is my sister Angie in the picture with me.

As the convoy of cars drive away from the The Frank Murphy Hall of Justice and we hit I-75 south bound headed for my house, we pass underneath the "Schaefer Street" exit sign, I blow my horn. Everyone starts blowing their horns, too! I look in my rear view mirror and I see all the cars of love for Kourtney. My phone will not stop ringing; the texts won't stop coming in. I got an awesome text message from one of the detectives from the River Rouge Police Department, too! Jaz phone is blowing up; it's just loud and emotional for everyone! My family who live outside the state are calling and texting and I'm trying to drive. I'm leading the group! I'm crying and driving! In my fantasy, Kourtney is flying above my car – he is right with us! I don't know if I'm happy or sad! I'm both, actually. I got the best I could get under the circumstances! I got the *most* I could get under the circumstances! Now, the final step will be sentencing day, March 12, 2008, which is the day I'll get to give my victim's impact statement. I have been working on it for about 8 months now. It will be my turn to talk without interruption. No arguments – just me with Kourtney's spirit right at my side. I ended up writing two statements. My first one was very hateful and derogatory, yet, still, I think it would have been okay to present. After all, look at what he did. Nonetheless, I created a new impact statement that I was more proud of. But, to this day, I still have a copy of my first speech.

I found out that the jury voted as soon as they got back to the room to deliberate. All of them raised their hands that he was guilty. Then they voted on 1st or 2nd degree murder. Everyone except one person voted yes on the 1st degree murder. The one juror that did not was hung up on whether it was premeditated or not. I understand that's when they asked to see the video again, a male juror brought it to everyone's attention that the video had been recording well before Kourtney made it to the gas station and that the murderer did NOT ever pump gas. Furthermore, another juror brought out that the gas pump was not even on the same side of the car. So, clearly, he was not there to pump gas...he was waiting on Kourtney to kill him! Premeditated! Powerful!

As soon as Kourtney pulled in, he is ambushed by nine bullets, one hit the area of his thumb and two penetrated to his heart and chest area. My first born son did all he could.... He still thought he had a chance as he drove away.... He probably thought he had gotten away.... I'm sure, with adrenaline pumping so fast, he did not realize that his life was ending. I bet he knew he was in trouble and needed help. That's why he pulled over next to that utility pole. But he did all he could do for himself. He died across the street from the gas station, near a utility pole. The cross streets of Schaefer and Bassett, which is borderline of the cities of River Rouge and Detroit, Michigan. The case could have gone to either River Rouge or Detroit, but River Rouge responded first to the crime scene.

Kourtney exited the Citgo across the street (in the background), pulled the Chrysler Pacifica into this grassy area right next to this pole. His life drifted away at "The Pole," which is why we decorate it in remembrance.

The infamous "Pole". That's what we call it now. Sometimes we call it "Kourtney's Pole". But, if someone says "the pole," instantly we know the location or what is meant by that name. From time to time we, decorate it. I understand that some of his friends visit, have a drink with him up there, and shed tears. We've had a couple balloon releases at this location as well.

Saturday, February 23, 2008, 9:17am

Trying not to think so much on recent revelations from the trial, such as Kourtney was still alive in the car when the police got there. They said he was unresponsive and in shock, but still.... "Unresponsive...." I'm told it does not mean "dead" and "shock" means one is not aware of pain or what is going on. But, still, thoughts of him gasping for air makes me sick to my stomach! Knowing that Kourtney trusted The Lord makes me feel he is safe now. I know he is safe...I know just where he is. He is with God. He was only *on loan* to me, I always remind myself.

Monday, February 25, 2008, 4:16pm

There are supposed to be threats on me and Jazmyn's lives now! These people are so damn dumb and stupid! They just don't learn, do they? He (the murderer) put *himself* in prison! He murdered Kourtney in a public place, was caught on video, and seen by eyewitnesses! They got the audacity to be mad at *me and my family*! For what!?! Still, I'm being careful...and so is Jazmyn. As careful as we can be, you know. I guess that if they want us dead, they will do it! What stopped him from killing Kourtney? He wanted to...and he did it! I'm so sick of all this mess. Damn, I can't even grieve my son's death.

Tuesday, February 26, 2008, 6:00pm

Today, a little better in terms of being nervous. I've been very busy today, so that's good. With so much behind me, I can start to re-focus my time and energy on other things. Next month, I'm going to start a new group with the national organization called Parent's of Murdered Children - Detroit Chapter. This chapter is located in the suburb of Southfield, Michigan. I'm going with my childhood friend, who also loss her son to a violent murder in November of 2007. I still want to start my own group. I have not heard anything from AVON. I see from the website that I can apply again on March 3rd. I will be submitting yet another application and essay questions. I hope and pray I get the grant. It's my intention to help another mother or father in some way.

Friday, February 29, 2008, 7:58pm LEAP YEAR!

I have not written in the past couple of days, but I've been thinking, that's for sure. The panic attacks started again when I think about Kourtney. I start breathing funny and something strange takes over me. It can be intense and scary. I don't like feeling as if I cannot breathe, dizzy and off balance. I miss Kourtney so much. I think about the last day he and I spent time with each other. I guess you don't know that the last time you see someone *will be* the last time you see him or her, huh?

Now I'm thinking about March 12th more and more. I've been working on my speech since July of 2007, trying to get my message across to this bum! It's not a curse out but, rather, some profound things and facts about Kourtney. He will never ever understand what he took from me. It's a horrible and sad reality to face day and night. But his fate is just about the same. He has a horrible and sad reality to face 24/7! Kourtney is really dead...he is gone! Oh my.... How will I ever be right again? I think, in time, I'm going to go crazy! I'm going to "check out." I try.... I really do try to be okay. But it's never enough. The truth is that most days, I give up. I'm still living, though. I have no choice but to move on. I know this, because I keep trying to fill my life with things that mean something to me and that make my life worthwhile. Like right now.... I'm looking for travel deals. I travel often, anyway. I guess I'm trying to do anything to feel normal again. Honestly, nothing helps. I may be okay for a little while. Inevitably, the sad feelings take over and I feel the void, accompanied with a headache or upset stomach or on the toilet with diarrhea, full of nervous energy, even when I have no energy at all! It can be a vicious cycle when I don't work extra hard to control my emotions or thoughts! Even though there are times when I smile and laugh – and it's genuine, too – inside I'm torn up and so heartbroken. It is a heart-wrenching truth to face-day to-day...all the time. I feel so damaged and let down. This is increasingly difficult to deal with. Wasn't this suppose to get better?

Monday, March 3, 2008, 5:44am

I'm headed to work. I'm expecting a busy week just like last week. Not sure if that's good for me or not. I'm not too sure of anything these days, other than I want my son back! I know my son loss his life on some real bullshit. Some fool hatin' on him. It was a personal attack and about nothing more. I am convinced. He's gone way too soon. All I have now is the "what if's" and the "I wish". But, as I will tell the murderer, "THERE ARE SOME THINGS WORSE THAN BEING DEAD!" Like his life I'm sure!

Tuesday, March 4, 2008, 5:51pm

Man, what a day! I got a subpoena last night to testify in Joseph & Terrence, trial! That courtroom is a zoo. The lawyers were cursing each other out, literally. They are now in the 10th week. I hope Joe & T make it out of this mess. It was hard for me to look at T in the courtroom. I had to point him out as proof that I know who he is. It truly saddened me. Although I knew I was there by force of the prosecution, it's my belief that I also helped the defense. It was difficult to be there. Kourtney was supposed to be T's alibi. I was really pissed off having to be there. Actually, I was pissed to the MAX! T said he was at my house with Kourtney, and that he had personally spoken with Jazmyn. Well, that became problematic because Jaz and I were in Phoenix, Arizona! However, it would not have been unusual for Kourtney to be at my house when I was not there. Many times, I've come home and Kourtney is there. No big deal.... Mama's house is always "home", right? I know it is. At least that's how it is for me and my family. But it made T look like he lied and not credible. Kourtney is not here for us to confirm any of this. Oh well.... It is what it is.

It used to trouble me from time to time, thinking about that day in their court case. I did not appreciate being subpoenaed by the prosecution! Frankly, I was mad as hell! Unfortunately for T, he put himself in that situation. And I was unable to help him out. I could not lie. They knew I was in Arizona during the time in question. I could not perjure myself and go to jail. I had nothing to do with what happened in that case. Unfortunately for me, I got pulled in it, nonetheless. The whole thing is sad. Everyone involved, and their families, have suffered great loss! Many things cannot be taken back or made right. I find that not even putting someone in jail makes it okay. For me it doesn't.

Sure, I'd much rather have the Justice, of course, but, at the start and end of every day since June 11, 2007, my son is STILL DEAD! As for my life, I'm doing all that I can to make good on a promise I made back in 2007: not to let my son's death be in vain! It's been an incredible journey, trying to figure out just how to handle that task. And the lessons continue....

Thursday, March 6, 2008, 8:35pm

It's been a crazy week. That unexpected court stuff threw my stress level over the edge! My secular work has been quite busy, too. Today has been a sad day. I found out earlier that they did convict Lil T of first degree murder. I cried. My heart is so heavy. I know these boys are not "killers". That's that street life...no rules! Another life – a young life – gone. I just wrote a letter to T and included a picture of him and Kourtney that was taken at my house. Joseph got a mis-trial and he will have to be tried again. Man, I'm hurt. Kourtney would be devastated. I hope that somehow he knows what has happened. I believe he does. I cannot really feel his spirit around today. He's probably trying to do what he can for T. I hope so.

Saturday, March 8, 2008, 6:34pm

Trying to get prepared for next Wednesday.... Sentencing.... Finally, a day that I have been thinking about for so long. Now, I'm just days from it. I get to speak my own words to the court regarding this horrible crime committed against my son, the crime that took him away. My blood starts to boil when I think about seeing that cold-blooded animal, and I get emotional. I do feel good about what I'm going to say. I like my revised statement. I'm ready, though. I saw someone at the mall today for a quick instance and I thought it was Kourtney. I'm still looking around for him, you know. In a matter of three seconds, my brain was like "Oh, there is Kourtney, I knew he would show up after all this time". That's just another one of those times when I can tell just how deep the hurt and missing him goes. I can only imagine what it will be like when he and I really do see each other again. I suppose that will happen when I die. I tell Kourt all the time that he better be there to greet me first, because I will never stop looking for him. Well, got to go.... I have a date tonight. This is something Ms. Jazmyn set up! She is so funny for doing this.

Yep. And life goes on, doesn't it? It does. Dating, working, shopping, bills, doing the laundry – still got to do the laundry – all the things that were done prior to the tragedy don't stop, even in the midst of the tragedy and it's aftermath. It's called "Life". When your child is murdered, it's called or becomes a "life-altered". So, let's pick up where I finally get MY DAY IN COURT!!

Wednesday, March 12, 2008, 4:49pm

Well, I let the murderer have it MY WAY TODAY!!!! I read my speech and free-styled some of it. I could not have told that bitch-ass nigga any better than how I told him to his face! For the first time, I got into an argument with one of "them" (the family) after it was all over! But I could not take it any longer! I guess it's true when they say that—you know "the truth hurts." I told all the truth today! Actually, "they" are really mad at the murderer and have displaced anger. But, finally, it is all over now. As I was delivering my powerful words, he continued to say "I did not do that shit." Yeah, whatever! He is so dumb and pitiful. But this is his life and he took Kourtney's life. Now he will pay for his decision with the rest of his natural life!

Check Fuckin'-mate! What a trade off. What a trade of places. He gave up his life to end Kourtney's life. No sense at all. I'm so sure he knows that by now. I told him that it's a "boomerang-type" plan he made, because it all came back on him! And it did. His plan backfired. He did not get away with it. As I'm sure he hoped he would. His limited intellect actually allowed him to believe he could kill Kourtney and not pay for his crime. Wrong! Or perhaps he was influenced by others to think he could do it and get away with it. WRONG, still! I told him that I'm sure he has no remorse for murdering my son. So all the more sweeter for me, and for Kourtney that HE GOT CAUGHT! I repeated, "You got caught!" three times. Each time, I shouted it louder and louder and pointed my finger directly at him in an upward and downward motion! I meant it. I let his ass know that I'm not offended because he hated or even hates Kourtney. I told him that because I'm sure Kourtney disliked him, too. So what? Does that mean you murder Kourtney? However, the fundamental difference between him and my son, I explained to him, is that my son valued his life! I went on to say and explain in detail how my son was able to ignore him. Kourtney knew he was a fool, running around with a gun with nothing to live for or nothing to lose! Kourtney wanted to live! He loved his life. He cherished his life and his family. He had plans that extended much further than what the streets could offer him. There is no parallel between the life of the murderer's and my son, the victim! None whatsoever! My son has peace now, while he has misery day-to-day and night after night – until he dies! He may live to be 100+ years-old. Sounds like the "walking dead" to me. I told him not to forget who put him in jail: Kourtney did!

As I continued to talk, he repeated, "I did not do the shit." Finally, I just yelled at him, as a mother yelling to a child! I said: "Shut the fuck up talking back to me with your disrespectful self!!." I heard mumbles from his side and out the corner of my eye, I could see that a sheriff's deputy went over there to warn them. The murderer lowered his head. The judge said nothing. He made no effort or comments to put an end to my relentless verbal onslaught! I was told after-the-fact this particular judge does not let anyone get away with what I did in his courtroom that day. But my feeling is that the judge agreed with what I was saying; what I was saying was so true. Further, I made no

attempts to get violent. I just spoke my words with strong conviction. I took up and represented for my son. The murderer had is back to the judge, so no one could really see him except me and some of my family members. It was weird how they set us up. His own attorney could not see him. Speaking of his attorney, how about this? The more I beat up on his client verbally, he could not stand it himself. So he jumps up and tries to "object!" Yeah, I said it right, he "objected!" Yeah, right! Oh my God, are you serious! Man, the judge shouted to him, "Sit down and shut up!" Right. Exactly! Sit down and shut up because his job was done. I felt he was really out of order for saying anything. After all, who interrupted or tried to stop that monster from robbing my son of his life? He had his 15 minutes, so I got mine for me and Kourtney!

I was able to get the murderer to be truthful about something. I had to ask him, because he seemed not to know the seriousness of the situation. I asked him directly "Do you like it here? You havin' fun?" I just glared at him. He humbled himself, lowered his head toward the floor and said "No." I threw my hands in the air and I said to him, "So what is the problem? What's going on out in these streets? I bet you can't even tell me why you don't like Kourtney or how this all started." He said "I had no problems with Kourtney. We squashed that." I yelled at him, "Stop telling that lie. You killed Kourtney! You wanted to do it – and you did it!" I went on to tell him, while looking back and forth between him and the judge, about the barbershop incident. I told him, "I bet you thought I didn't know about that." I explained to him how I knew that six months prior to the murder, he pulled a gun on Kourtney as he was getting a haircut and told him he would not make it to the summer. Further, that the employees of the barbershop had been threatened and were afraid to come forward and testify. I told him that I understood and was not mad at them because they have to live and work in that neighborhood. Of course, he tried to act like he did not know what I was talking about.

There were so many other points I made and many more that I wished I made. But I'm pleased with how I handled it. Even my "freestyle" portion of the speech was compelling, if I must say so myself, because it was right off my heart and unexpected. I was not emotional. I didn't come off too angry, either. I told myself that morning that however I presented my speech, it will be okay. If I cry or scream, it will be okay. When I presented my information, I was more so confused about his lifestyle, lack of love, how he has mismanaged his life, the negative impact of all of his bad decisions, and about how all of his horrible baggage has spilled over into me and my son's life. I also spoke on how my strength comes from the fact that I know that I raised a good son. I also told him about the promise that God makes to us about death. I certainly spoke on the type of guy Kourt was, how proud of him I am, and how Kourtney knew that he was loved. I told him that Kourt had my complete love and devotion since

July 20, 1984, when he entered this world, and that the same love continues to this very moment. How Kourtney brought no shame to me or our family. After I was done speaking, everyone was hugging me. There were tears and emotions all over the room. There were also accolades of "Congratulations!" bestowed upon me. An attorney who was sitting in on the case came up to me and said he wanted to hire me to do his opening and closing remarks! I felt so good. I felt that I had said pretty much all that I could say in the time allotted. With that time, I felt that I had made known to the murderer "MY IMPACT STATEMENT" on behalf of my son and myself. I tried to say words to make him think, so that he would be ashamed of himself. Not words to make him feel sorry for me. Like I told him, "I'm okay, because of the promises from God about death." I felt good when we left. I should also mention that I had my heart-shaped urn wrapped around my wrist.... I held Kourtney's ashes tight within my left hand as I spoke. I told you he would be right at my side...and he was. As mentioned earlier, when we left the courtroom, we went directly to "The Pole" and had a balloon release. That was the one time I did not have my camera with me. We did a second release at Honey's house about an hour later for those who had missed it. Of course, we captured some pictures with our cell phones.

Thursday, March 13, 2008, 5:50pm

I start a new group tonight. It's called Parent's of Murdered Children, located in Southfield, Michigan. My friend found out about it last month and told me. I'm happy to learn that an arrest has been made in the case of her son's murder. I'm so tired after yesterday. It was hard to make it work, but I made it. I want a beach getaway so bad - or any kind of getaway. Maybe I'll just go to my favorite spa and get a few body treatments.

Friday, March 14, 2008, 10:42am

I'm working from home today. I am mentally EXHAUASTED!!! I tried to visit with T today, before they ship him off to who-knows-where. However, he had taken my name off the visitor's list. I understand because they can only have five names on at a time. I feel so bad for these guys and about all that has happened. Seeing Joseph the other day behind bars just made me hurt all over for Kourtney, knowing how he felt about them and how they feel about him.

7:40pm

I got a call from the prosecutor a little while ago. She told me that Kourtney's murderer has also been convicted of first degree murder for the other guy he killed while on the run from Kourtney's case. So, that's two! That boy totally fucked up his life. I hope people can see that now. It's not something to celebrate! He did it to himself. It's not a conspiracy; no one is picking on him. Good fuckin'-BYE!

Saturday, March 15, 2008, 9:16pm

Ummm.... Today...a regular kind of day I suppose. Been thinking about Kourtney. But what's new, huh? Not feeling emotional, though. It seems that I'm in one of those cycles, where I can look at his pictures and smile and not get upset. That makes today a "close-to-all-right" day. I wonder if I will be in these cycles of grief until I die? I just don't see how I can feel the way I did prior to the tragedy. I know it would be impossible not to feel the void and loss even 20 years from now. My son is gone...my first born...and he was very much a part of my life. He will always be apart of my life. Strange how I think about him now in his death. In my mind, when he was alive, I knew he was okay for the most part. Sure, I worried from time to time, as any parent would as a child gets older. But, I never felt or knew he was in trouble, or having issues with anyone. I often think about the dream I had a few nights before he was killed. I feel sorry for Kourt at times, you know, because of how his life turned out. How sad is that -- to be shot up and ultimately killed in a car. Tragic! I never imagined any of this, as I'm sure he did not. I would have to say that I'm sure he realized some dangers living that type of lifestyle. It's so weird not talking to him in all this time. That's the hardest part to get used to: not hearing from him. It's like he has disappeared. But, then, I know he did not disappear. Rather, he was taken away in a violent manner. *Untimely*, as far as I'm concerned. I know, as he pulled away from Honey's, for what would be his last time, his mind was not on being dead in about 20 minutes. I would love to know what was on his mind as he drove through River Rouge into the gas station. I wonder. I know that I will always wonder. I try not to ponder on it too much. It's another one of those things I will never be able to change. (Deep sigh.)

Sunday, March 16, 2008, 9:36am

I had a dream about Kourtney the other night. I've been meaning to type it out. Actually, I've had two dreams about him within the past week. One dream was okay. He was alive. That's all I know. The other dream was about the funeral and Jazmyn and I getting dressed. That was a sad dream. I hate the autopsy that was performed on him. They removed a portion of his head, like, towards the back of his head that touched the pillow. It was a small circle carved out. Jaz and I could see the gauze and padding. Personally, I was afraid to remove it totally. Did not want to see what I didn't want to see! I don't understand why they had to do that. But, anyway, back to the dream. In this dream, Kourtney was floating in the air, and I said to Jazmyn, "Put the small circle piece back on his head because Kourtney is floating away." He was lying on his back. However, he was not in a casket. He was in thin air and floating away.

I truly appreciate the dreams I have about him. It doesn't matter, though... alive, dead, as a young adult, little boy.... It doesn't matter. All the dreams help me in some way. I wish Kourtney could let me know with his own mouth that he is okay. But, at the same time, I know that he is okay. That's just me yearning to talk to him.... I miss him. Oh well.

Monday, March 17, 2008, 7:00pm

A life unfulfilled! That's how I feel about Kourtney's life. Maybe I'm wrong. In many ways, I hope that I'm wrong. In an effort to calm myself, I think and say to others: "Well, his life's mission was complete." I don't know what to believe, really. Should I? I don't even have an answer for that. All I do know is that my first born son is so far away from me.... Hard to conceive. Hard to breathe. Within the past few days, all I can think about is how unbelievable this has been. This whole experience. Funny how times flies when YOU'RE NOT THE ONE HAVING FUN!!! It's coming up on one year. In a few days, it will be spring. Kourtney was taken from me in the spring of 2007. I hate thinking about his life, you know. It all brings me to his last day on earth...his last day of life. My God, how could any of us ever contemplate what was to come? Just thinking about his last full week...his last month...his last drive in a car...his last time coming over to my house...the last meal I cooked for him...the last time we talked on the phone...his last slice of pizza...the last time he took a shower...the last time he looked at his own reflection in the mirror.... JESUS! All these "last events" in his life haunt me now. I do well not to think on it so much. Tears I don't fight, not in private, anyway. But my thoughts... hey, that's another story. I have to maintain control. It's too easy to go too far.

I had an early dinner tonight with Jaz and John John and thought to myself: "I'm having dinner with my two kids, even though I know I have *three* kids that should be here. But one is gone now...my first born is gone." No life. Does he exist is some form? I believe that he does. Speaking of being haunted, I've been seeing them damn Chrysler Pacificas all day long, in the color he was driving. Honestly, I've been turning my head. Sometimes, I just go ahead and look and get what's coming to me. If it's going to be a panic attack, then, oh well.... If it's going to be crying while I'm driving, then, oh well. Come on with it! I know the downward spiral into the emotional pit is inevitable! When I reach the "pit," I may cry for days, have bouts of depression, coupled with uncontrollable shaking. I'm starting to think that I must face all of these physical and emotional symptoms...all the things that make me feel worse...just to get to what will make me feel better. Now, how crazy is that? (Deep sigh.)

Oh, I made a big accomplishment last week by going to the site where Kourtney's life ended. We call it "The Pole". I had been avoiding it. At first, I would drive nowhere near it. If I'm in the car with others, I would ask them to please take another route. I was scared to be there. The tire tracks of the Pacifica he was driving stayed very long, I understand. Wow. Was he driving that fast, I wonder? Yeah, probably. Being there was not so bad. It was the day of sentencing. I cried and examined the area. Other people had been going up there, putting up balloons, teddy bears, and momentos. I appreciate that. I had to realize that although I hated what took place there, my Kourtney was there after all. He was there...and I should go there, too. Also, I should stop being afraid of the gas station. Now, I'm ready to get his clothes back from the police. Well, maybe not. All of these things are a part of his life. They also represent an event in his life. No matter how tragic, it was still his life. I have to realize that he did not plan for these things to happen, but they did happened. It's all apart of Kourtney's life. I know that I miss my son. If I were to write a book, I think the name of it would be entitled *A Life Unfulfilled*. That's so appropriate.

One day I found that driving pass the Citgo gas station was something I could handle, too. I had told myself that I would NEVER drive by that gas station. I made myself believed it to be taboo, or simply just something I should not do. In some twisted way, I felt I was holding this high honor for Kourtney. But I did make the drive by. I don't remember when it happened. I just remember being in my car alone and looking at the gas station from a distance. I looked in my rearview mirror to see if I could back up my car and turn it around. I was changing my mind about this "therapeutic exercise". I had driven there on purpose. I stayed at the stop sign and thought about this being the street Kourtney pulled out on to as he drove right across the street to the gas station. It seemed likely, since many of the streets in River Rouge are one way. As I prepared to drive away from the stop sign, it felt empowering to think about Kourtney at that very moment. I took my foot off the brake and slowly accelerated. At the same time, I talked out loud to God and Kourtney, not sure if I would have a panic attack, or worse. Maybe get the nervous breakdown that I believed I was gearing up for or even wanted! Within in a few seconds, I was in front of the gas station where it all started. I took a quick glance in my rearview mirror and tapped my brake just a little since there was no traffic behind me. The gas station was busy with people pumping gas and walking in and out the store part. Then, suddenly and without plan, I blew my horn and smiled! I said out loud "It's okay, Kourtney! I'm okay! Thank you, Jesus!" And, before I knew it, I was at the pole. As I drove by, again, I blew my horn and shouted "Kourtney!" And, to this day, late March of 2009, that is my little private ritual. When I find myself driving pass the gas station and the pole, I always toot my horn lightly two to three times as an acknowledgement and a small but large tribute to my Kourtney. And, although I'm crying a little bit as I type this section early this morning, my tears are not all tears of sadness or burden. They are tears of progress and recovery. I know that I've come a long way. Yeah, I still have more work to do. But I'm out of the danger zone....

In the distance is the gas station where Kourtney was shot. Here is how far he made it (to the pole) and pretty much where his life ended on June 11, 2007.

Did I say "PROGRESS"! I believe that I did!

Mothers, our work never ends....

Conclusion & Afterthoughts

AND THERE IT IS - some of it, anyway. I wake up almost every morning and say to myself "He still dead." Yeah, he is. I had to get over the fact that he could actually die. I never thought Kourtney – nor any of my kids – could die (not before me). But, he did; it happened. It's heartbreaking, but true. When I would be in the denial phase, I would ask myself over and over "Kourtney can die?" As if he could not die. That's weird, huh---even after he had been dead for several months. For me to say "He still dead" is representative of the void that I feel. Kourtney is that missing person in my life; he is that void. So, since he is still dead, it comes to how to deal with it, how to deal with it second-to-second...minute-to-minute...hour-to-hour... day-to-day...week-to-week...month-to-month...year-to-year.

As one might imagine, there are many levels and waves of emotions that I have conquered. Yet there is still more to be managed. I use the word "managed" because I don't believe that a mother or father ever "gets over" the death of a child. What members of "the club" do is manage our emotions and learn how to fit into our new lives. My biggest fear was doing what other people told me all the time: Let it go. I had to find out on my own that letting go did not mean to forget him, or to no longer miss him, or stop loving him. "Letting go" places one at the final step of the grief process, which is "Acceptance". But, it takes some time to get there. Some grief experts agree that Acceptance takes about two to five years to achieve. To make it to Acceptance means that the other levels of grief have been dealt with or experienced at one time or another. There are five distinct levels of grief, which are: *Denial, Anger, Bargaining, Depression and Acceptance*. In the *Denial Phase*, we refuse to believe what has happened. In the *Anger Phase*, we simply get angry! The anger can come out in many ways. Experiences of emotional outbursts are common, even turning the anger inward on oneself. Then there is the *Bargaining Phase,* where we try to work out a deal with God to bring our loved one back. Now comes *Depression*. This phase is very difficult for many of us that dealt with the loss of any kind...a child, a parent, etc. It is a feeling that you have no purpose, no joy. Feeling tired all the time. Even, experiencing thoughts of guilt and suicide. And, finally, *Acceptance*. This is where we know – we realize – that life has to go on. And, we can move on and make plans for our future. We accept the loss. Grief is a personal process. No one can tell another person how to do it or how long it should take or make statements like "Shouldn't you be over that by now?" Believe it or not, there are people who feel that way. What I have found out is that reading and professional counseling has helped me to identify my feelings, to know that what I was going through was normal and that I'm not alone. None of the phases of grief are easy.

To this day, in the spring of 2009, I continue to write in my journal. My journal has been the one constant and reliable outlet in my life. A few months back, I decided on a stop date for the book: March 31, 2008. I felt that ending time was good because everything had happened: the tragedy itself, the arrest, justice, and my day in court. What I noticed, as I read my notes for the remainder of March of 2008 and beyond, is that, even though I had survived so much, I still had days of extreme sadness that came out of nowhere...and I still have unanswered questions. Also, planned fantasies of suicide intensified over the coming months. I was even slipping back to the denial phase, because I could never stick with what had happened. Who wants their son or daughter to be murdered? No one. I think to myself, my son was shot and killed in a car. I thought about many things for Kourtney, but I had not considered death for him. Not in my life time, anyway. That alone is a tremendous burden to "accept". I also see from my notes that I wondered about me being truly happy again, about feeling that my heart was wiped out, and that I had nothing else to give. At that time, and presently, I'm trying to hold on to Kourtney's life. I have physically held on to so much of his life, such as being unable to put away his shoes and some clothing. Also, I still have not completed the funeral flower compost pile. I have many pictures that sit out in my home one way or another. As for the latter, I have pictures in collages, scrap books, on my computer screensaver, in the kitchen--two in the kitchen, to be exact. It's just *the love*. That's all I can say. And I keep a picture on my desk as I write this book or pay a bill online. I want to see his face. This way I can glance at him...give him a wink or a smile...cry...shake my head in disbelief. Like I said, *it's just the love.*

Kourtney meant so much more to us than being my first born son, or a big brother.... In my home, he was our Protector! We had to get used to being women with no alpha male. Many times, we felt – Jaz & I, primarily – that we were vulnerable to anything. Who was going to come to our rescue now? We were wide open for anything - and we were afraid, literally. Sure, we had John John, who was only 12-years-old at the time and already 6' 3''. (John John lives full-time with his dad). But Kourtney had made his place with us and knew where he stood. He took his role seriously, too. We miss that. In my mind, Kourtney was untouchable. Not like he was a superhero, but he could take care of himself in any situation for the most part. I knew he would call on me when he needed me, and he did. At 22-years- old, I was allowing him to grow up and seek out the independence of a young man. I backed off and tried not to ride his back so much about the changes he and I both understood that he needed to make. Further, I had set an example of things for him to avoid, coupled with the example of having good work ethic for him to mirror to some degree. As his mother, I knew I had instilled some good values in him, and he had been raised in a home with love and trust. That's what kept him affectionate and kept his heart open towards little kids. It kept them knocking on Honey's door, looking for him. There were kids on my street that did not even say hello to me, but they knew him for sure. I've seen him from time to time slow down and stop and talk for a few minutes with the kids. He was like a magnet. They were drawn to him, "like a moth to a flame." Most days, when they saw him pull up, before he could even park his car, they would run to him for candy or ice cream money. He could not say no. And he didn't. The condition of his heart would not allow him to do so. Those acts of kindness were the core of his character. I remember when I had arranged a job interview for him, one where he would be cooking for preschool-aged kids. (Kourt had a desire to be a chef and had some culinary training.) I knew it would be a good fit for him; he did, too, as the constant smile on his face made it evident when I described the work environment and how the children would learn his name. The truth of the matter is that he adored little kids. Maybe he (or me) did not know why.... He just did.

You know, just when I thought I had given up and let my sense of self-destruction take over me, I realized that *I owe.* As I sat at my desk on January 29, 2009, thinking about the possibilities of this book, I became so excited of what it could mean. That day, I cried for Kourtney. I also cried for the *faith in my heart*. This book was a way that I could pay Kourtney back, a tribute to all the good things he did for me, such as the way he helped me with Jazmyn and John John. He recognized the importance of family. One of his friends wrote a letter to Jaz. I happened to read it the night before the funeral. In part, he said, "Kourtney is the first real nigga to show me what family is all about and morals." As a result, I had his letter copied in the middle of the night and attached to the obituary. Kourtney meant a lot to people. I feel that God has allowed his spirit to reach out to me so that, together, we can help others. After all, in my opinion, his life was all about that, anyway. I know that deep down, with all my dark thoughts, had I acted on any of them, Kourtney would have been so disappointed that I had given up. So, when I can't do it for *me*, I do it for Kourtney, Jazmyn and John John. I repeat: WHEN I CAN'T DO IT FOR ME, I DO IT FOR KOURTNEY, JAZMYN AND JOHN JOHN! That's who I owe. I also owe myself, my family, my community, and God.

I had to learn how to maintain control over my life. I had to make a choice: to either be pitiful or to empower myself and move forward! To this day, I fall off the wagon, but I get right back up. I know it can mean trouble if I stay down. I keep in mind that *I owe.* Disappointments in life are inevitable, but being miserable and giving up is *an option*. I want to use the time that God has given me to work towards being better and accomplishing goals, not being stressed and worried. I want that spirit of being free and peaceful within in me. I know what it feels like, too. Since the beginning of 2009, my life has changed for the better. I had to go through what I went through. Those experiences have shaped me. This tragic event that happened to me and my son – and the fact that God has kept me – has revealed to me that there is so much more, and that these little and big pieces of my life are just pieces of my life puzzle. God knows that complete picture. I, eventually, will, too. I'm thankful and blessed. On this side of the world, Kourtney's life puzzle was complete on June 11, 2007.

So, whatever I do or accomplish, I now know that I'm not leaving Kourtney behind. He is always with me. He is a gift from God. I relish that gift in the past, present and future – that's how it is and will be. And, although I still feel that he is gone too soon, I'm still grateful and feel Divinely blessed that I was entrusted to be his mother. Remember: Our kids are only *on loan* to us. They – we all – belong to God. A woman at church who loss two baby boys quoted a scripture to me that said, in essence, God provides us with a legion of Angels. As she and I cried, she added, "How blessed I am to be able to call one by name!" In her case, two! Praise God!

You know, people find their way into our lives and back out again. Sometimes there are hurt feelings. But, in time, we get over that person and move on to the next, discovering new friends and relationships. Those special feelings no longer exist. But there are some people that we will never lose it for...like a person in my life, my son, my first born, my Kourtney. I'm so overwhelmingly delighted to confirm that IT IS IMPOSSIBLE to lose that special love for a son or daughter that has gone before us. That true and unconditional love, an eternal bond that we found from the beginning will always be the complete circle of love between Me, Kourtney and God...there is no end....

Cherished Memories

Jazmyn & Kourtney in a wedding, 1991

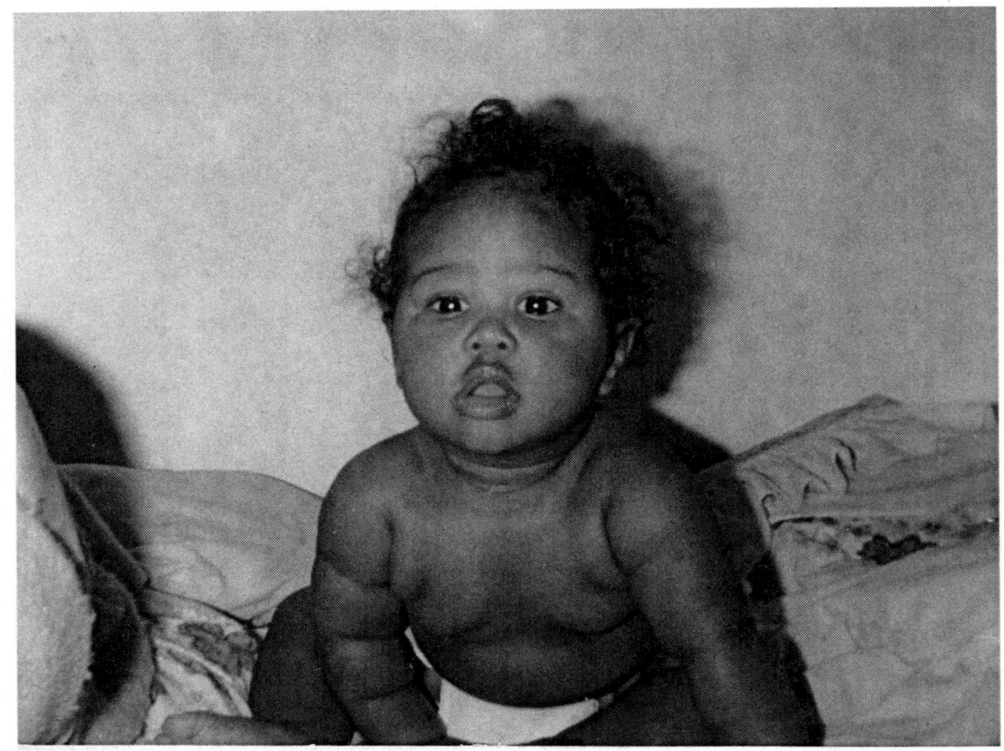

Kourtney, 6 months old. He was absolutely adorable from day one. I recall walking to the nursery, some hours after he was born, to see my newborn baby boy. There were four nurseries "A", "B", "C", and "D". My baby boy was in Nursery D. I noticed a crowd of people at the last nursery which was Nursery D. No one was at the other nurseries. Since I was in hospital attire, it was clear to see I was a new mommy; as I walked up the hallway, people started to make room for me. What I heard made me blush. People were talking about: how cute and "Eskimo-like" Baby Boy Duffie looked. I said out loud "That's my baby" as I made it up to the glass window. They were all admiring him and I felt proud of my bouncing baby boy. Folk were telling me congratulations and about how he is "so fat and adorable." Indeed, he was weighed in at 7lb 2oz and 17 ½ inches long. He had this jet black hair, layers of it that whipped in a circle around his head. He was so cuddly and made you want to kiss his cheeks. He never changed is whole life....

Kourtney, 6mos, Detroit Tigers won the World Series that year, 1984.
Grandma Honey helping Kourt to walk!

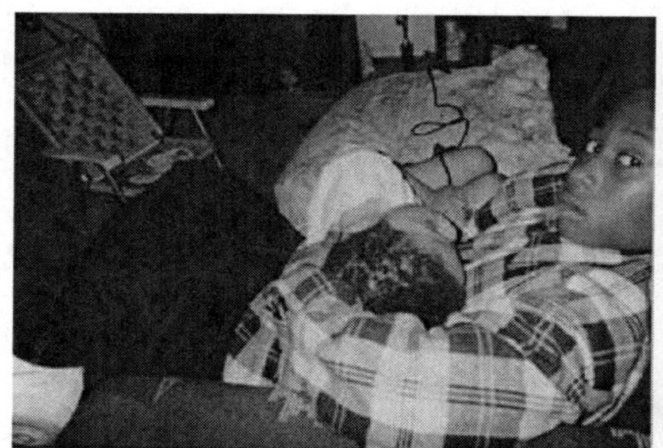

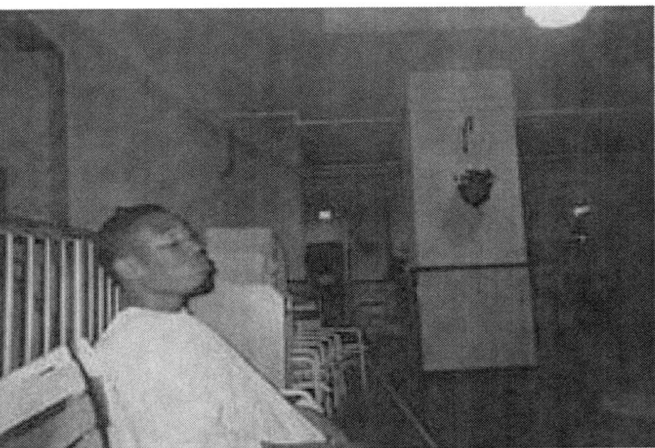

CHEVY

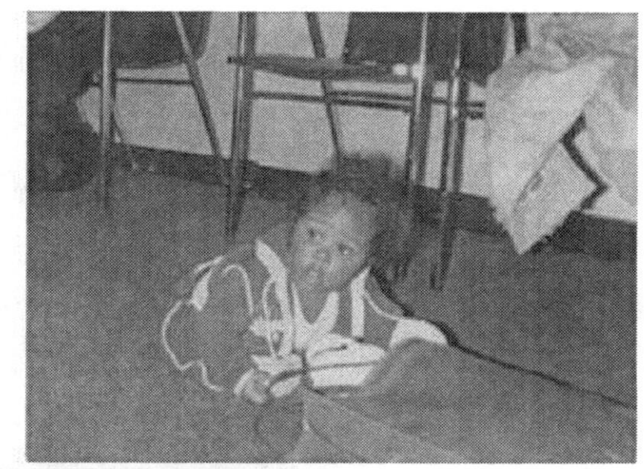

Grief Support & Resources

National Organizations

Parent's of Murdered Children
"For the Families and Friends of Those Who Have Died by Violence"
www.pomc.org

The Compassionate Friends
"Supporting Family after a Child Dies"
www.compassionatefriends.org

M.A.D.D.
"Mothers Against Drunk Driving"
www.MADD.org

Local/Metro Detroit, Michigan Organizations

Parent's of Murdered Children (POMC)
Group Sessions held Monthly/2nd Thursday,
Meeting Times
6-6:30pm Check in
6:30-8:30pm Support Meeting
St. David's Episcopal Church
16200 W. 12 Mile, Southfield, MI
(between Southfield and
Greenfield)
Contact: Sylvia Banks, Team Leader
248.989.4200
sbanks@advomas.com

The Compassionate Friends - Detroit Chapter
Group Sessions held Monthly/1st Tuesday, 7-9pm
New Greater Baptist Church
10636 Tireman, Detroit, MI
Contact: Kelly, stanfordk8@comcast.net

The Compassionate Friends – Metro Detroit – Ann Arbor Chapter
Group Sessions held Monthly/3rd Sunday, 2-3:30pm
1st Presbyterian Church
1422 Washtenaw, Ann Arbor, MI
Contact: Valerie, 734.769.0496

Journey Through Grief
Sponsored by Howe-Peterson Funeral Services
Dearborn & Taylor, MI
6 Weeks Series (no summer sessions), 6:30-8pm
Contact: 313.561.1500
www.howepeterson.com

S.O.S.A.D.
"Save Our Sons and Daughters"
www.SOSAD.org

Triumph Missionary Baptist Church
"Where the Word is the Word" – Pastor Solomon Kinloch, Jr.
Main Campus, Liddesdale, Detroit, MI 48217
313.386.8044
www.triumphch.org

Contact me: klduffie@yahoo.com, subject line: BOOK
Karen Lynne Duffie, PO Box 1056, Southgate, MI 48195

*"Bring all that I am, to all that I do, is all that I need.... ACCEPT – ADJUST – ADVANCE"
*(quote that I adopted years ago from a motivational seminar I attended)

... not in vain Kourtney

KAREN LYNNE DUFFIE, is a first time author. The motivation and love for her fallen son inspired this project. She credits her strength, energy and determination to God for seeing this very special publication through to completion. She is the proud mother of three, one daughter and two sons.

Karen & Kourtney, Thanksgiving 2005

LaVergne, TN USA
18 May 2010
183139LV00001B/43/P

9 781426 918957